THE NINTH
GARFIELD
TREASURY

THE NINTH
GARFIELD
TREASURY

BY: JIM DAVIS

BALLANTINE BOOKS • NEW YORK

A Ballantine Book
Published by The Random House Publishing Group

The Sunday strips appearing here in color were previously in black and white in
GARFIELD LIFE IN THE FAT LANE #28, GARFIELD TONS OF FUN #29,
GARFIELD BIGGER AND BETTER #30, and GARFIELD HAMS IT UP #31.

Published in the United States by Ballantine Books, an imprint of The Random
House Publishing Group, a division of Random House, Inc., New York, and
simultaneously in Canada by Random House of Canada Limited, Toronto.

www.ballantinebooks.com

Library of Congress Catalog Card Number: 97-93768

ISBN: 0-345-41670-8

First Edition: November 1997

10

Printed in China

THE NINTH
GARFIELD
TREASURY

In A Perfect World...

...You Could Vaporize Annoying Drivers

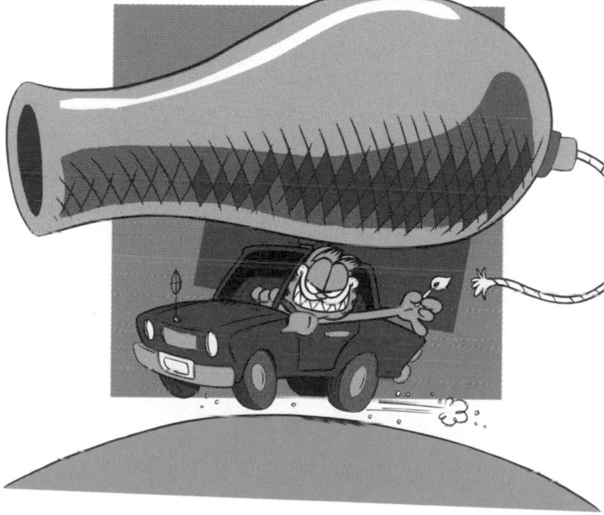

...It Would Be Okay Not To Act Your Age

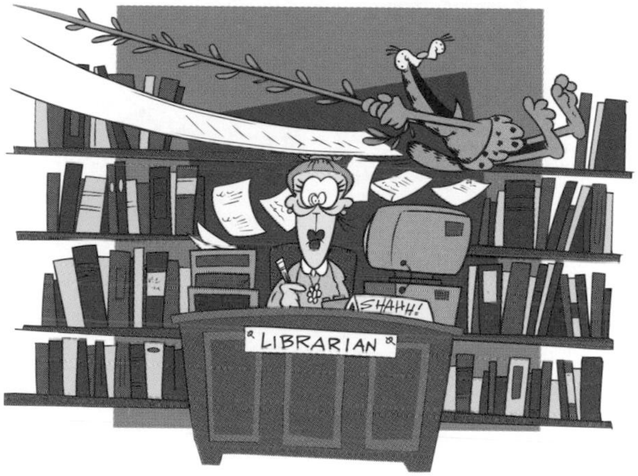
LIBRARIAN

...Oranges Would Have Zippers

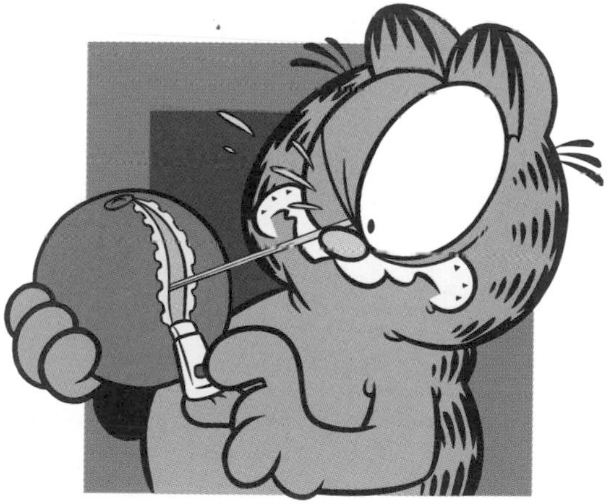

...Elves Would Do Your Chores

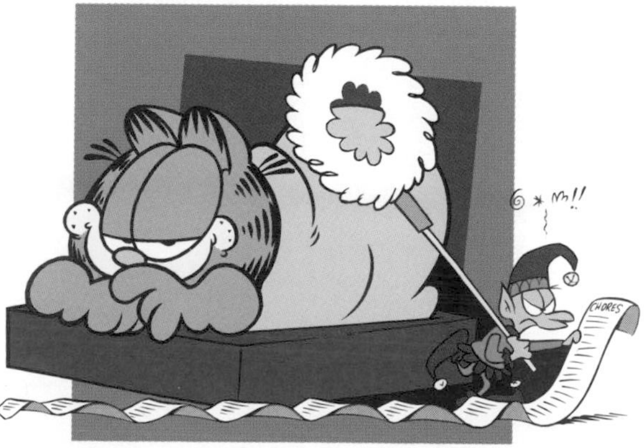
CHORES

...The Coffee Would Always Be Hot

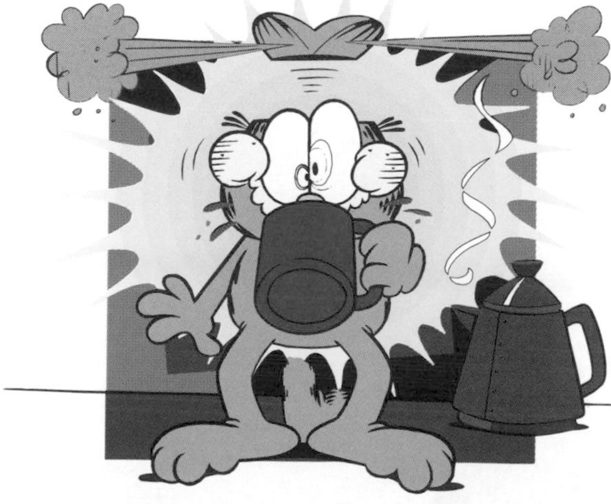

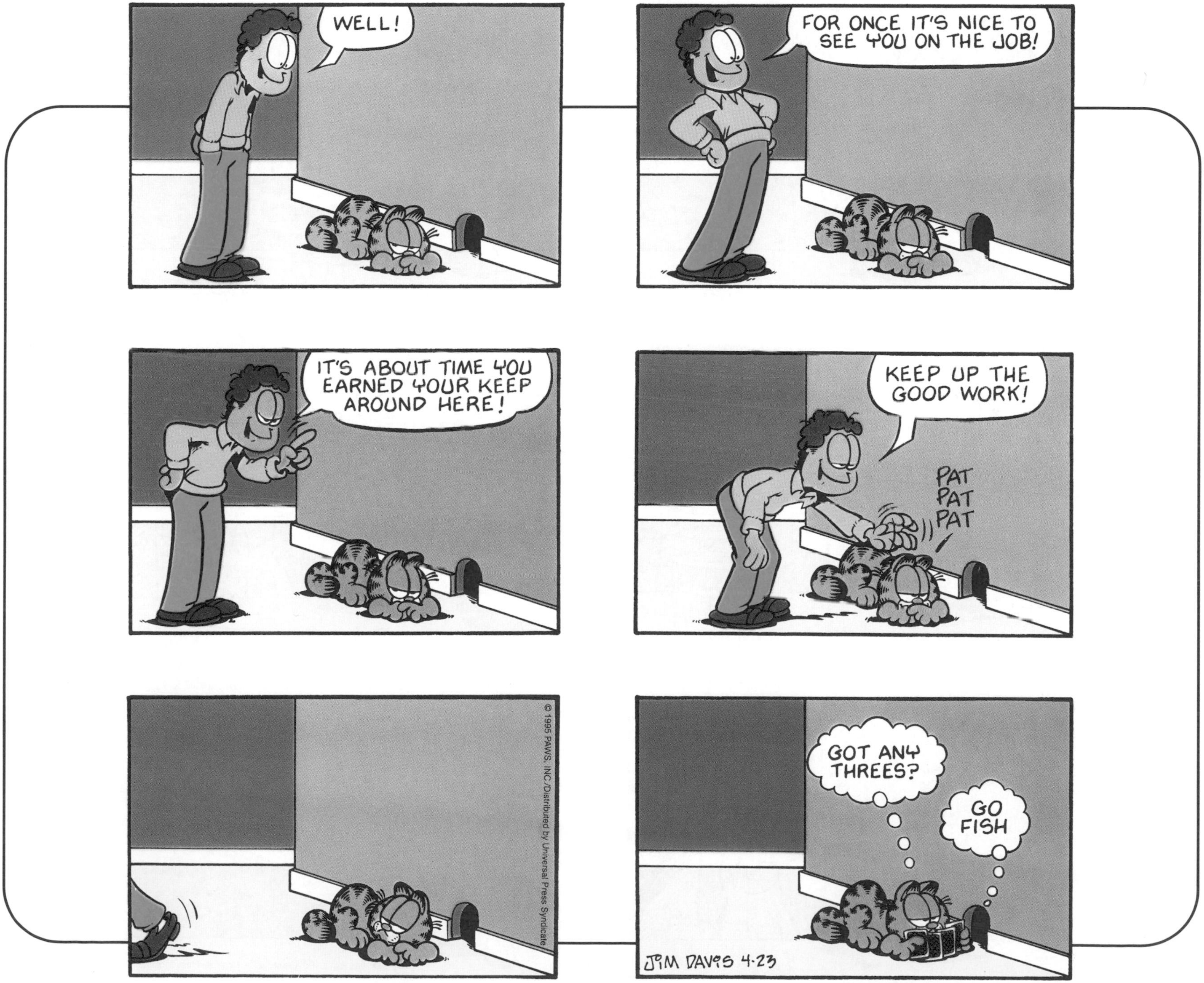
WELL!
FOR ONCE IT'S NICE TO SEE YOU ON THE JOB!
IT'S ABOUT TIME YOU EARNED YOUR KEEP AROUND HERE!
KEEP UP THE GOOD WORK!
PAT PAT PAT
© 1995 PAWS, INC./Distributed by Universal Press Syndicate
GOT ANY THREES?
GO FISH
JIM DAVIS 4-23

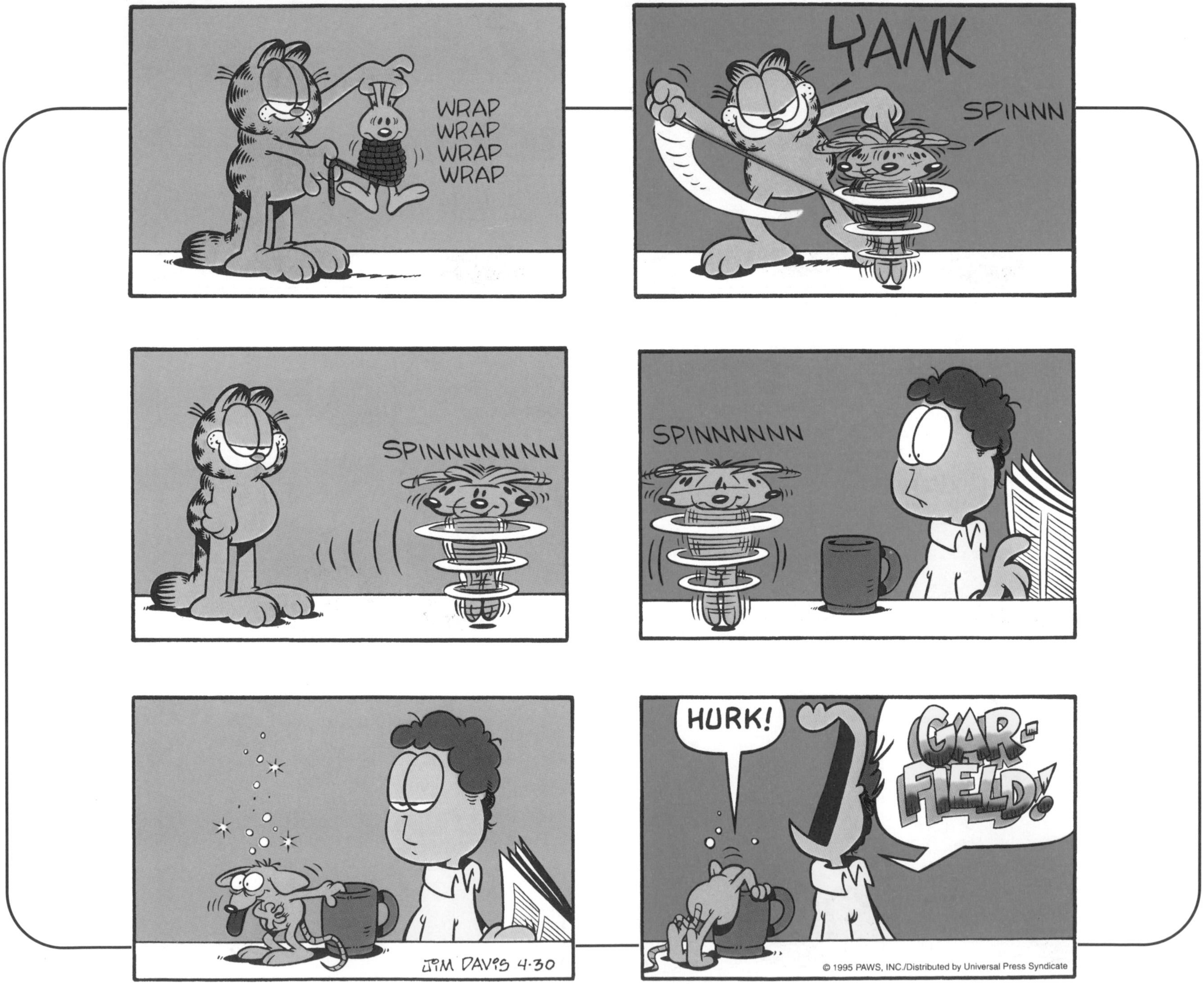
WRAP
WRAP
WRAP
WRAP
YANK
SPINNN
SPINNNNNNNN
SPINNNNNNN
JIM DAVIS 4·30
HURK!
GAR-
FIELD!
© 1995 PAWS, INC./Distributed by Universal Press Syndicate

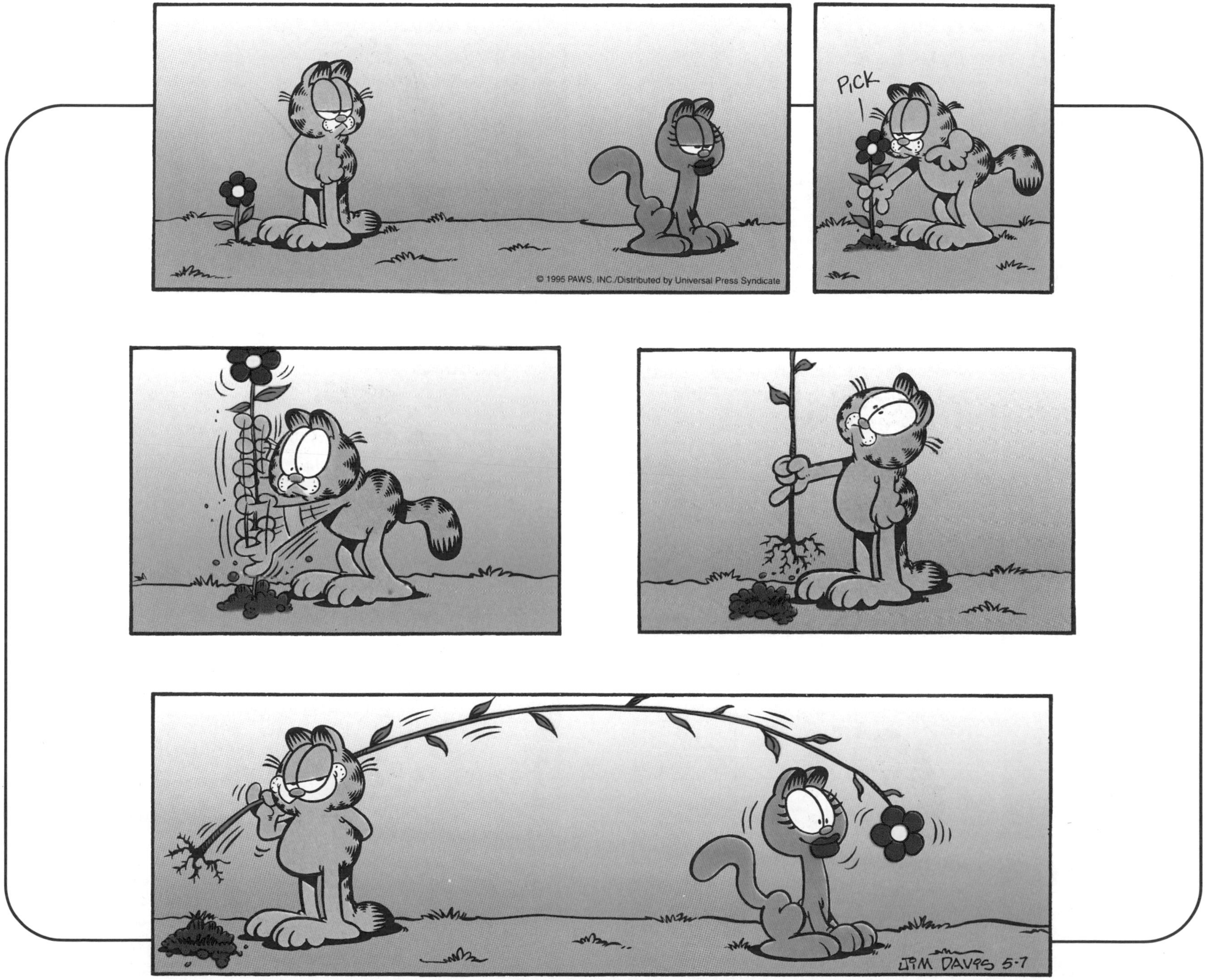
© 1995 PAWS, INC./Distributed by Universal Press Syndicate
PICK
JIM DAVIS 5-7

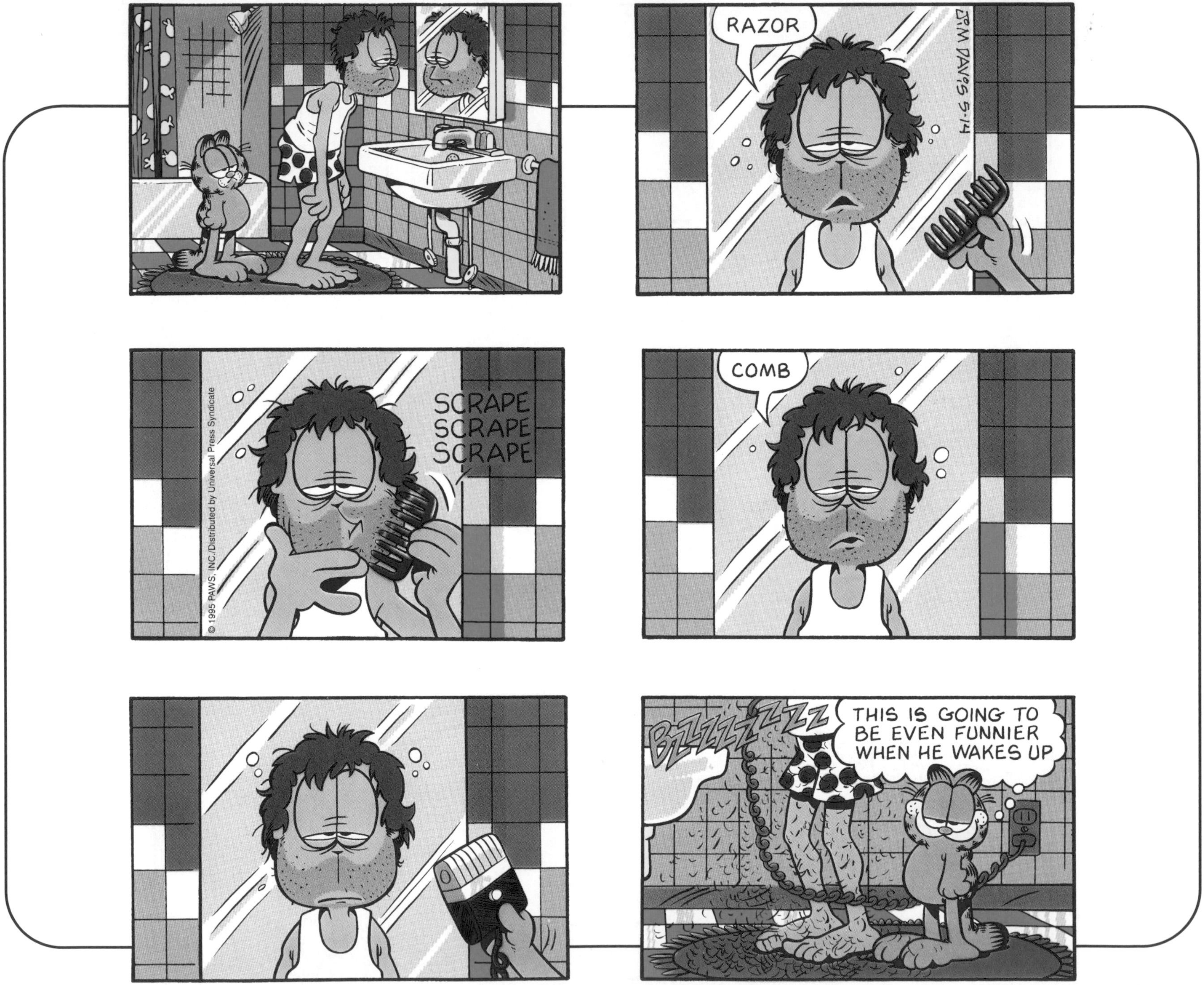
RAZOR
JIM DAVIS 5-14
© 1995 PAWS, INC./Distributed by Universal Press Syndicate
SCRAPE
SCRAPE
SCRAPE
COMB
BZZZZZZZZZ
THIS IS GOING TO BE EVEN FUNNIER WHEN HE WAKES UP

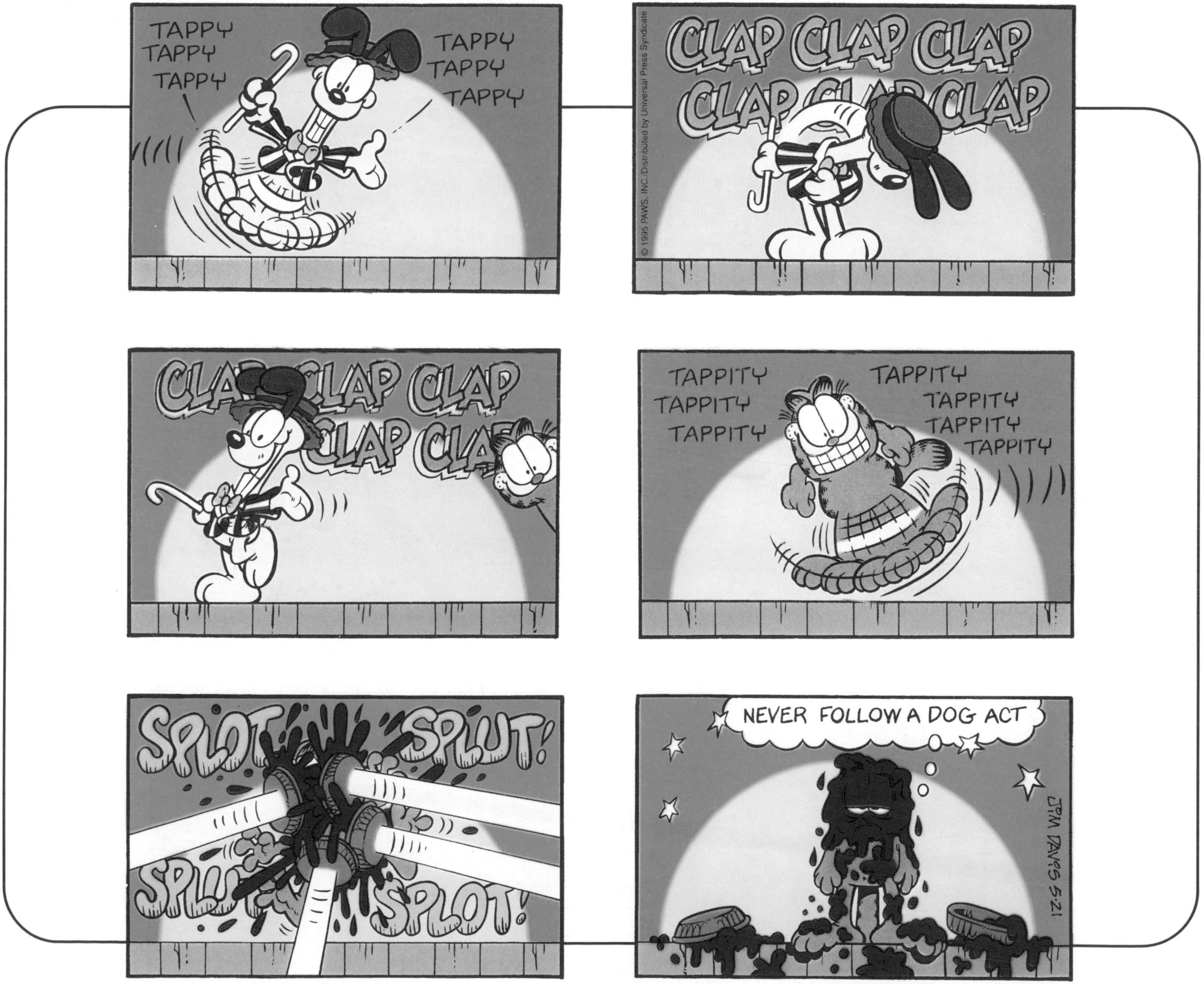
TAPPY
TAPPY
TAPPY
TAPPY
TAPPY
TAPPY
© 1995 PAWS, INC./Distributed by Universal Press Syndicate
CLAP CLAP CLAP
CLAP CLAP CLAP
CLAP CLAP CLAP
CLAP CLAP
TAPPITY
TAPPITY
TAPPITY
TAPPITY
TAPPITY
TAPPITY
TAPPITY
SPLOT! SPLUT!
SPLUT! SPLOT!
NEVER FOLLOW A DOG ACT
JIM DAVIS 5-21

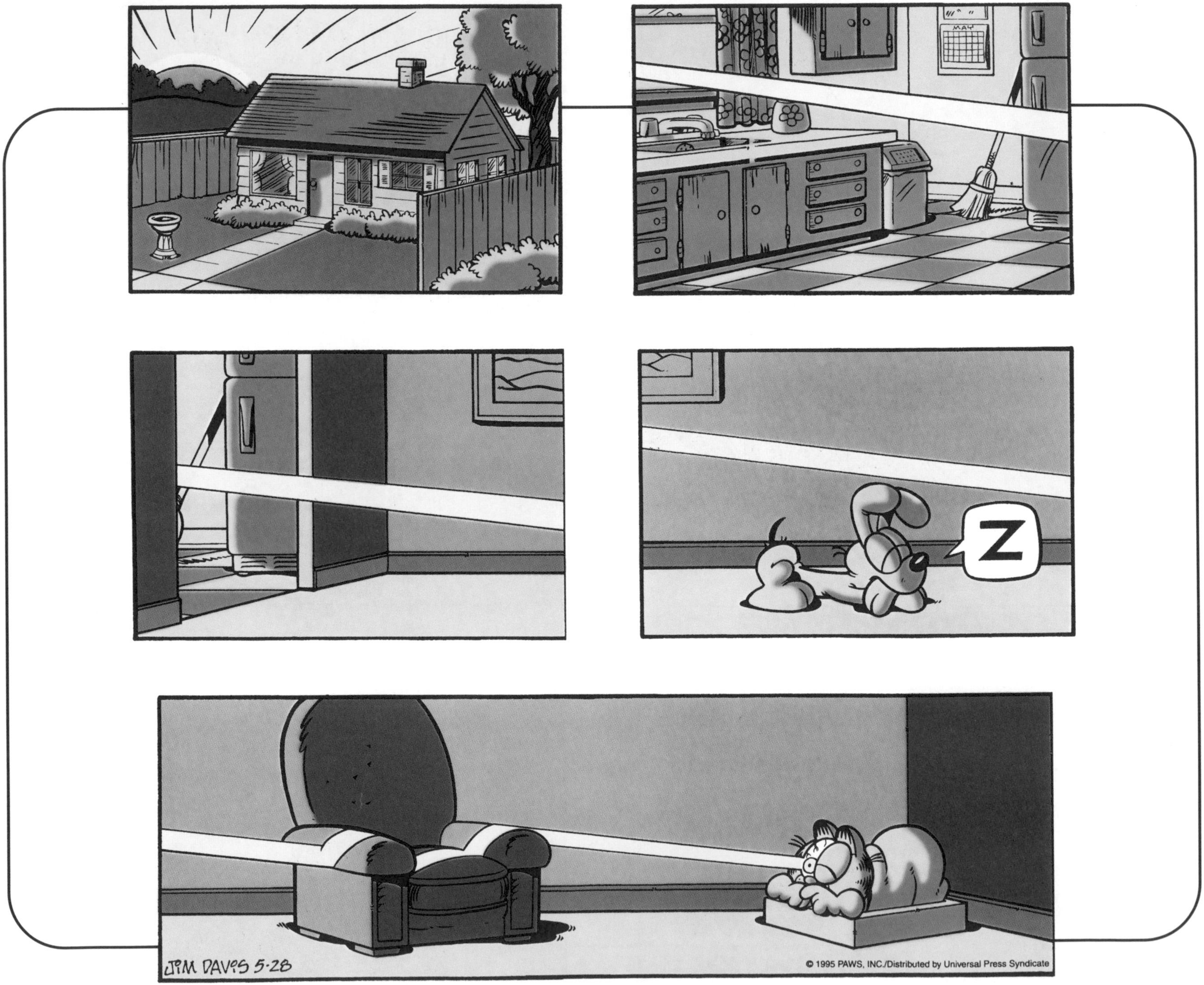
Z
JIM DAVIS 5-28
MAY
© 1995 PAWS, INC./Distributed by Universal Press Syndicate

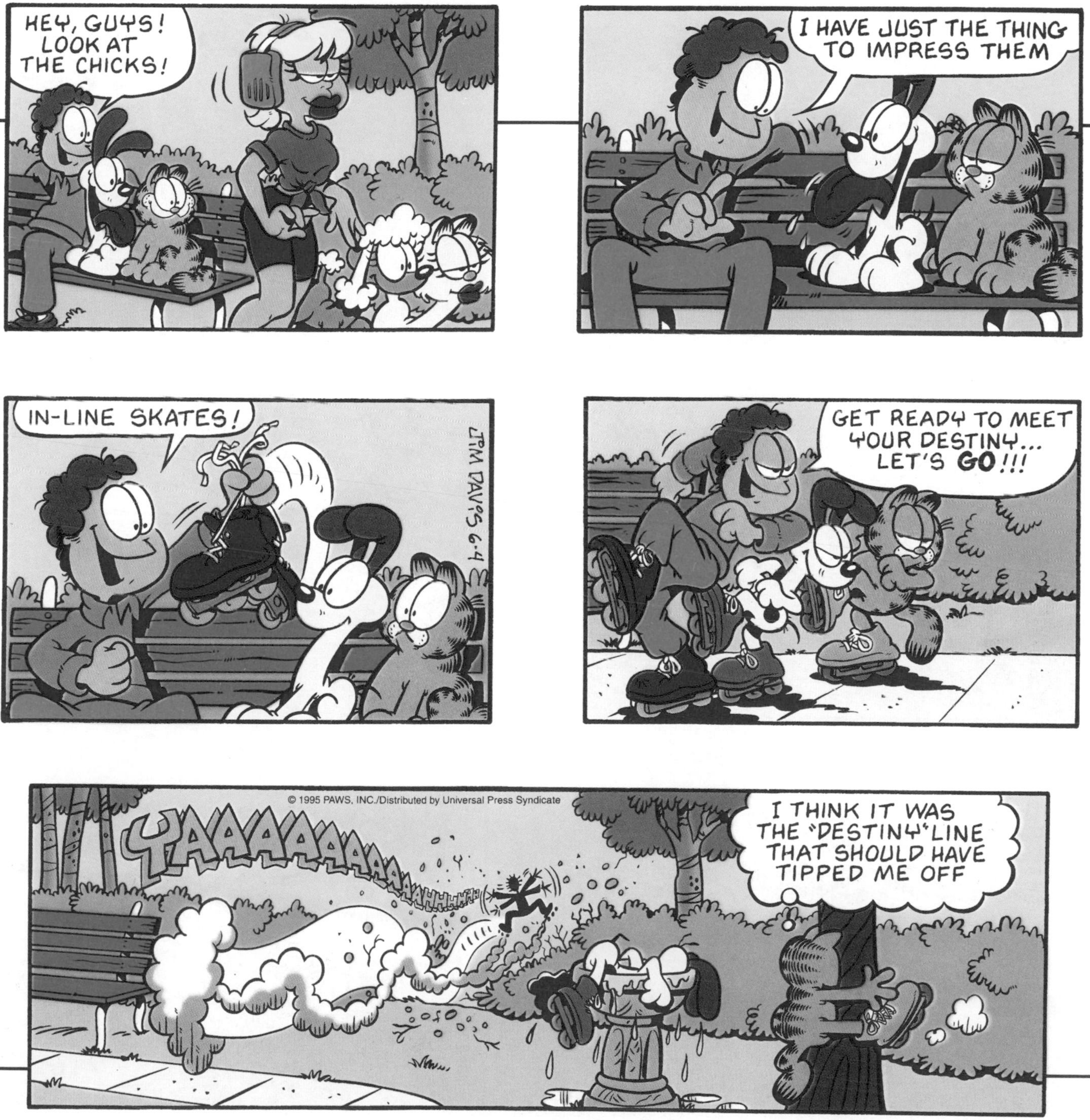
HEY, GUYS! LOOK AT THE CHICKS!
I HAVE JUST THE THING TO IMPRESS THEM
IN-LINE SKATES!
JIM DAVIS 6-4
GET READY TO MEET YOUR DESTINY... LET'S GO!!!
© 1995 PAWS, INC./Distributed by Universal Press Syndicate
YAAAAAAAAAAAHHHHHH
I THINK IT WAS THE "DESTINY" LINE THAT SHOULD HAVE TIPPED ME OFF

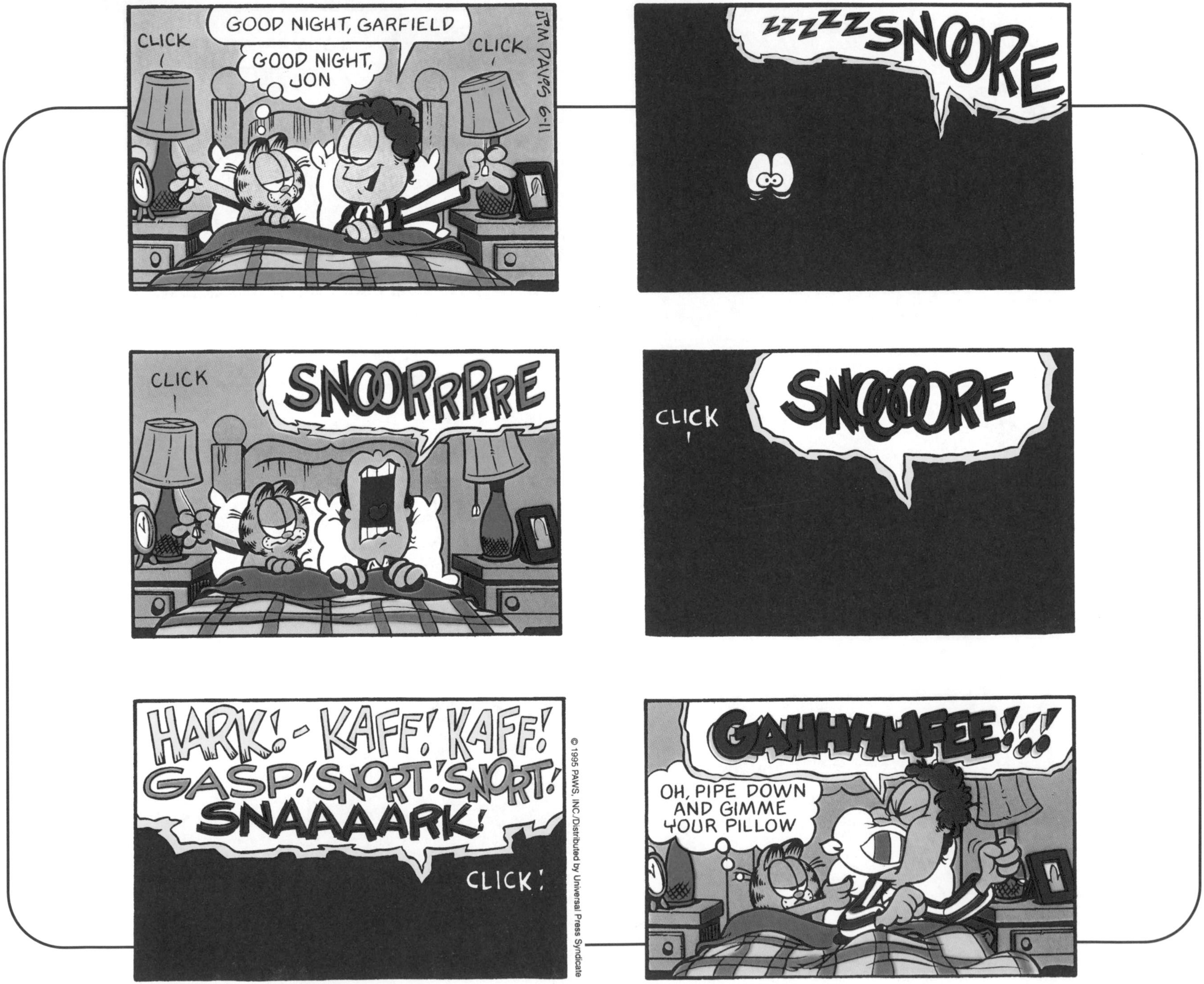
JIM DAVIS 6-11
CLICK
GOOD NIGHT, GARFIELD
GOOD NIGHT, JON
CLICK
ZZZZZSNOORE
CLICK
SNOORRRRRE
CLICK
SNOOOORE
HARK! - KAFF! KAFF!
GASP! SNORT! SNORT!
SNAAAAARK!
CLICK!
GAHHHHFEE!!!
OH, PIPE DOWN AND GIMME YOUR PILLOW

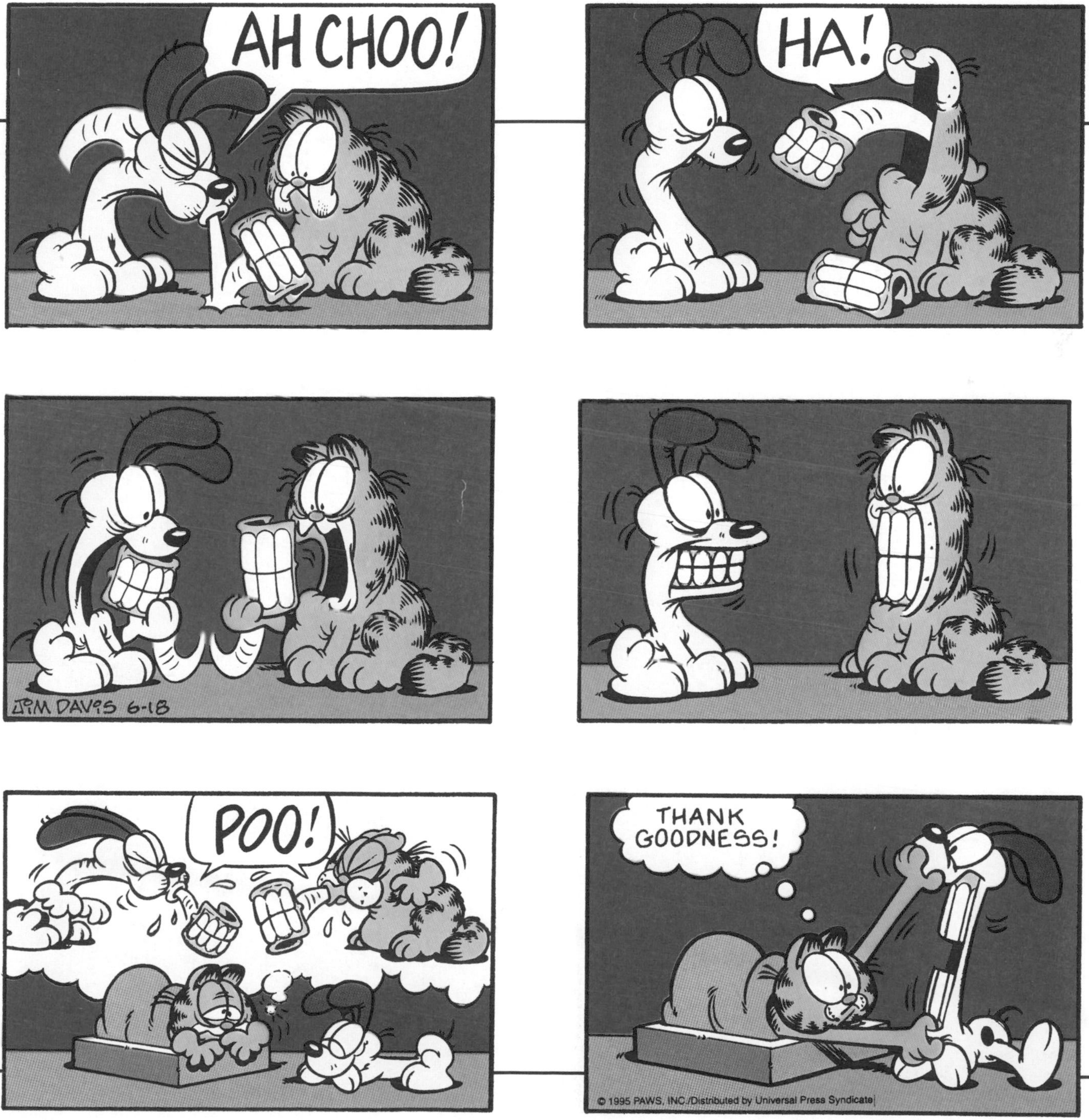
AH CHOO!
HA!
JIM DAVIS 6-18
POO!
THANK GOODNESS!
© 1995 PAWS, INC./Distributed by Universal Press Syndicate

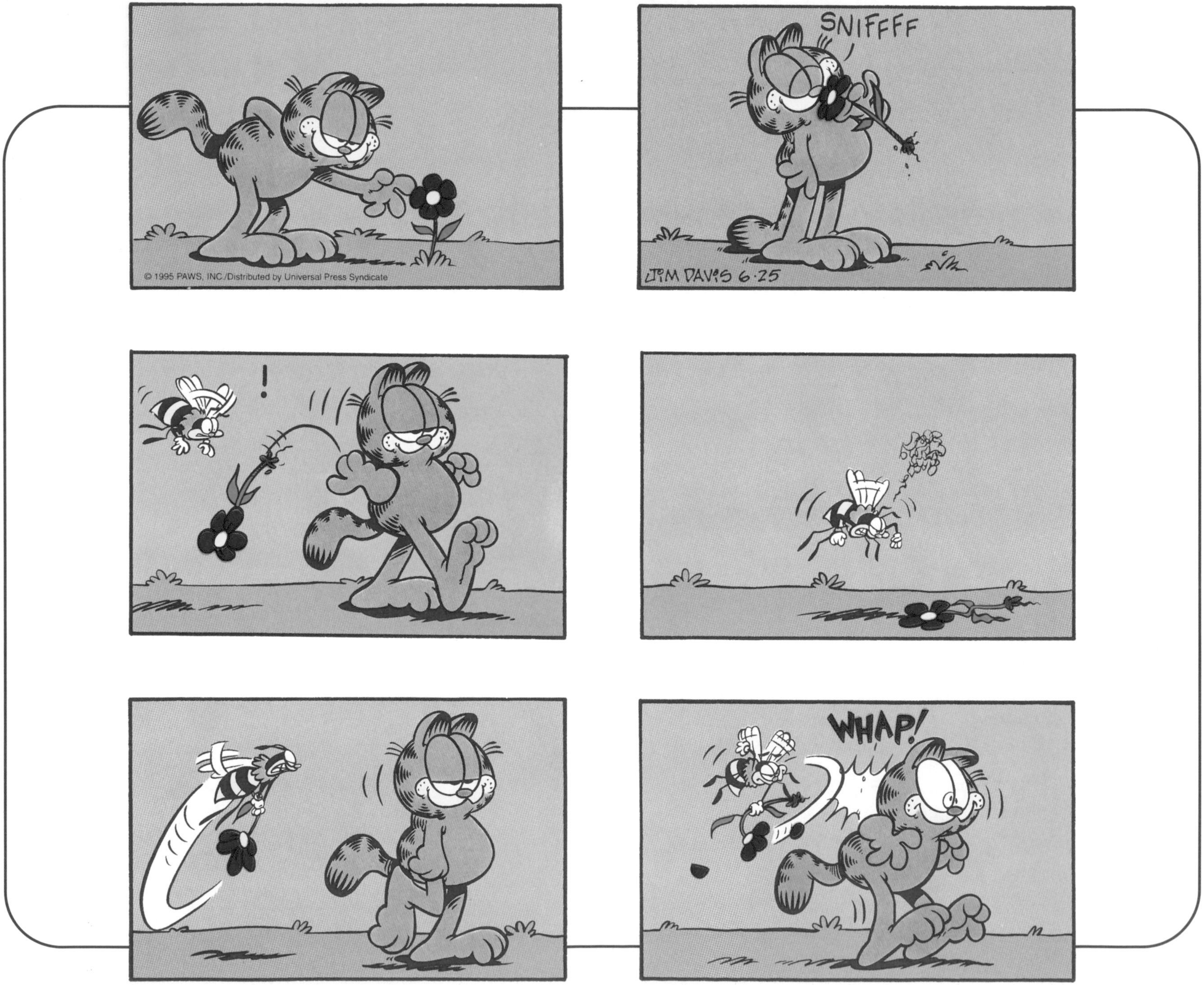
© 1995 PAWS, INC./Distributed by Universal Press Syndicate
SNIFFFF
JIM DAVIS 6·25
!
WHAP!

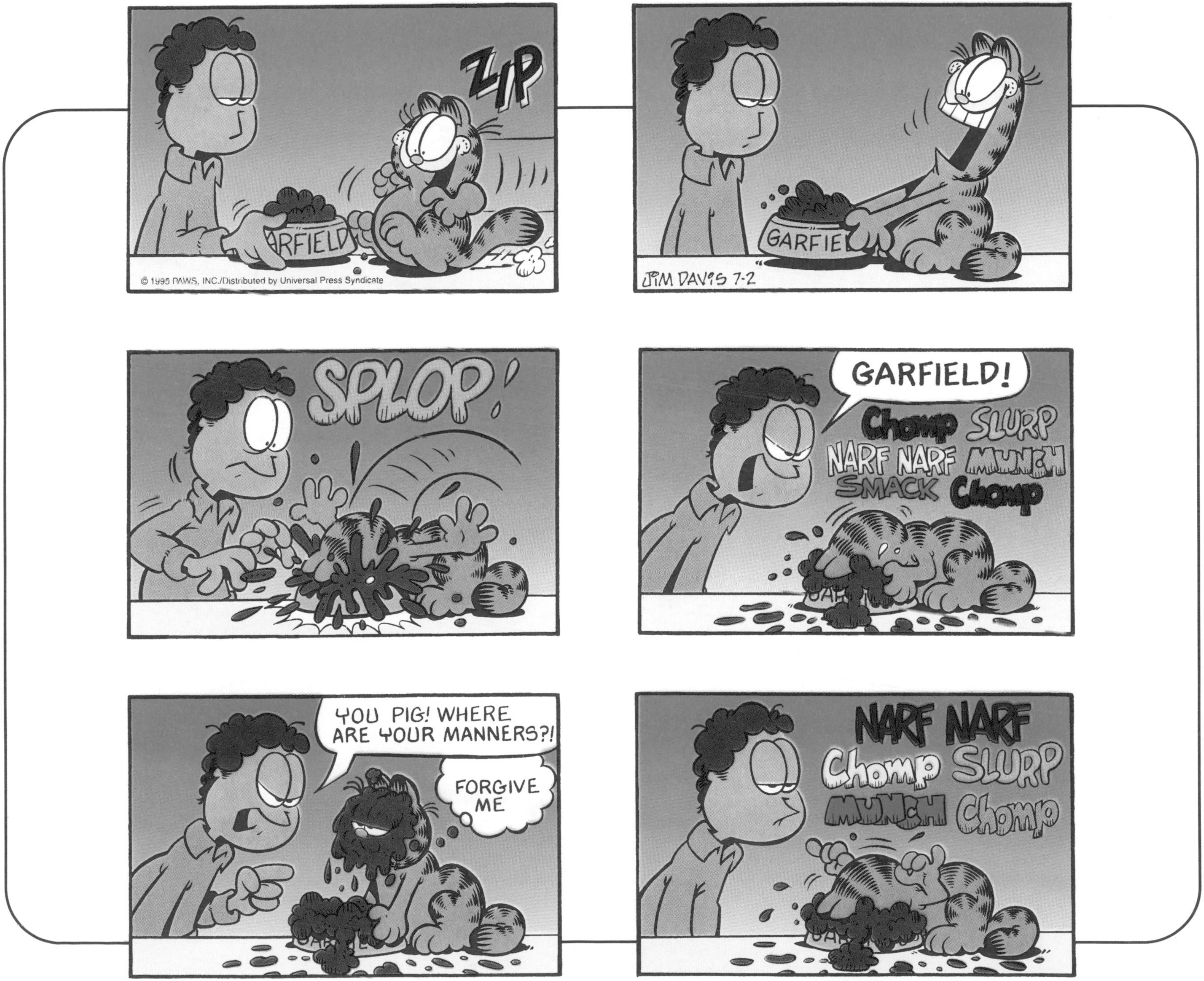

ZIP
© 1995 PAWS, INC./Distributed by Universal Press Syndicate
GARFIELD
JIM DAVIS 7-2
SPLOP!
GARFIELD!
Chomp SLURP
NARF NARF MUNCH
SMACK Chomp
YOU PIG! WHERE ARE YOUR MANNERS?!
FORGIVE ME
NARF NARF
Chomp SLURP
MUNCH Chomp

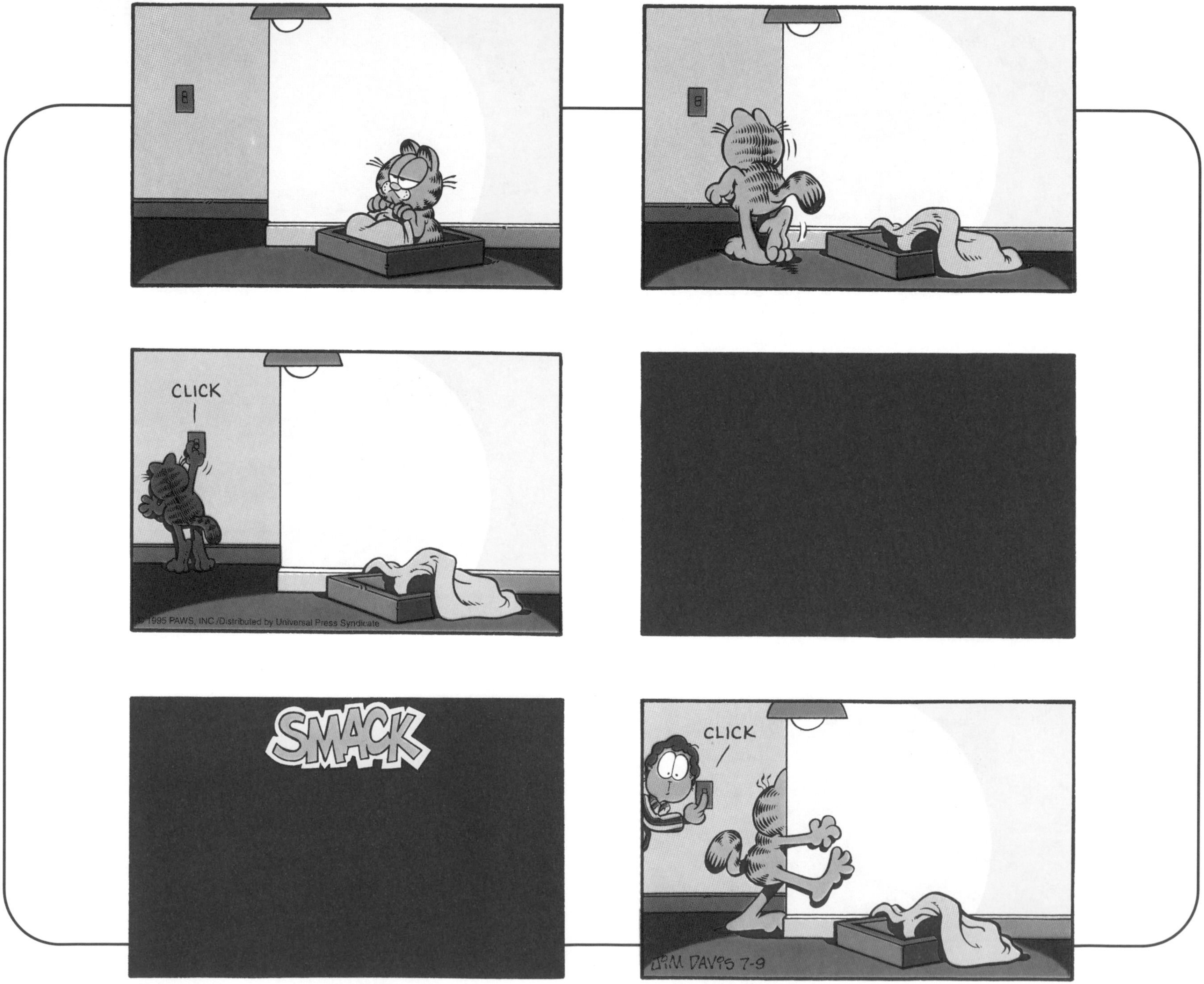
CLICK
© 1995 PAWS, INC./Distributed by Universal Press Syndicate
SMACK
CLICK
JIM DAVIS 7-9

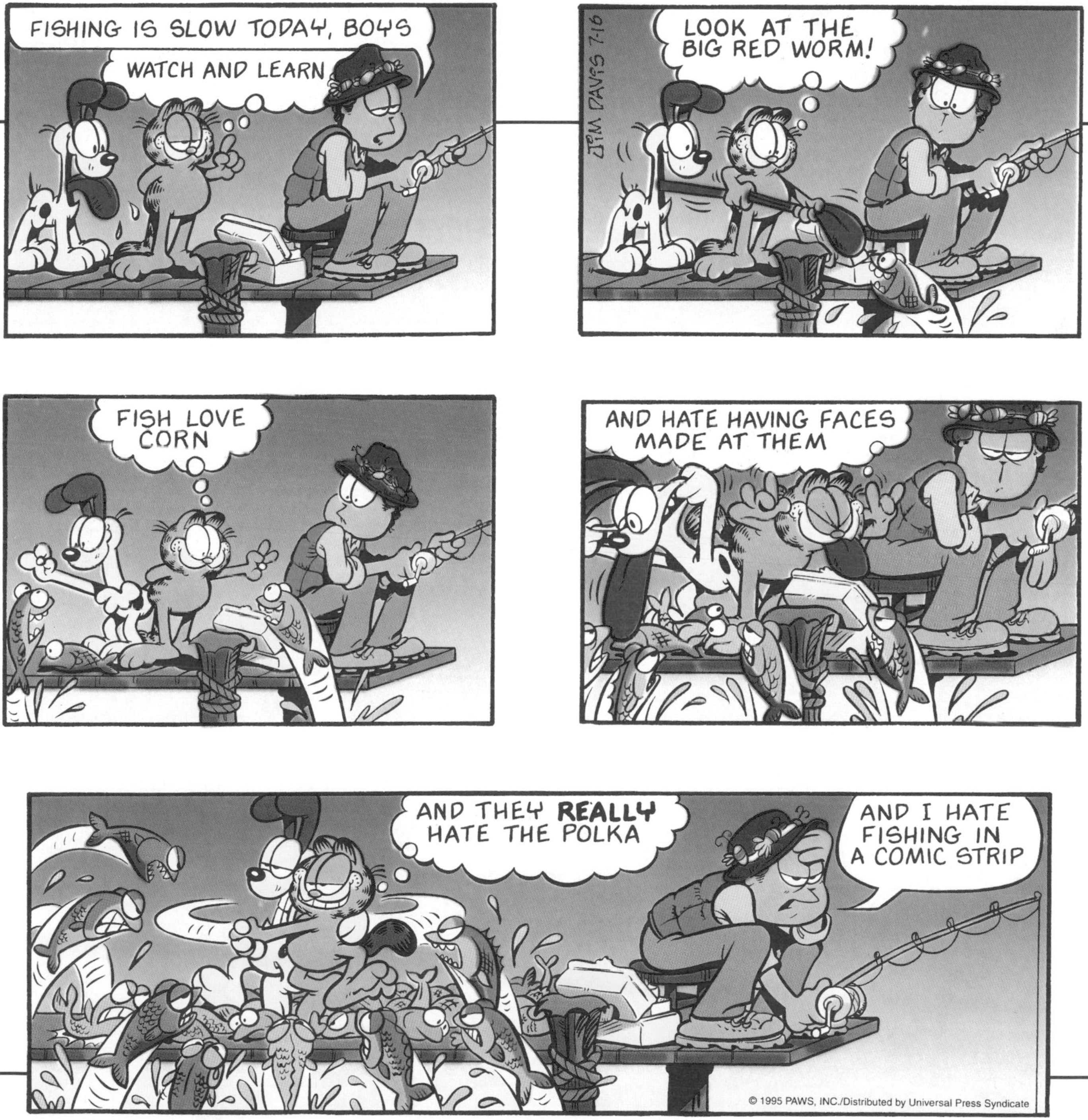
FISHING IS SLOW TODAY, BOYS
WATCH AND LEARN
JIM DAVIS 7-16
LOOK AT THE BIG RED WORM!
FISH LOVE CORN
AND HATE HAVING FACES MADE AT THEM
AND THEY REALLY HATE THE POLKA
AND I HATE FISHING IN A COMIC STRIP
© 1995 PAWS, INC./Distributed by Universal Press Syndicate

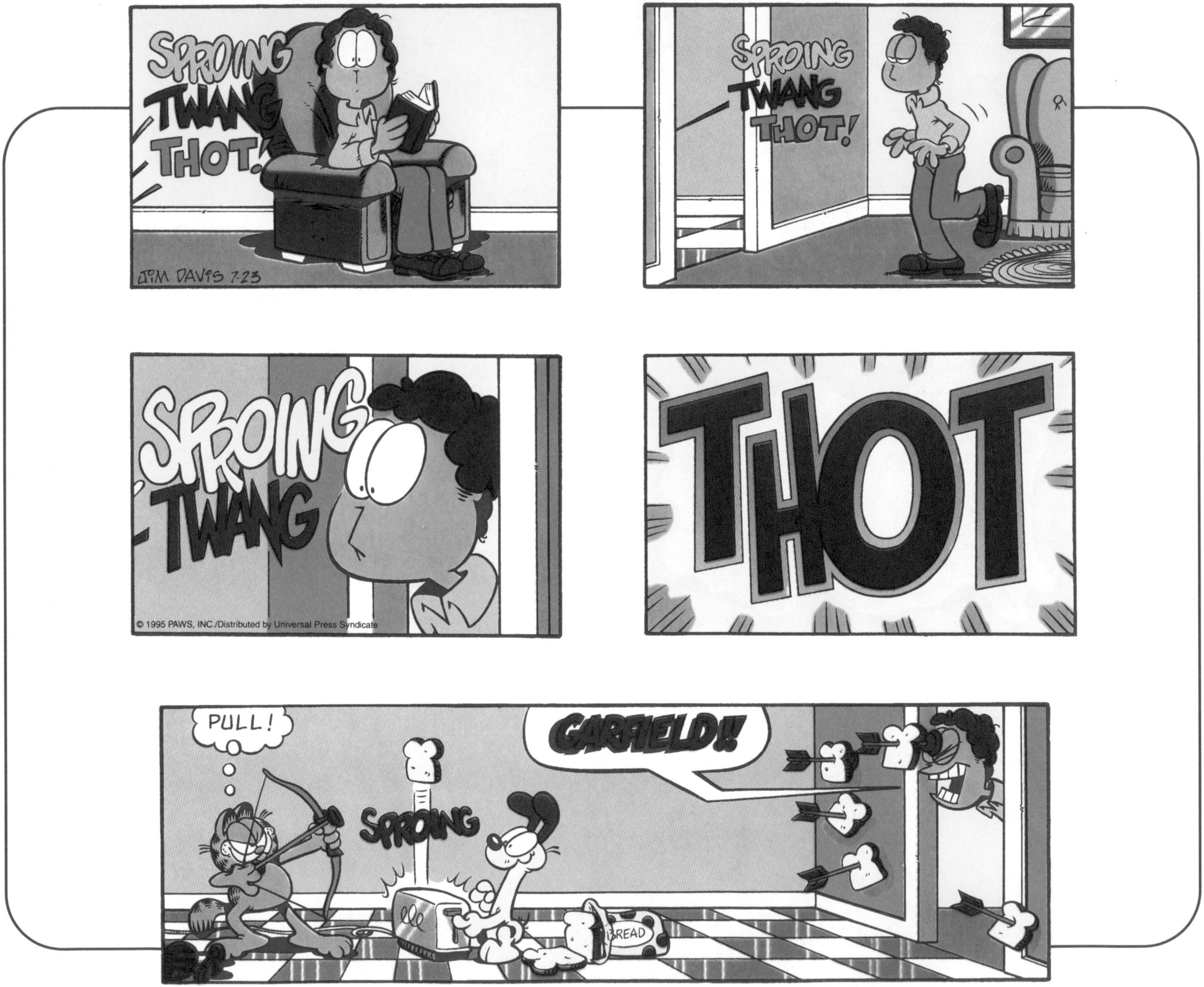
SPROING
TWANG
THOT!
JIM DAVIS 7-23
SPROING
TWANG
THOT!
SPROING
TWANG
© 1995 PAWS, INC./Distributed by Universal Press Syndicate
THOT
PULL!
SPROING
GARFIELD!!
BREAD

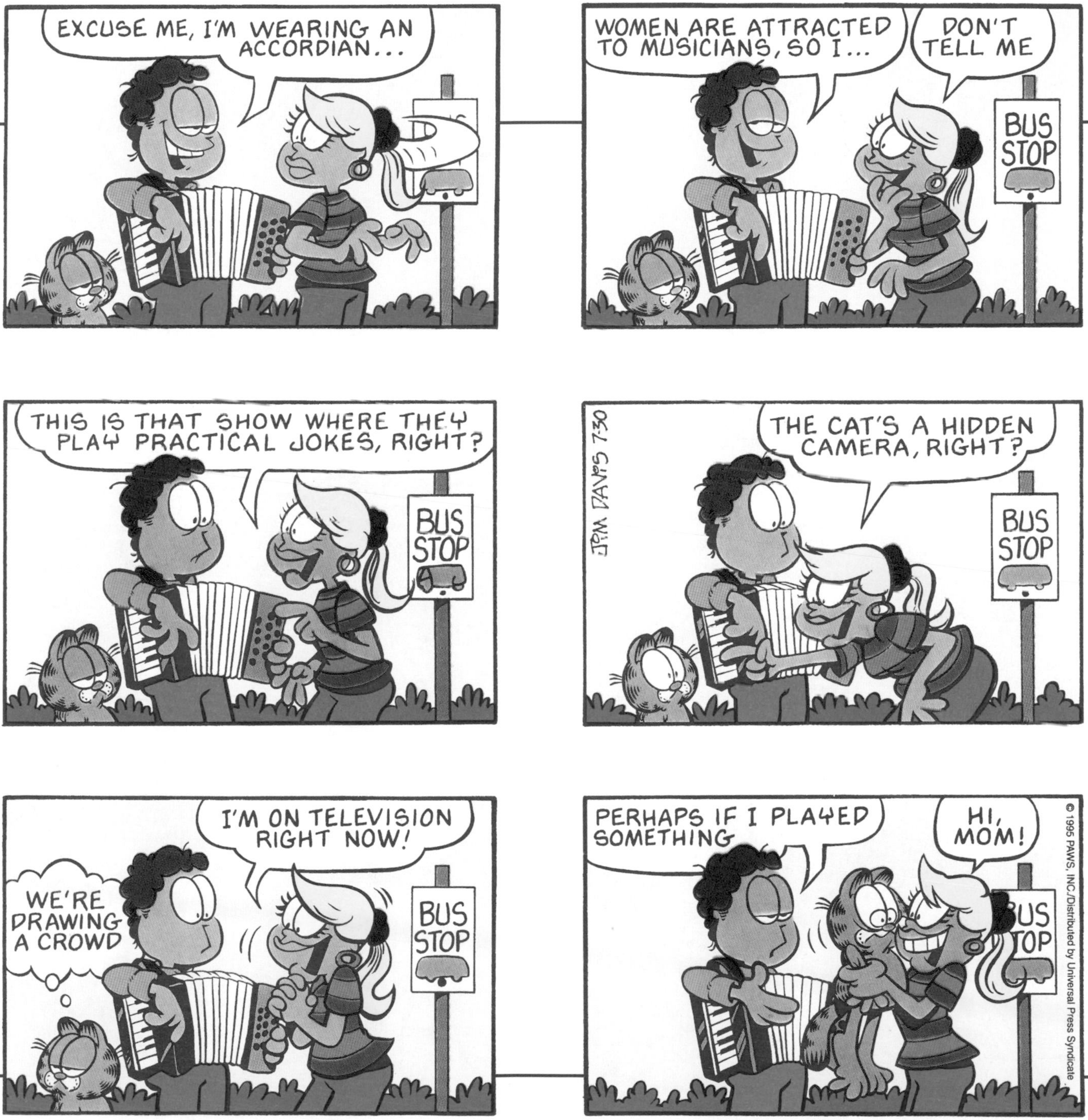
EXCUSE ME, I'M WEARING AN ACCORDIAN...
WOMEN ARE ATTRACTED TO MUSICIANS, SO I...
DON'T TELL ME
BUS STOP
THIS IS THAT SHOW WHERE THEY PLAY PRACTICAL JOKES, RIGHT?
BUS STOP
JPM DAVIS 7-30
THE CAT'S A HIDDEN CAMERA, RIGHT?
BUS STOP
I'M ON TELEVISION RIGHT NOW!
WE'RE DRAWING A CROWD
BUS STOP
PERHAPS IF I PLAYED SOMETHING
HI, MOM!
© 1995 PAWS, INC./Distributed by Universal Press Syndicate

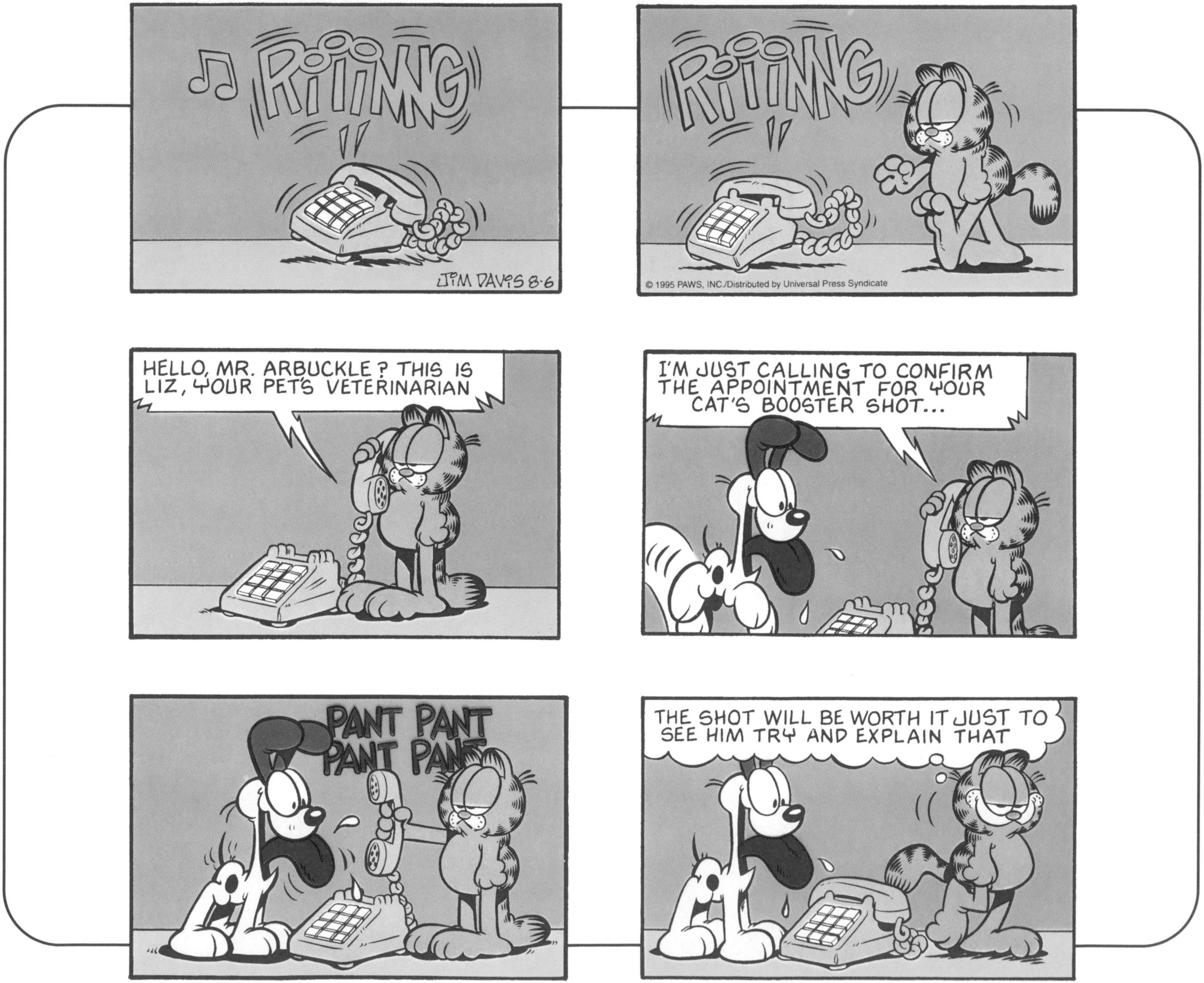
RiiiiNNG
RiiiiNNG
HELLO, MR. ARBUCKLE? THIS IS LIZ, YOUR PET'S VETERINARIAN
I'M JUST CALLING TO CONFIRM THE APPOINTMENT FOR YOUR CAT'S BOOSTER SHOT...
PANT PANT PANT PANT
THE SHOT WILL BE WORTH IT JUST TO SEE HIM TRY AND EXPLAIN THAT
JIM DAVIS 8-6
© 1995 PAWS, INC./Distributed by Universal Press Syndicate

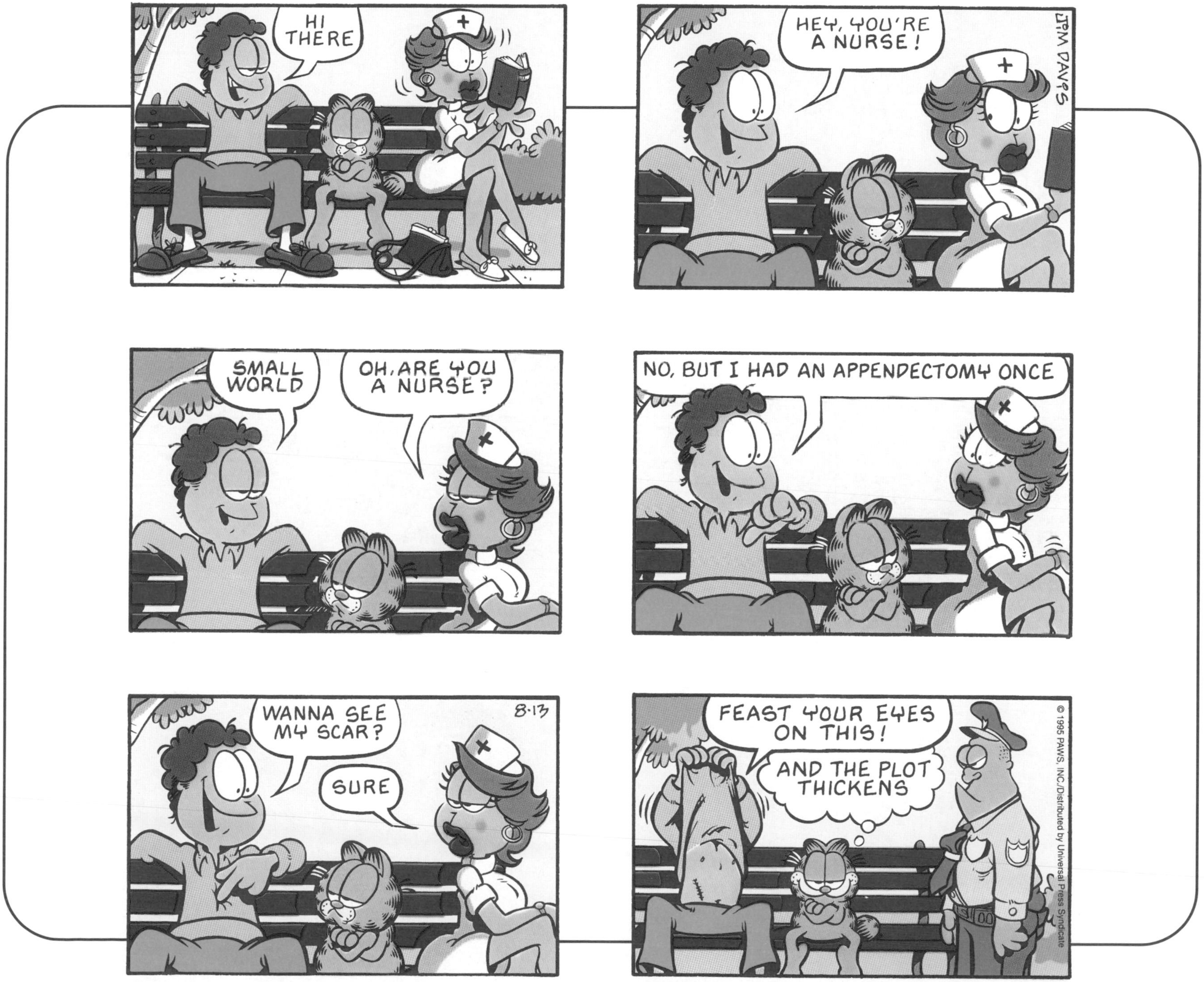
HI THERE
JIM DAVIS
HEY, YOU'RE A NURSE!
SMALL WORLD
OH, ARE YOU A NURSE?
NO, BUT I HAD AN APPENDECTOMY ONCE
WANNA SEE MY SCAR?
8·13
SURE
FEAST YOUR EYES ON THIS!
AND THE PLOT THICKENS
© 1995 PAWS, INC./Distributed by Universal Press Syndicate

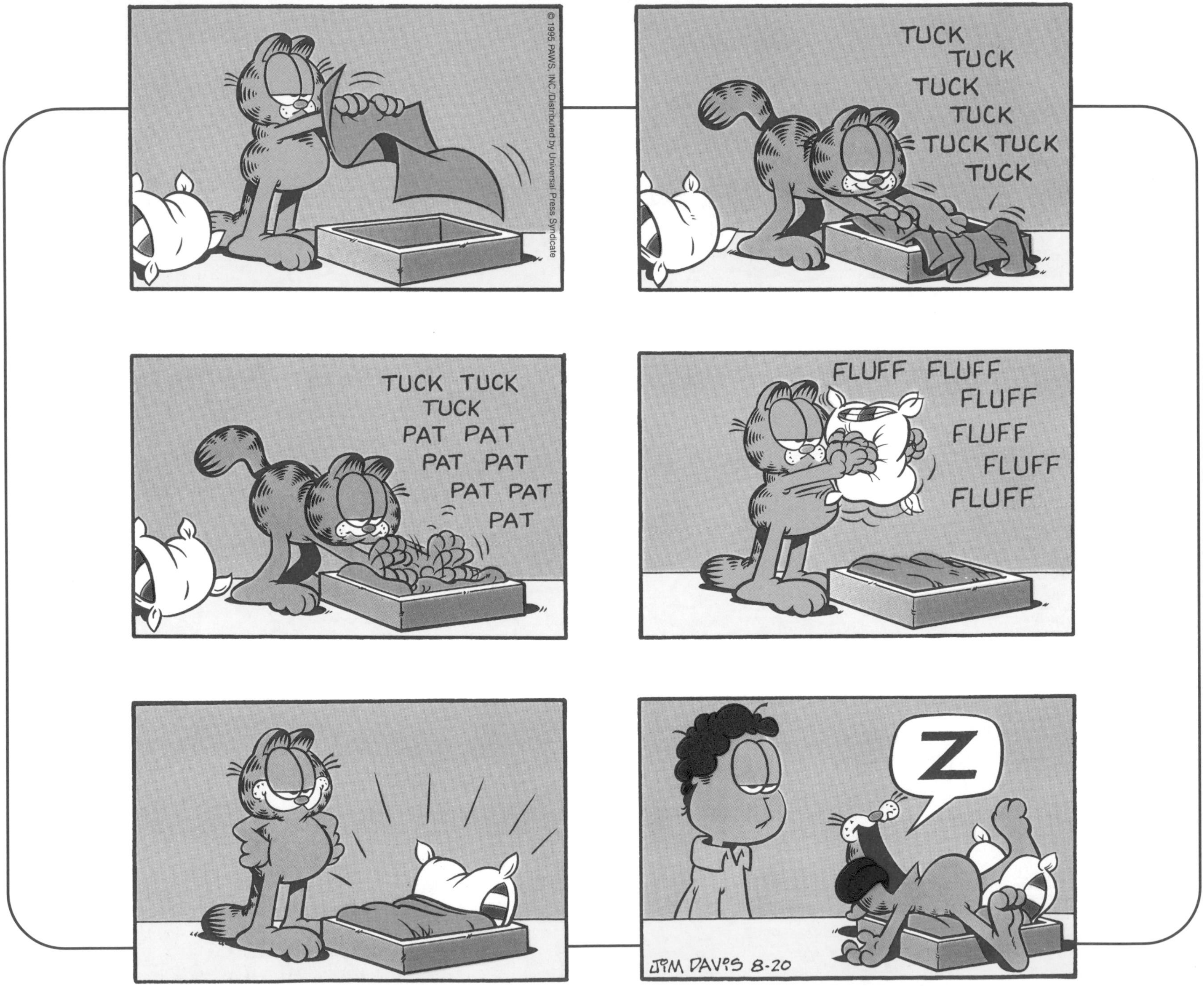
© 1995 PAWS, INC./Distributed by Universal Press Syndicate
TUCK TUCK TUCK TUCK TUCK TUCK TUCK
TUCK TUCK TUCK PAT PAT PAT PAT PAT PAT PAT
FLUFF FLUFF FLUFF FLUFF FLUFF FLUFF
Z
JIM DAVIS 8-20

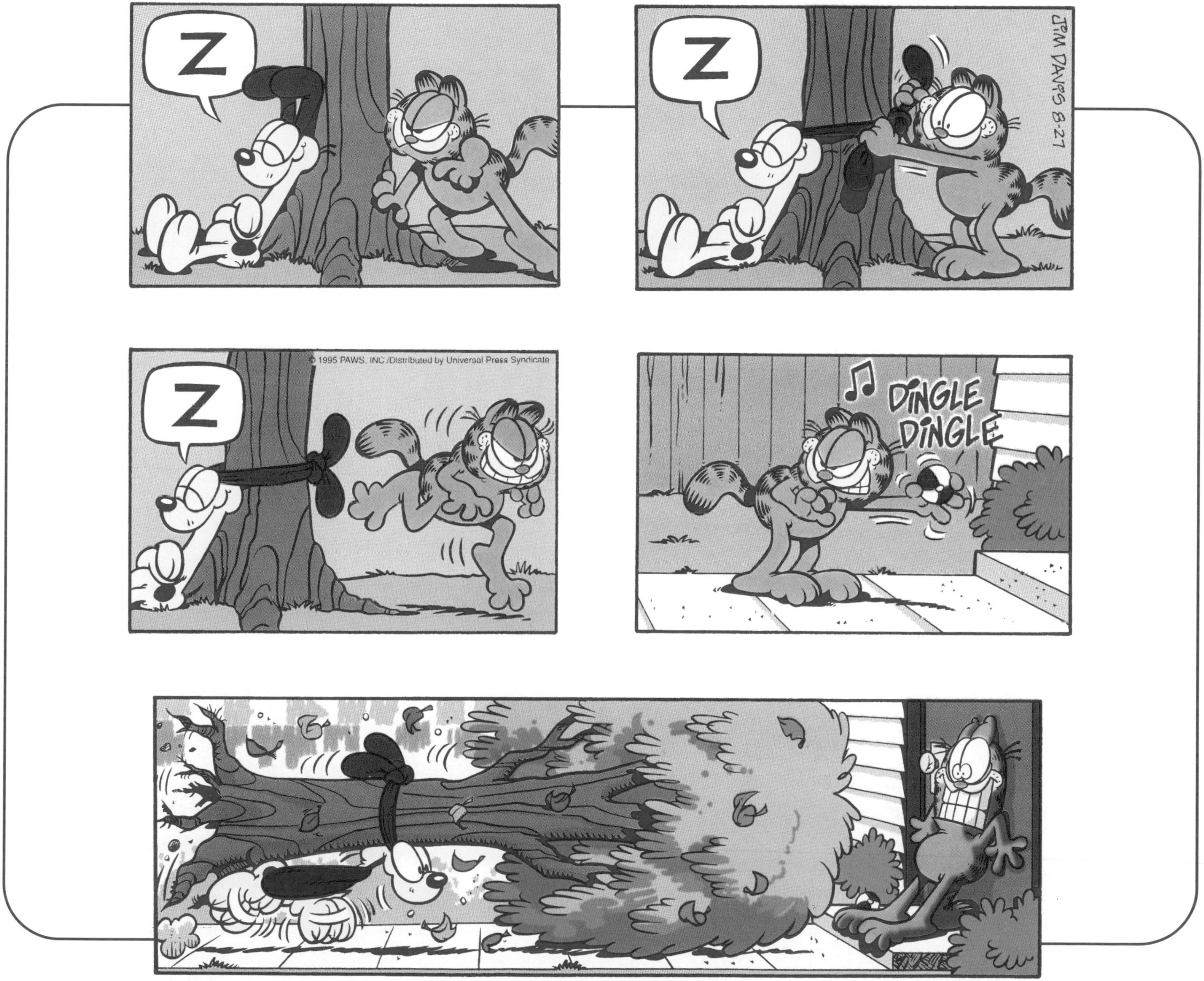
Z
JIM DAVIS 8-27
Z
© 1995 PAWS, INC./Distributed by Universal Press Syndicate
Z
DINGLE
DINGLE

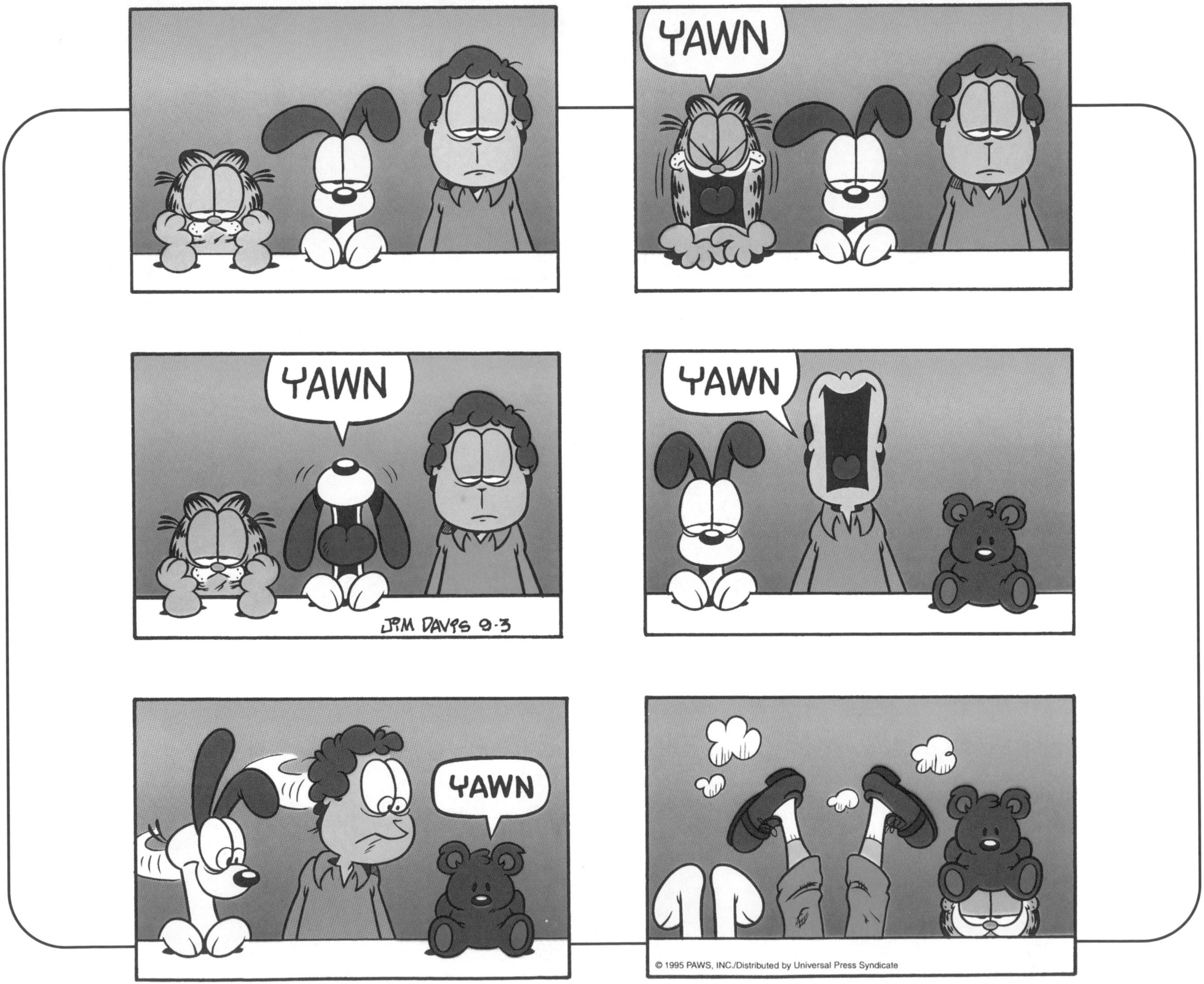
YAWN
YAWN
JIM DAVIS 9-3
YAWN
YAWN

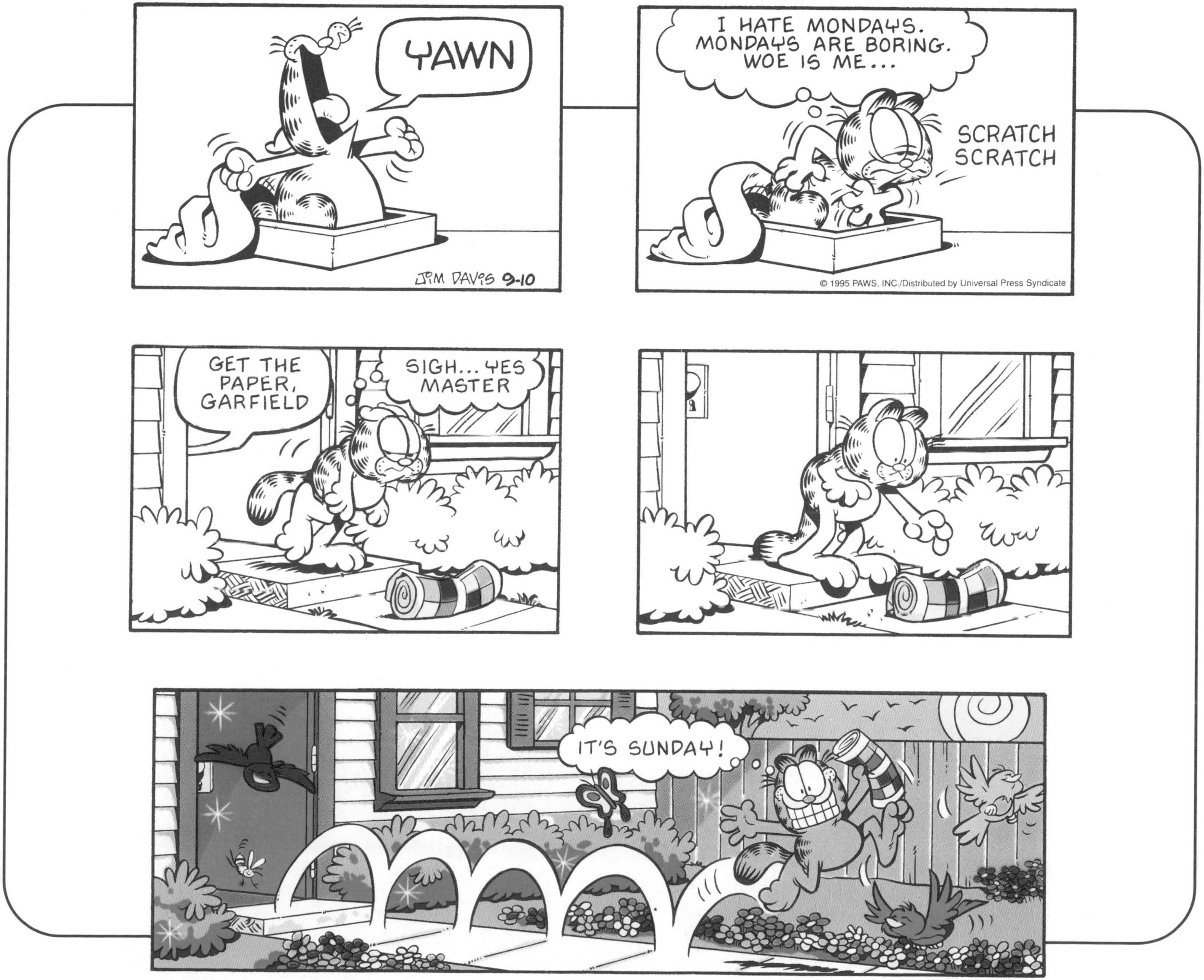
YAWN
JIM DAVIS 9-10
I HATE MONDAYS. MONDAYS ARE BORING. WOE IS ME...
SCRATCH SCRATCH
© 1995 PAWS, INC./Distributed by Universal Press Syndicate
GET THE PAPER, GARFIELD
SIGH... YES MASTER
IT'S SUNDAY!

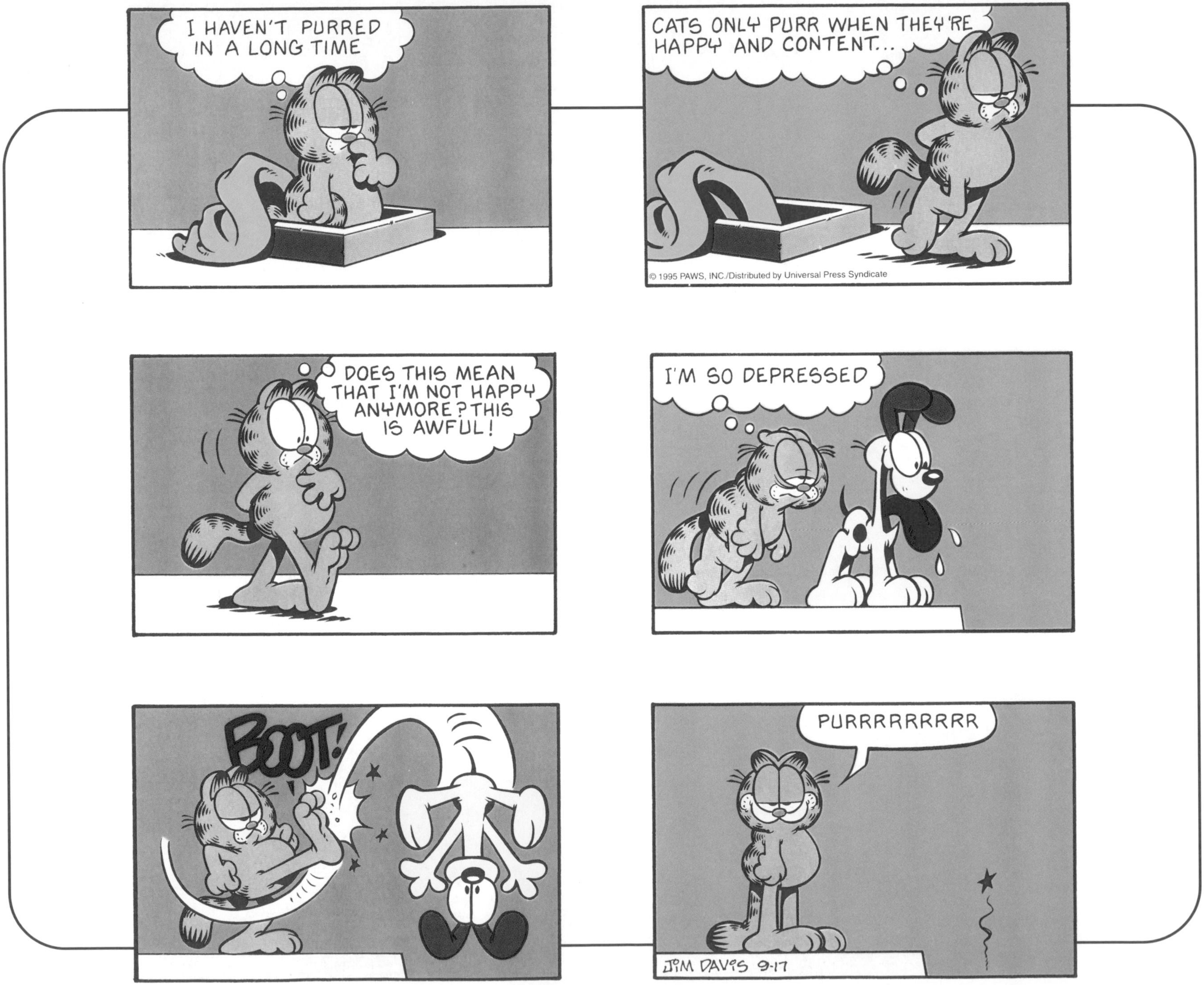
I HAVEN'T PURRED IN A LONG TIME
CATS ONLY PURR WHEN THEY'RE HAPPY AND CONTENT...
© 1995 PAWS, INC./Distributed by Universal Press Syndicate
DOES THIS MEAN THAT I'M NOT HAPPY ANYMORE? THIS IS AWFUL!
I'M SO DEPRESSED
BOOT!
PURRRRRRRRRR
JIM DAVIS 9-17

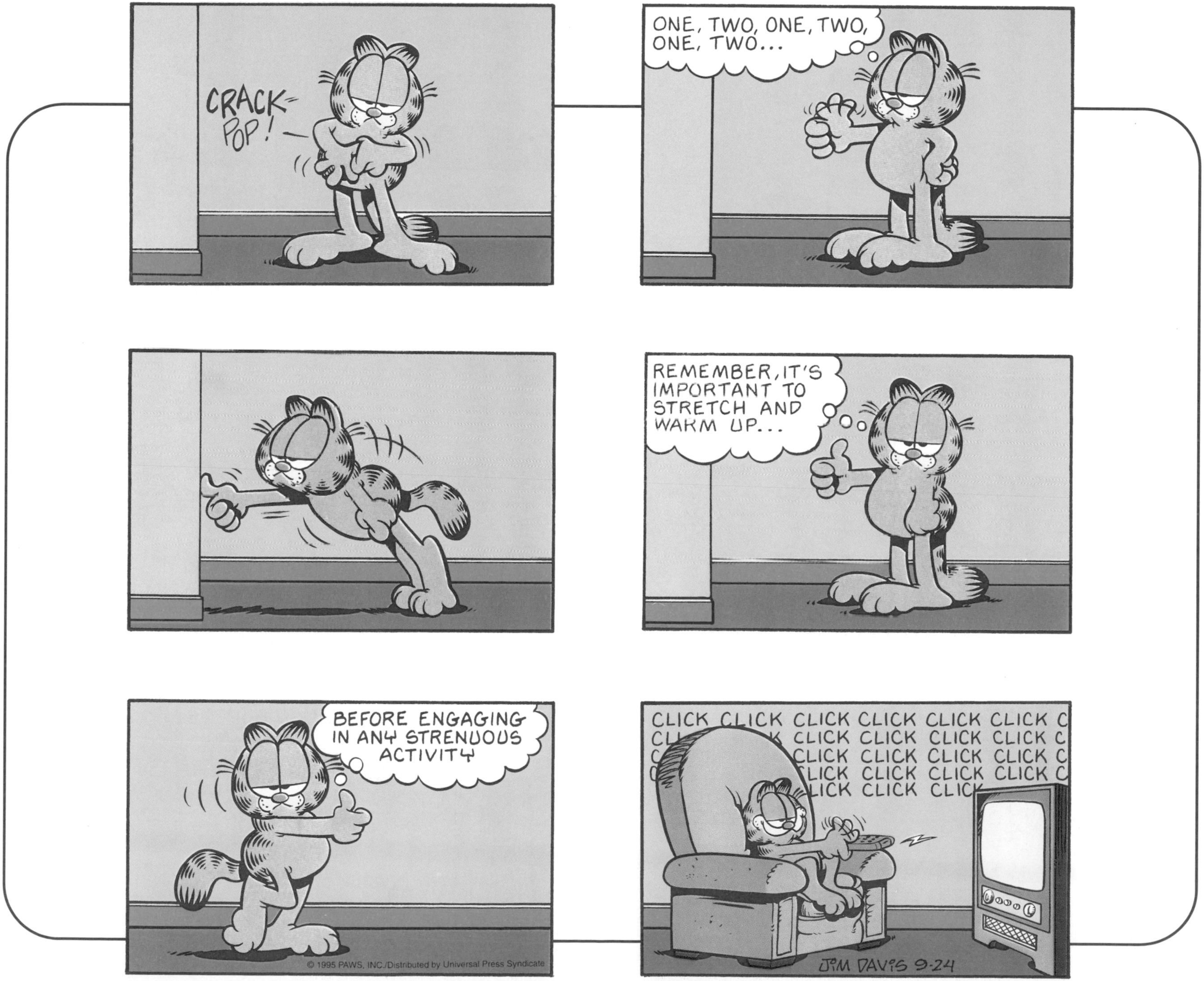

CRACK POP!
ONE, TWO, ONE, TWO, ONE, TWO...
REMEMBER, IT'S IMPORTANT TO STRETCH AND WARM UP...
BEFORE ENGAGING IN ANY STRENUOUS ACTIVITY
CLICK CLICK CLICK CLICK CLICK CLICK
© 1995 PAWS, INC./Distributed by Universal Press Syndicate
JIM DAVIS 9-24

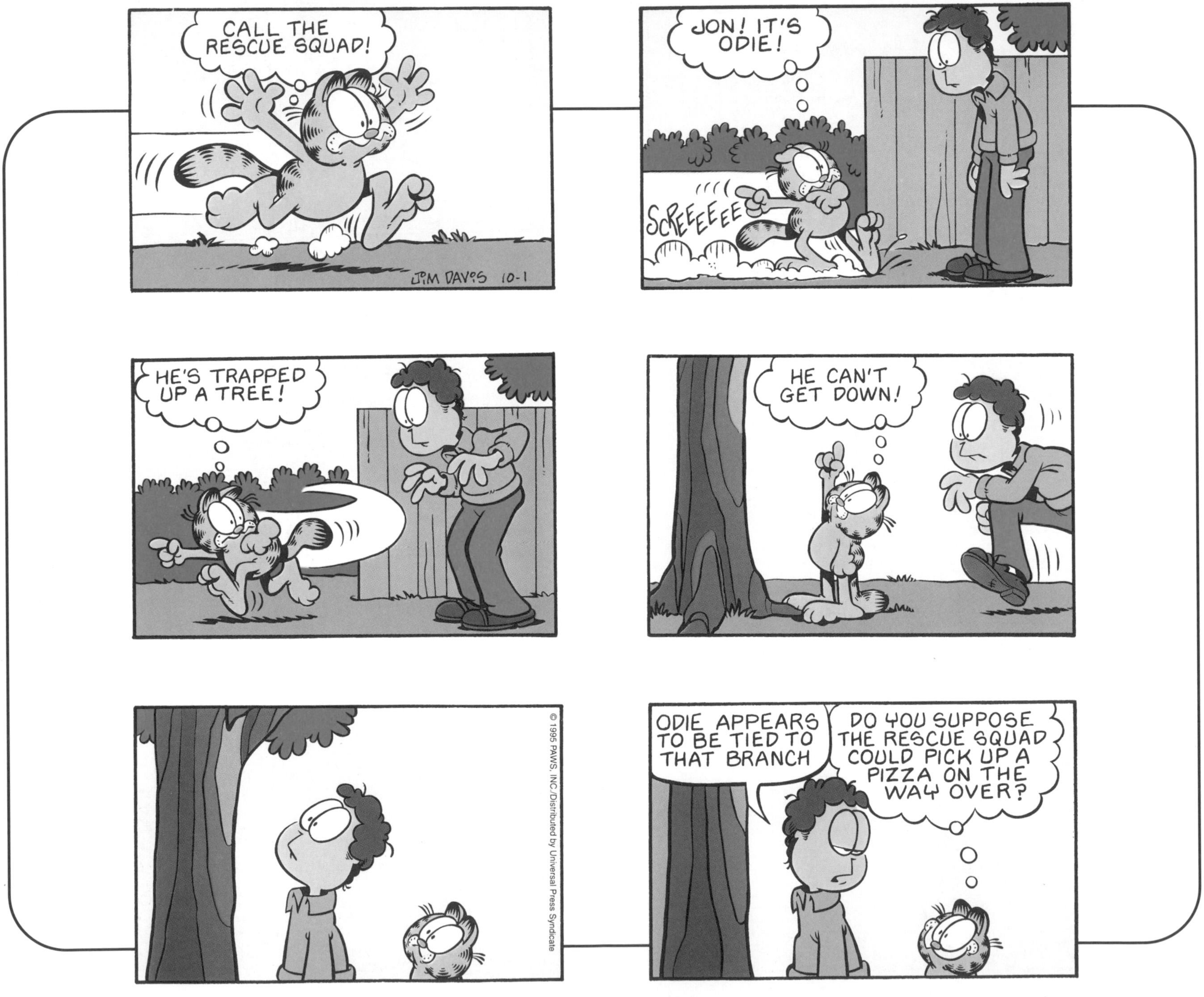
CALL THE RESCUE SQUAD!
JIM DAVIS 10-1
JON! IT'S ODIE!
SCREEEEEEE
HE'S TRAPPED UP A TREE!
HE CAN'T GET DOWN!
© 1995 PAWS, INC./Distributed by Universal Press Syndicate
ODIE APPEARS TO BE TIED TO THAT BRANCH
DO YOU SUPPOSE THE RESCUE SQUAD COULD PICK UP A PIZZA ON THE WAY OVER?

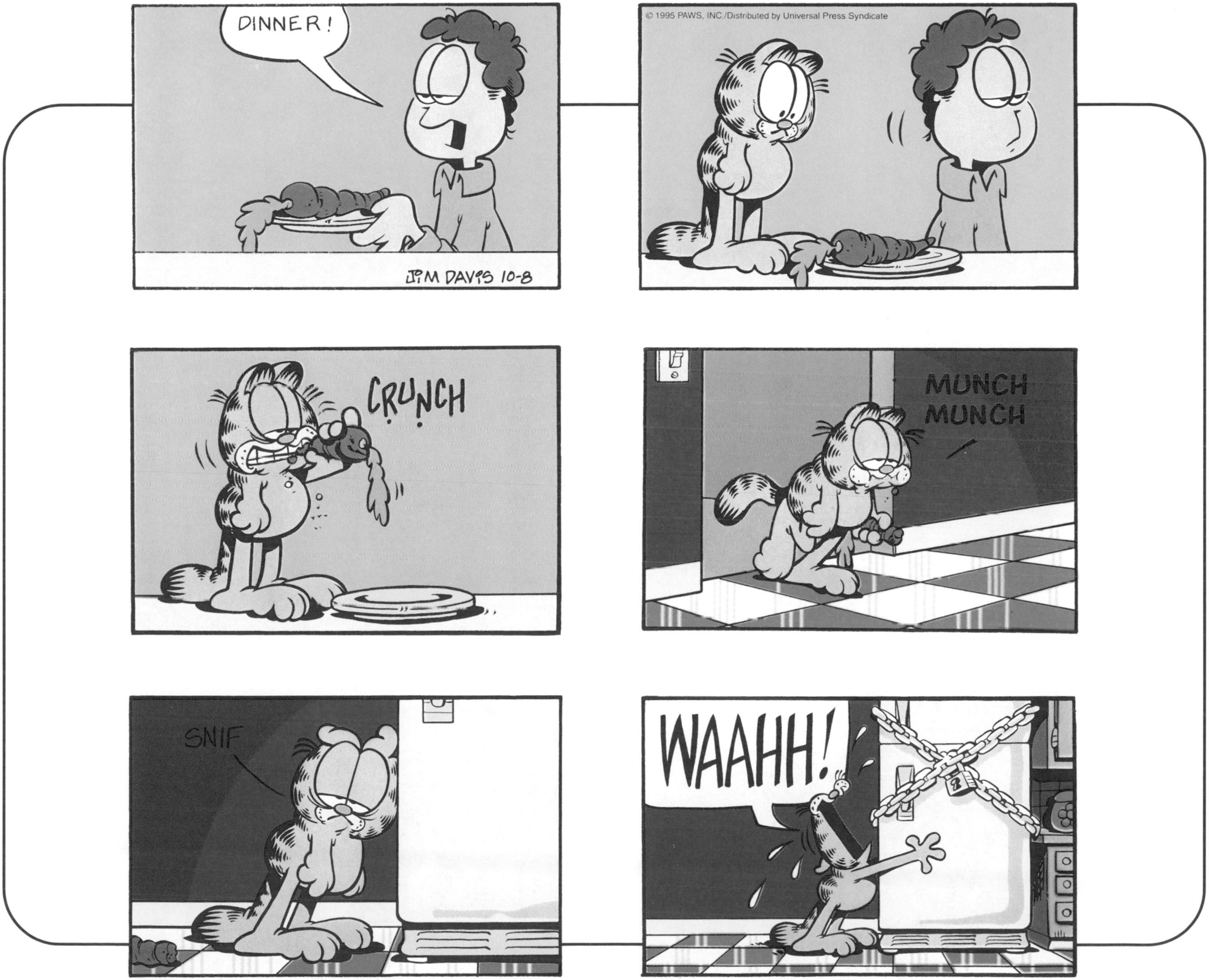
DINNER!
JIM DAVIS 10-8
© 1995 PAWS, INC./Distributed by Universal Press Syndicate
CRUNCH
MUNCH
MUNCH
SNIF
WAAHH!

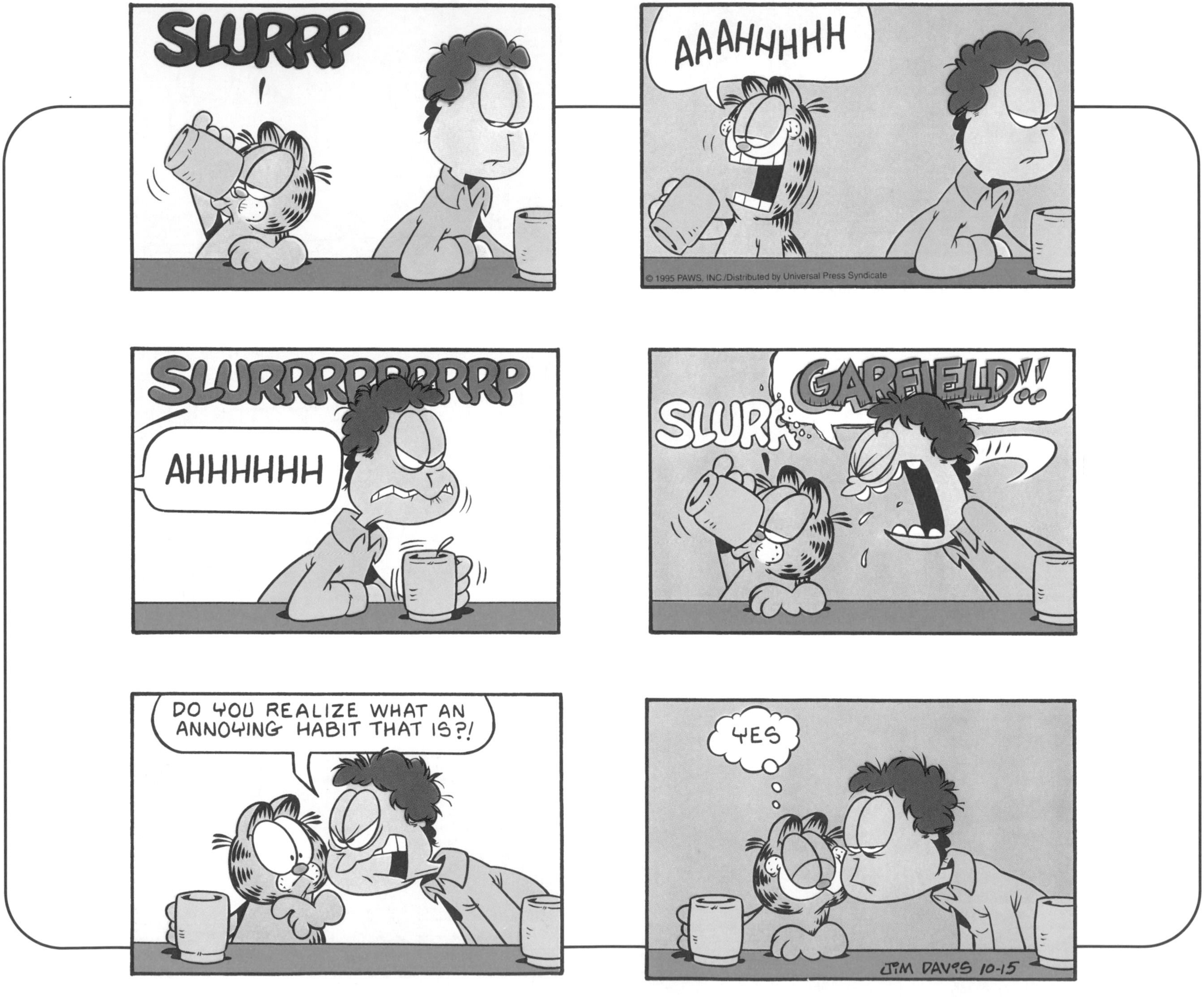
SLURRP
AAAHHHHH
© 1995 PAWS, INC./Distributed by Universal Press Syndicate
SLURRRRRRRRP
AHHHHHH
SLURR
GARFIELD!!
DO YOU REALIZE WHAT AN ANNOYING HABIT THAT IS?!
YES
JIM DAVIS 10-15

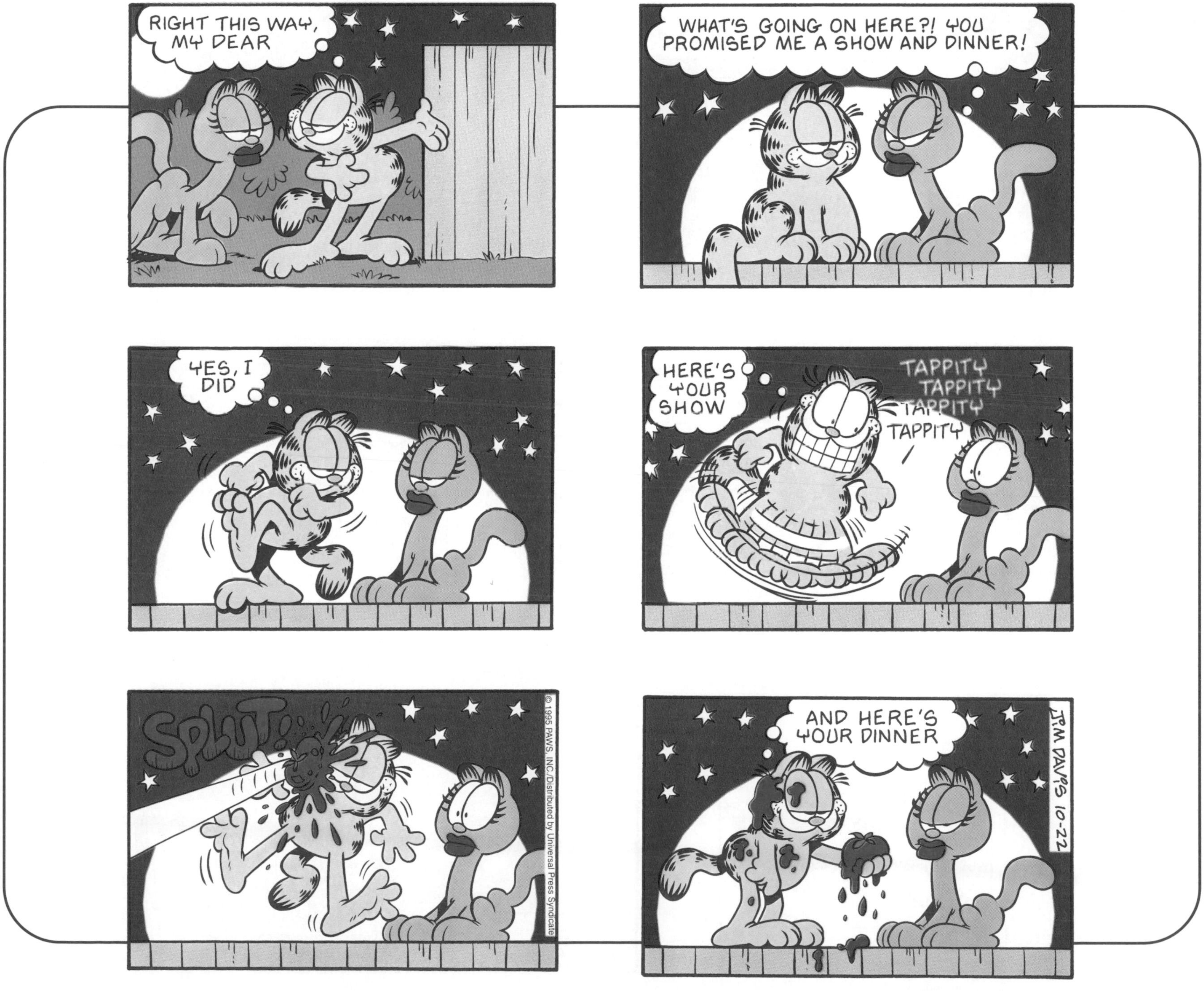
RIGHT THIS WAY, MY DEAR
WHAT'S GOING ON HERE?! YOU PROMISED ME A SHOW AND DINNER!
YES, I DID
HERE'S YOUR SHOW
TAPPITY TAPPITY TAPPITY TAPPITY TAPPITY
SPLUT!
© 1995 PAWS, INC./Distributed by Universal Press Syndicate
AND HERE'S YOUR DINNER
JIM DAVIS 10-22

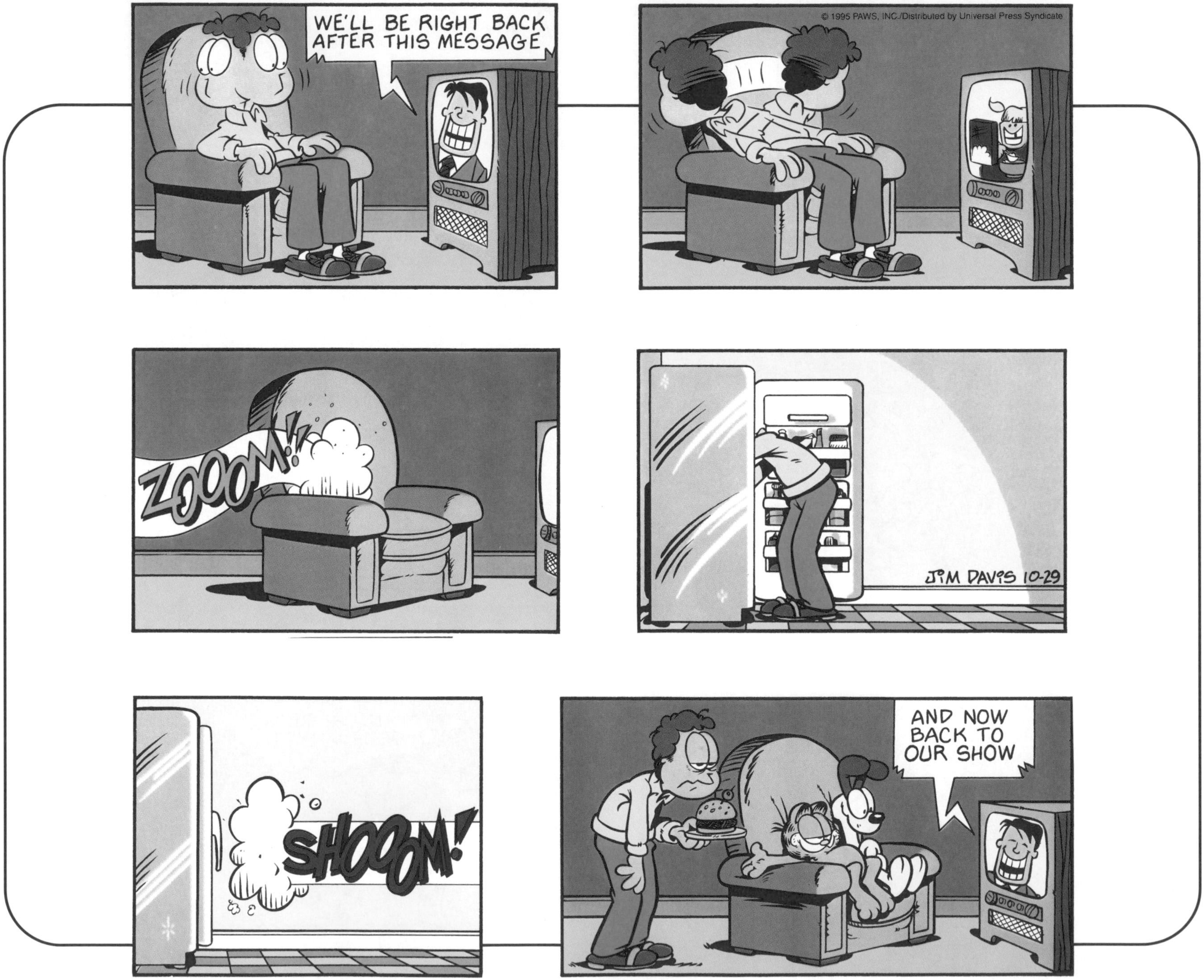
WE'LL BE RIGHT BACK AFTER THIS MESSAGE
© 1995 PAWS, INC./Distributed by Universal Press Syndicate
ZOOOM!!
JIM DAVIS 10-29
SHOOOM!
AND NOW BACK TO OUR SHOW

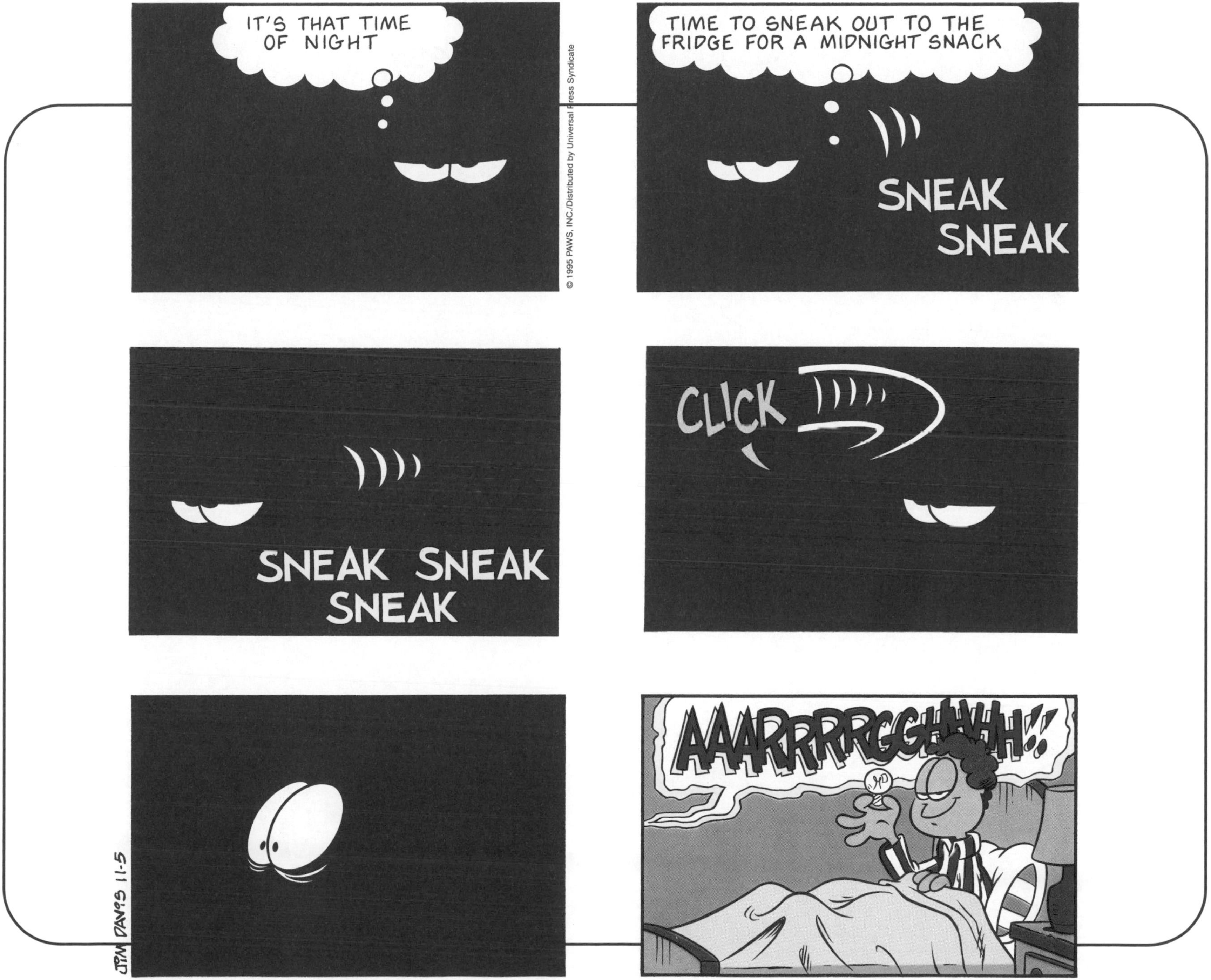
IT'S THAT TIME OF NIGHT
TIME TO SNEAK OUT TO THE FRIDGE FOR A MIDNIGHT SNACK
SNEAK SNEAK
SNEAK SNEAK SNEAK SNEAK
CLICK
AAARRRRRGGHHHH!!
JIM DAVIS 11-5

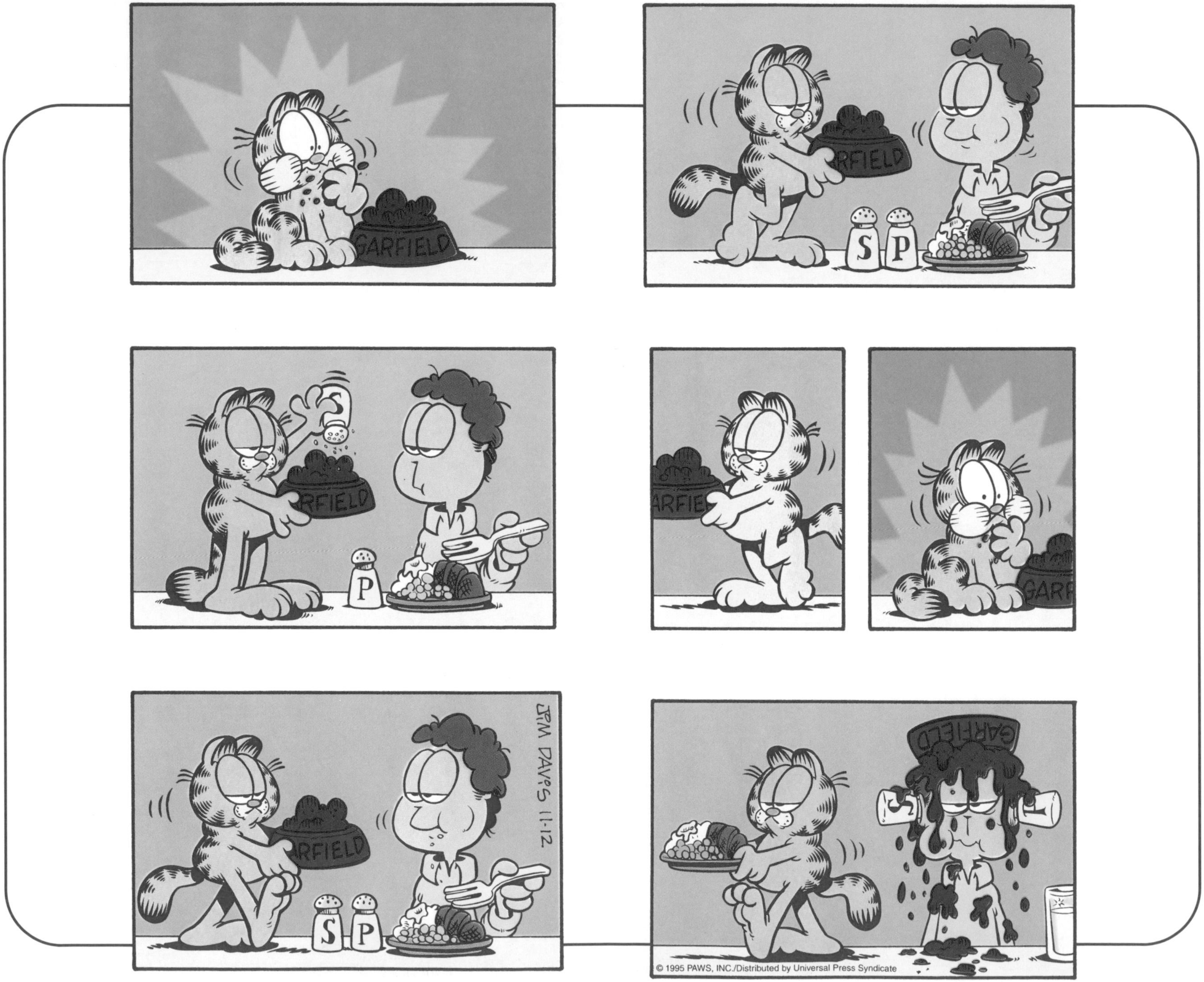
GARFIELD
S P
JIM DAVIS 11-12

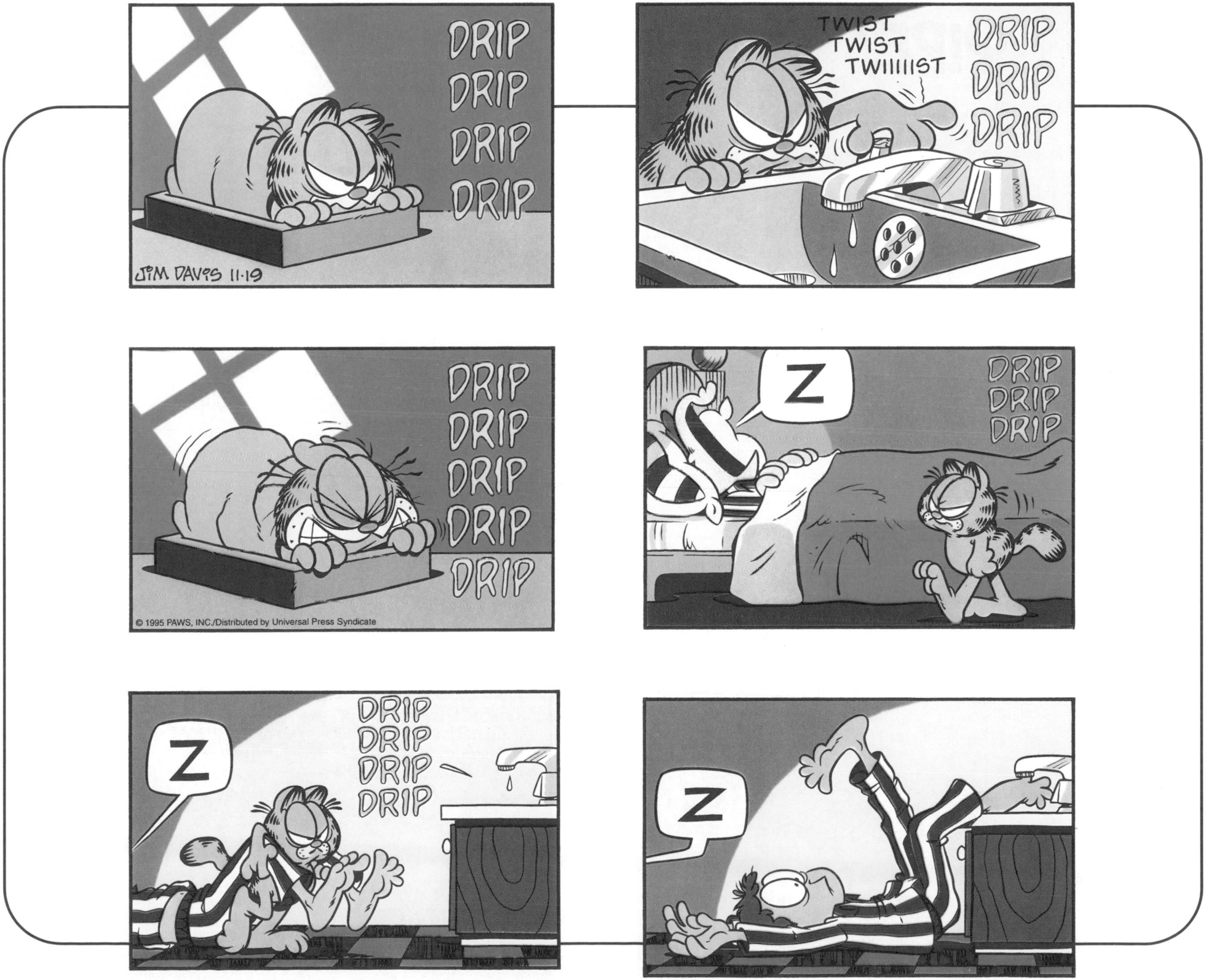
DRIP
DRIP
DRIP
DRIP
JIM DAVIS 11-19
TWIST
TWIST
TWIIIIIST
DRIP
DRIP
DRIP
DRIP
DRIP
DRIP
DRIP
DRIP
Z
DRIP
DRIP
DRIP
Z
DRIP
DRIP
DRIP
DRIP
Z

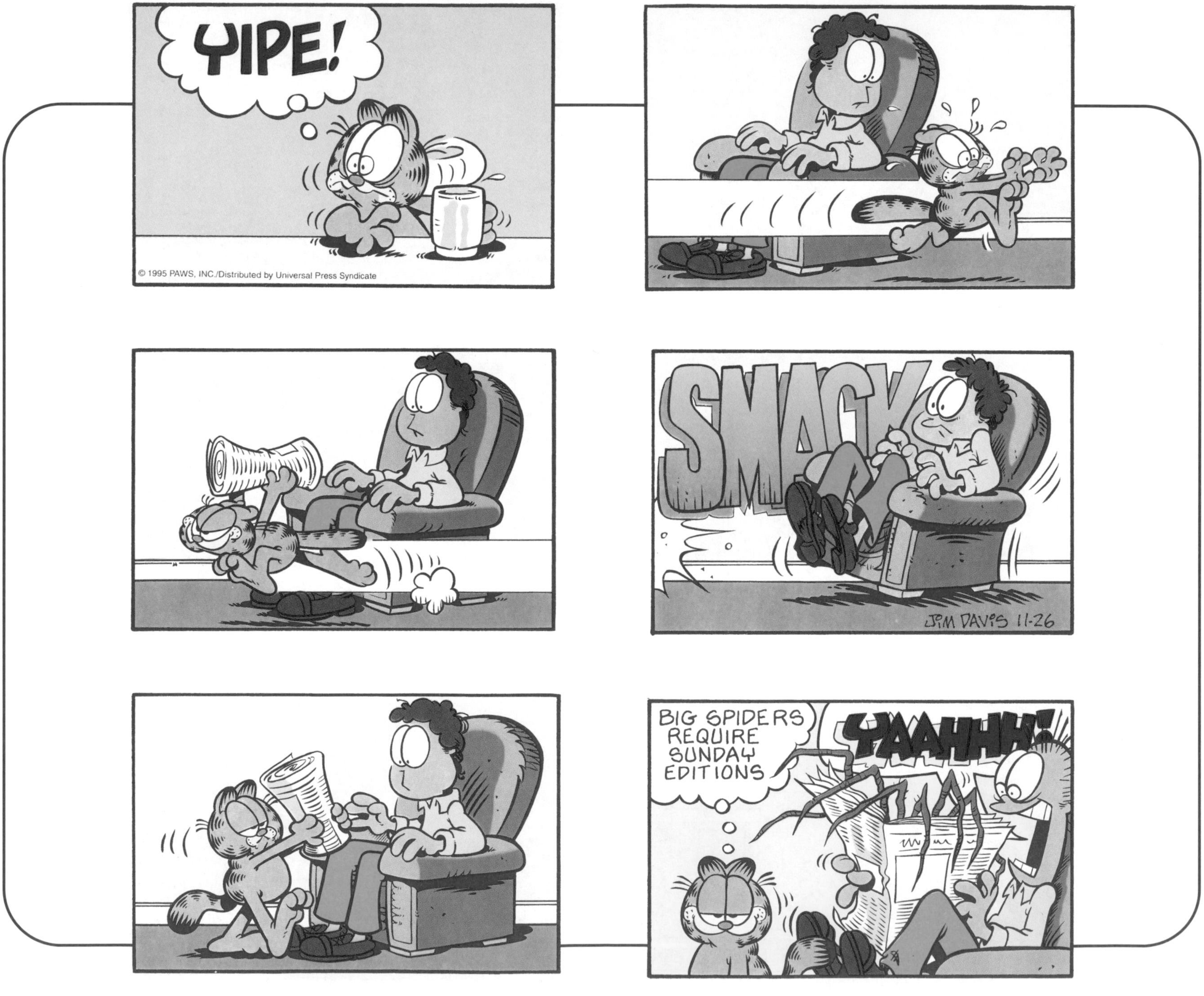
YIPE!
© 1995 PAWS, INC./Distributed by Universal Press Syndicate
SMACK
JIM DAVIS 11-26
BIG SPIDERS REQUIRE SUNDAY EDITIONS
YAAHHH!

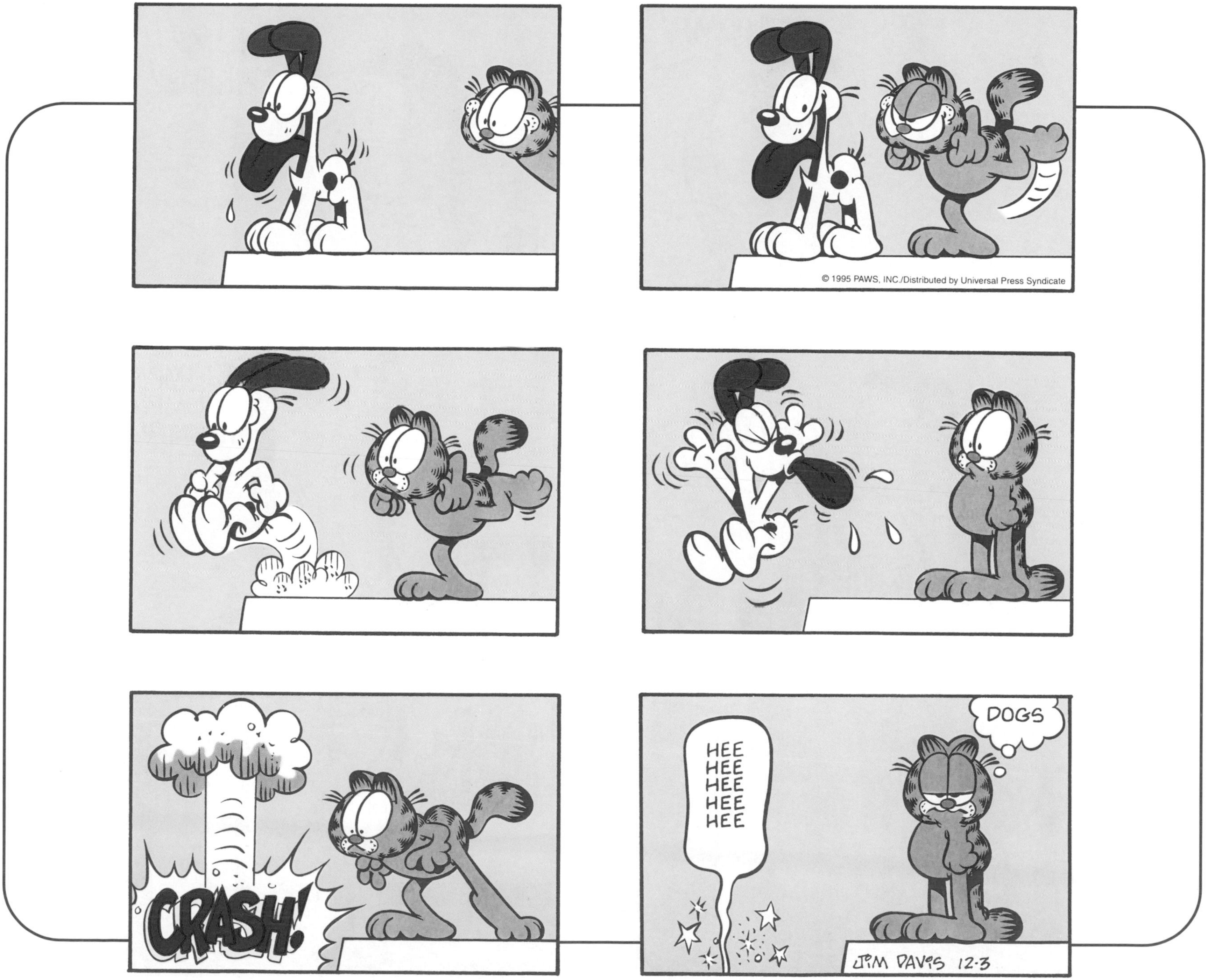
© 1995 PAWS, INC./Distributed by Universal Press Syndicate
CRASH!
HEE HEE HEE HEE HEE
DOGS
JIM DAVIS 12-3

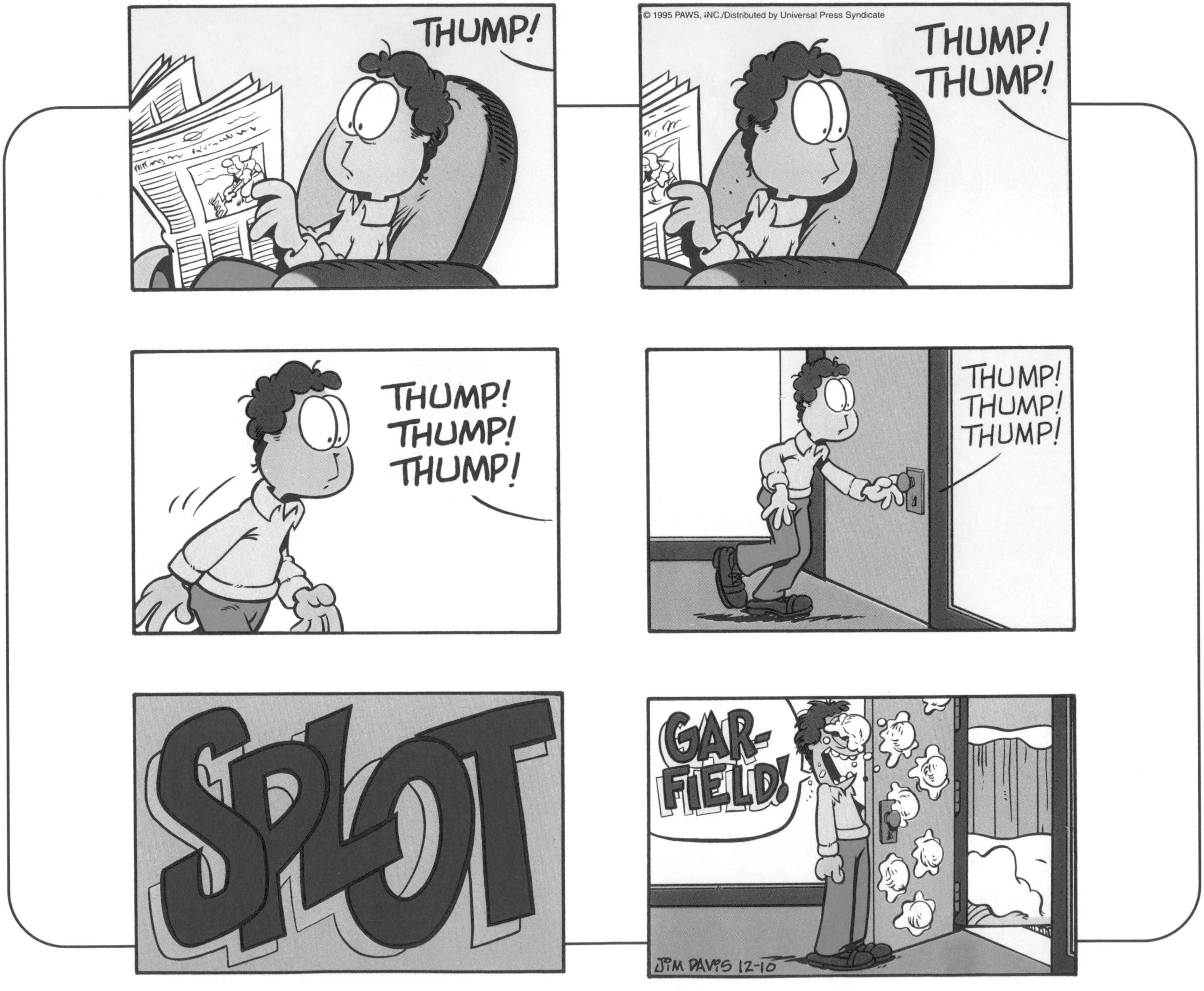
© 1995 PAWS, INC./Distributed by Universal Press Syndicate
THUMP!
THUMP! THUMP!
THUMP! THUMP! THUMP!
THUMP! THUMP! THUMP!
SPLOT
GAR-FIELD!
JIM DAVIS 12-10

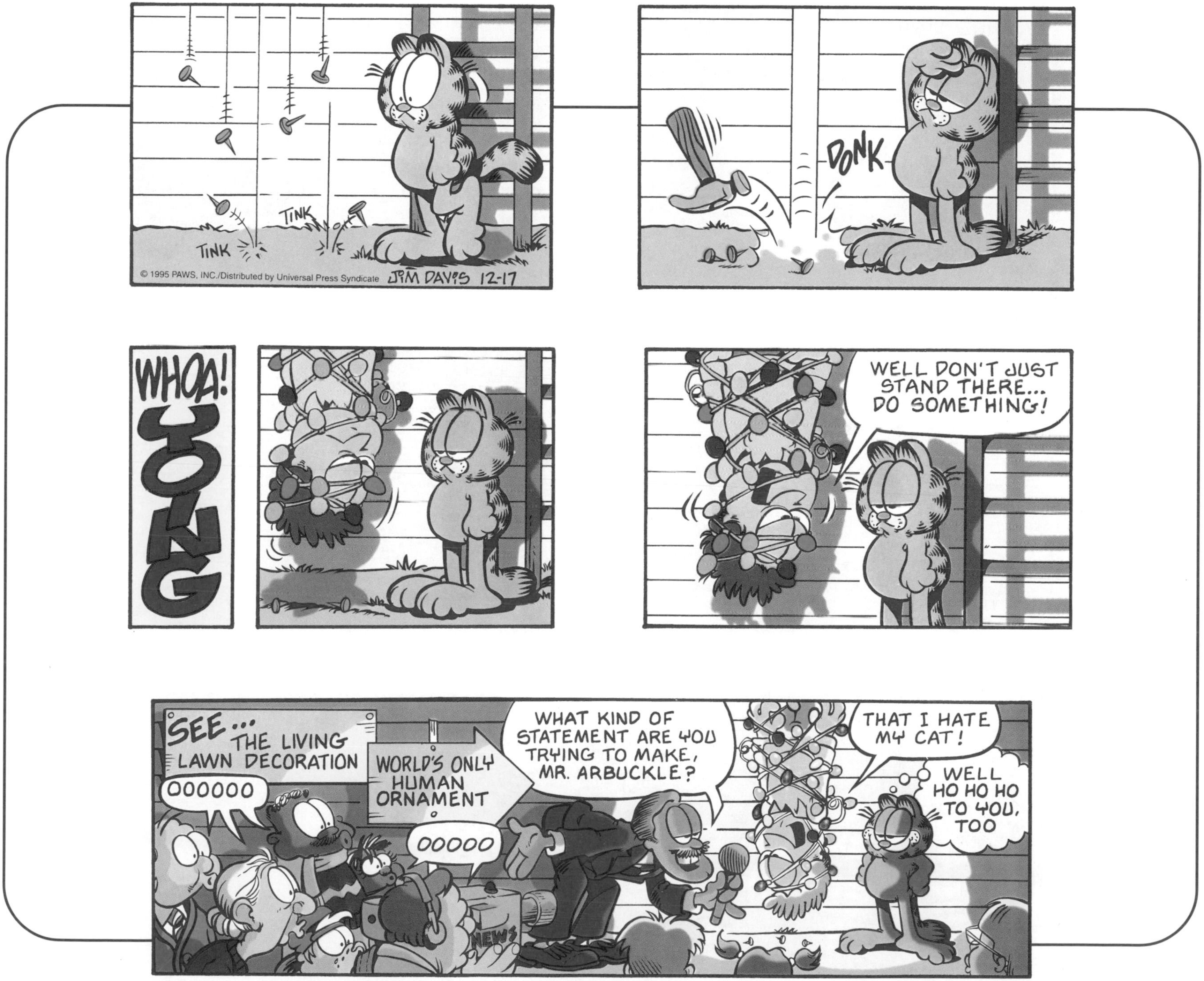
TINK
TINK
© 1995 PAWS, INC./Distributed by Universal Press Syndicate JIM DAVIS 12-17
DONK
WHOA!
YOING
WELL DON'T JUST STAND THERE... DO SOMETHING!
SEE... THE LIVING LAWN DECORATION
WORLD'S ONLY HUMAN ORNAMENT
OOOOOO
OOOOO
WHAT KIND OF STATEMENT ARE YOU TRYING TO MAKE, MR. ARBUCKLE?
THAT I HATE MY CAT!
WELL HO HO HO TO YOU, TOO
NEWS

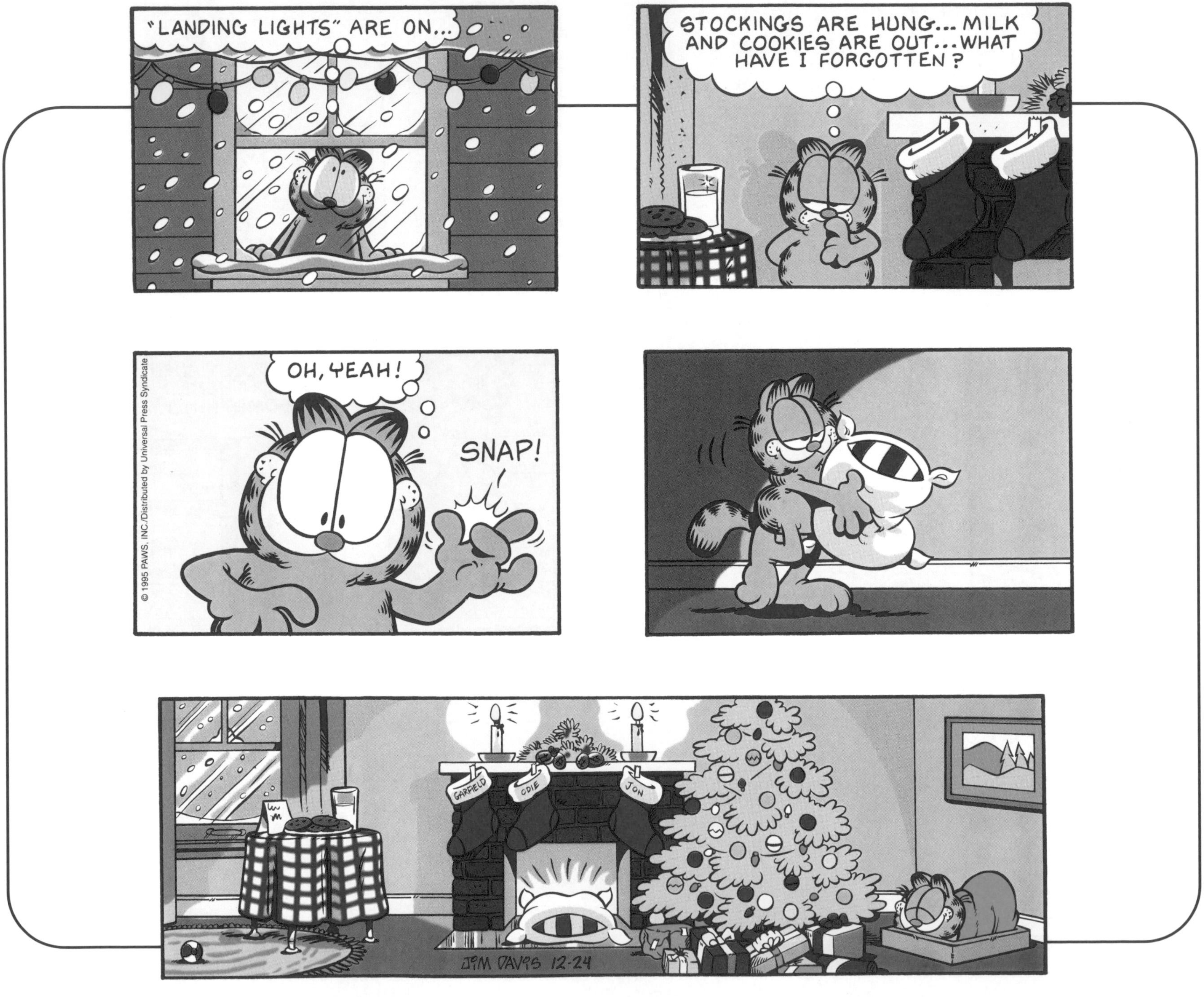
"LANDING LIGHTS" ARE ON...
STOCKINGS ARE HUNG... MILK AND COOKIES ARE OUT... WHAT HAVE I FORGOTTEN?
OH, YEAH!
SNAP!
GARFIELD
ODIE
JON
JIM DAVIS 12-24

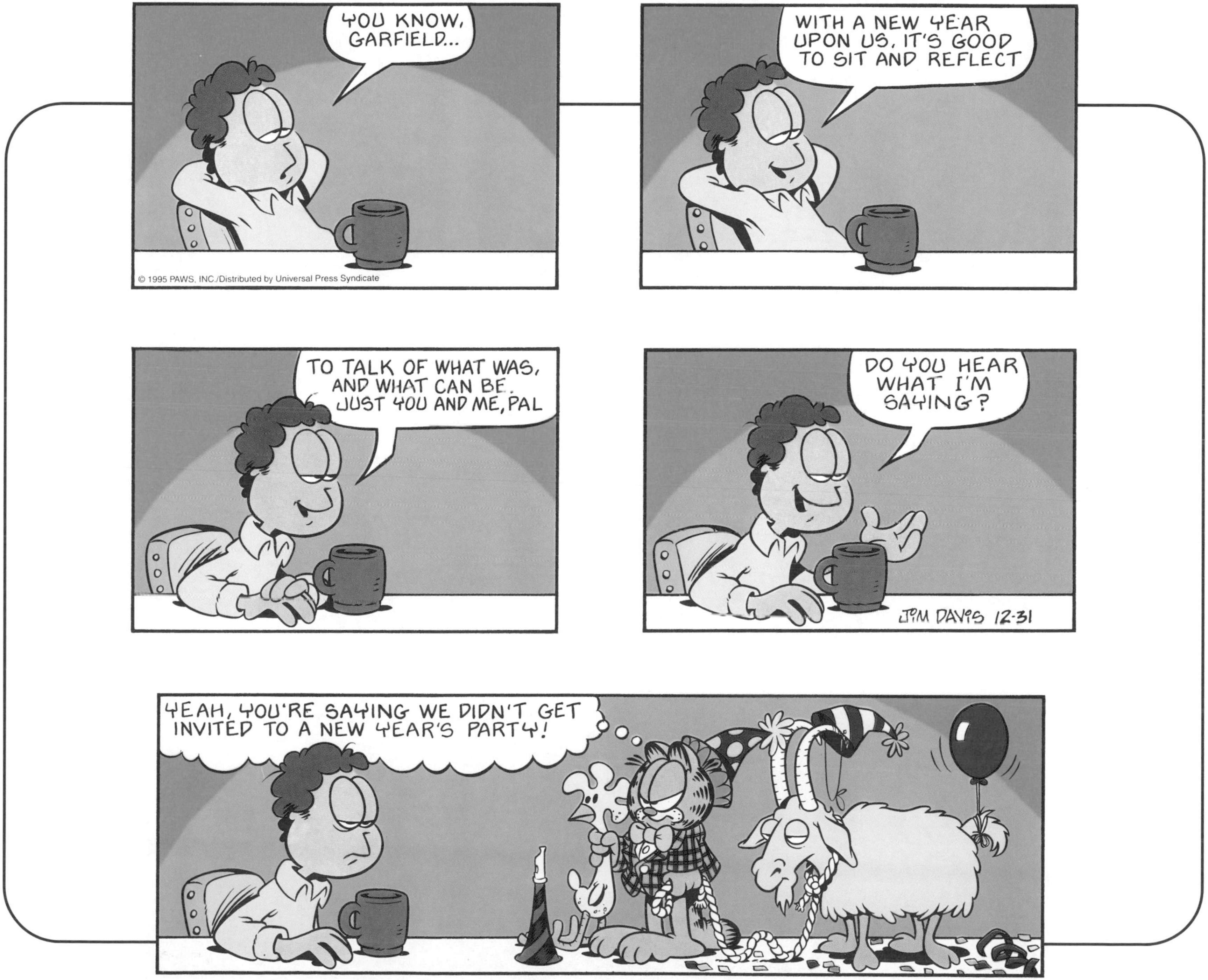
YOU KNOW, GARFIELD...
© 1995 PAWS, INC./Distributed by Universal Press Syndicate
WITH A NEW YEAR UPON US, IT'S GOOD TO SIT AND REFLECT
TO TALK OF WHAT WAS, AND WHAT CAN BE. JUST YOU AND ME, PAL
DO YOU HEAR WHAT I'M SAYING?
JIM DAVIS 12-31
YEAH, YOU'RE SAYING WE DIDN'T GET INVITED TO A NEW YEAR'S PARTY!

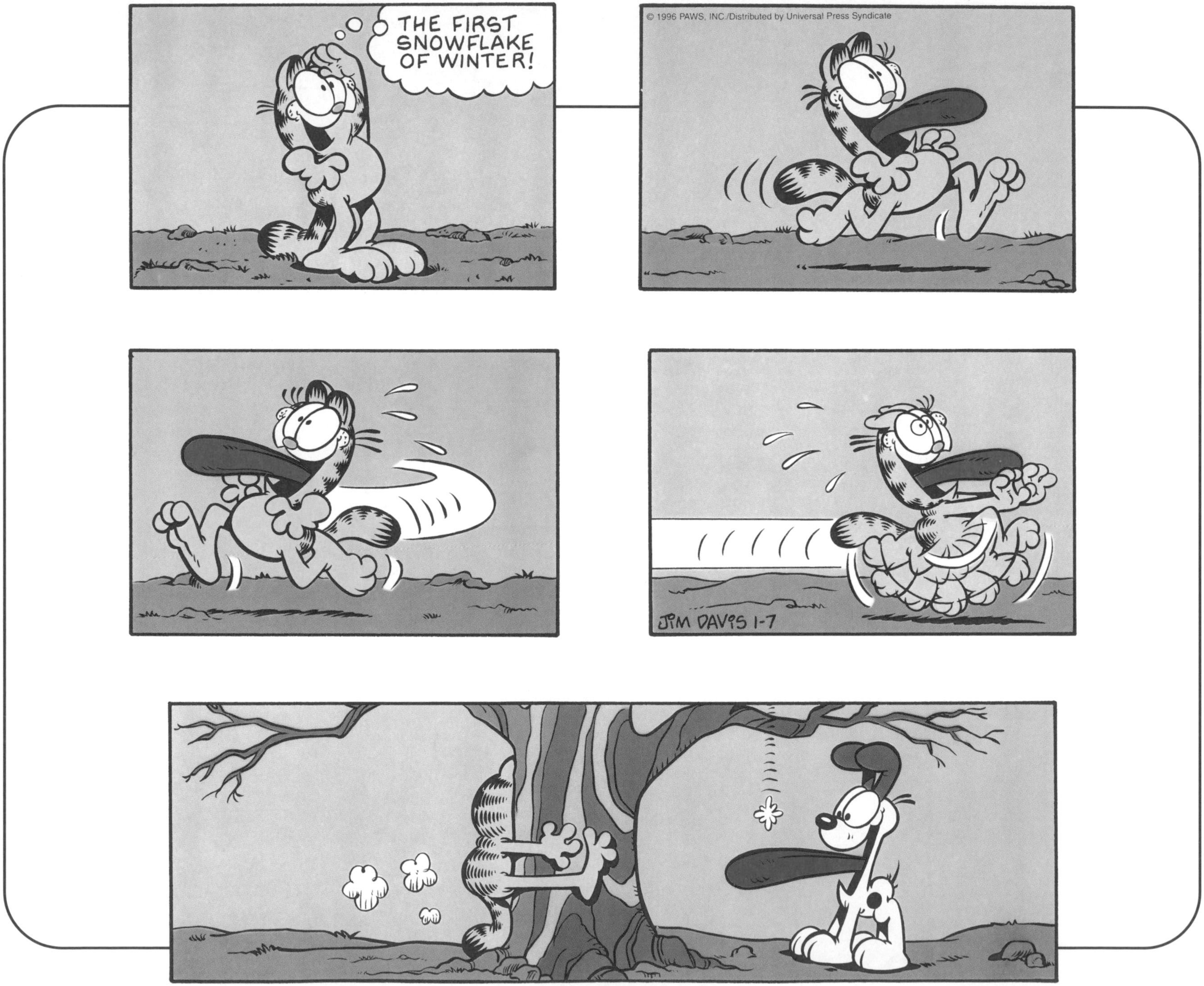
THE FIRST SNOWFLAKE OF WINTER!
© 1996 PAWS, INC./Distributed by Universal Press Syndicate
JIM DAVIS 1-7

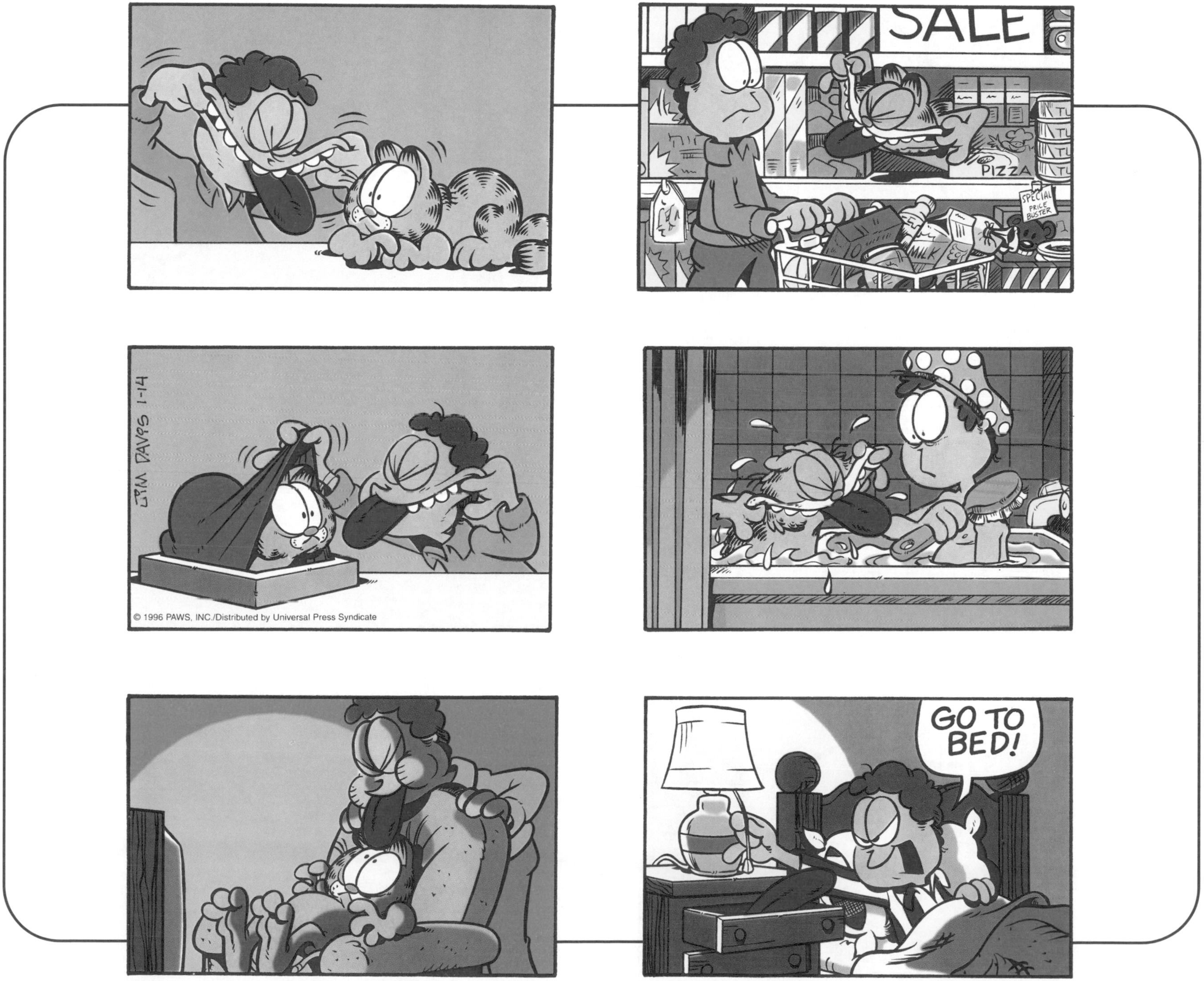
SALE
PIZZA
SPECIAL PRICE BUSTER
MILK
© 1996 PAWS, INC./Distributed by Universal Press Syndicate
GO TO BED!

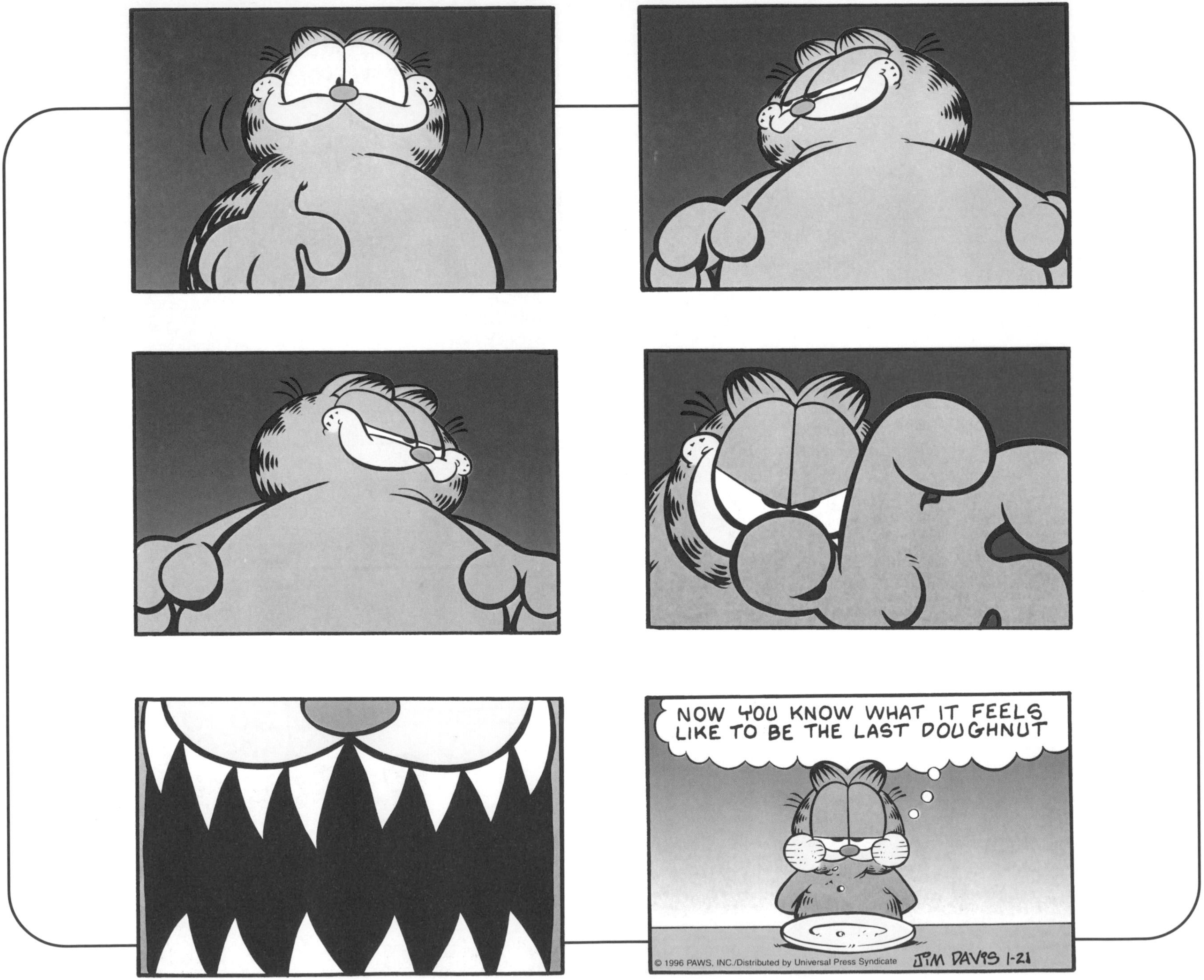
NOW YOU KNOW WHAT IT FEELS LIKE TO BE THE LAST DOUGHNUT
© 1996 PAWS, INC./Distributed by Universal Press Syndicate
JIM DAVIS 1-21

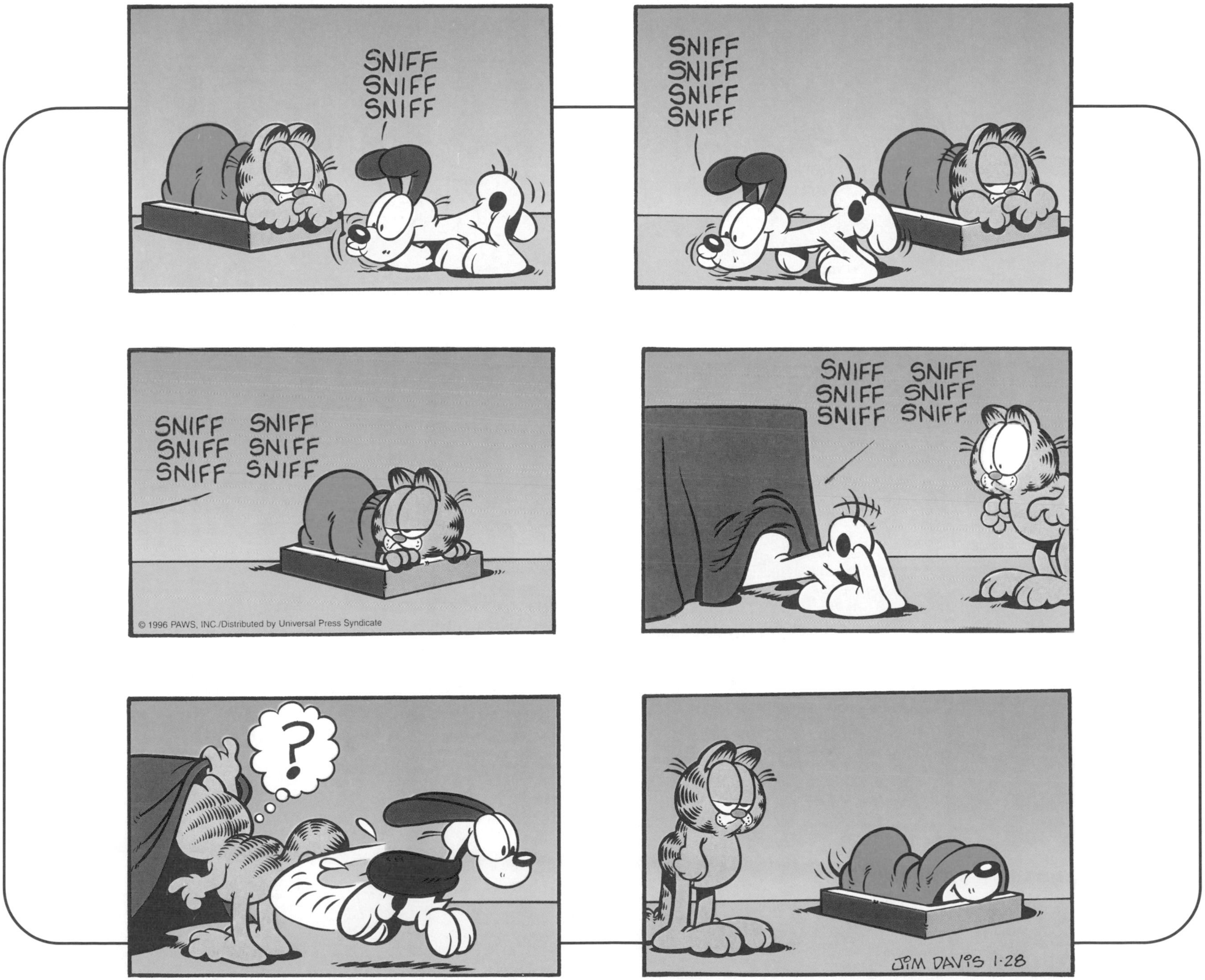
SNIFF
SNIFF
SNIFF
SNIFF
SNIFF
SNIFF
SNIFF
SNIFF SNIFF
SNIFF SNIFF
SNIFF SNIFF
© 1996 PAWS, INC./Distributed by Universal Press Syndicate
SNIFF SNIFF
SNIFF SNIFF
SNIFF SNIFF
?
JIM DAVIS 1·28

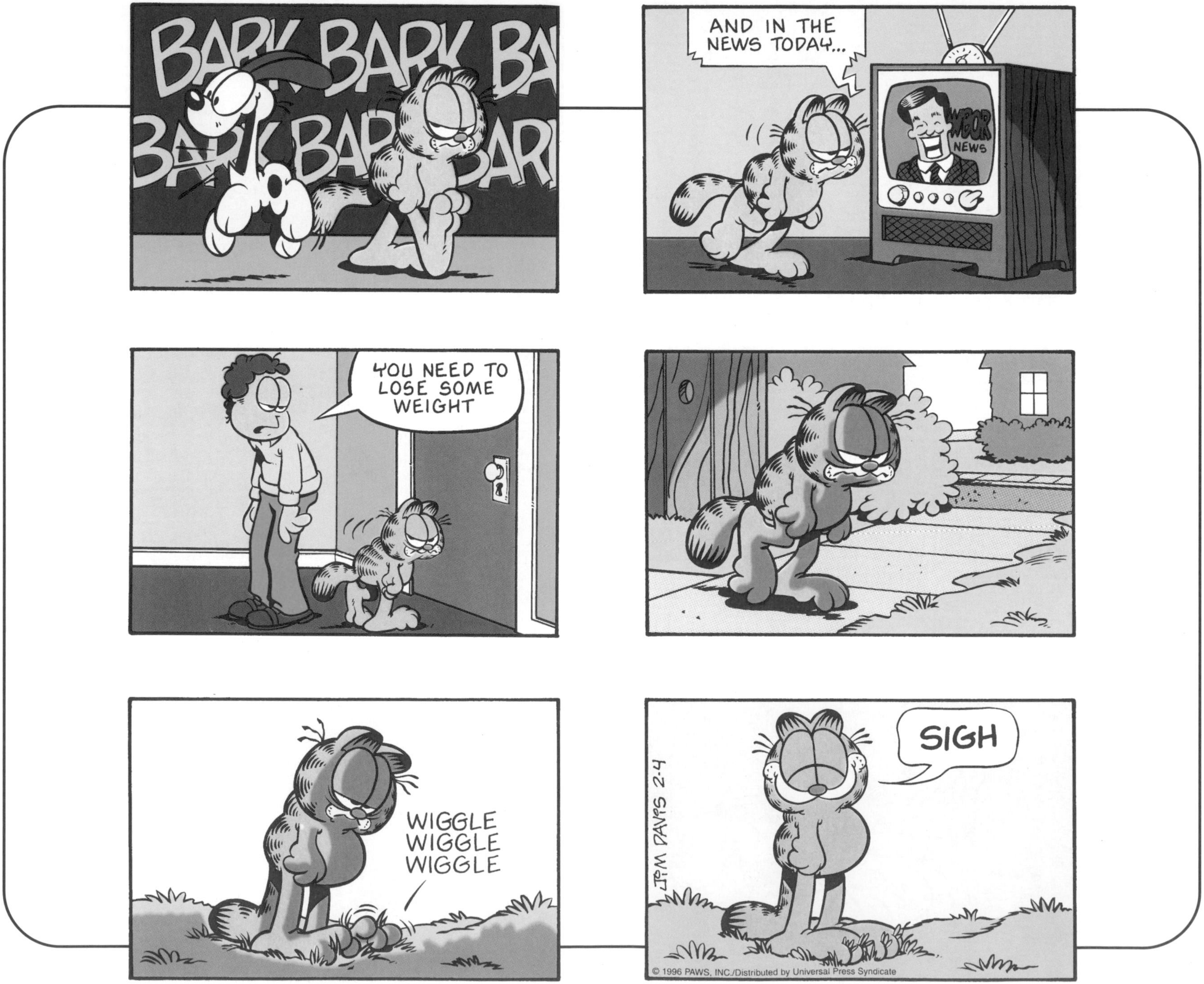
BARK BARK BA
BARK BARK BARK
AND IN THE NEWS TODAY...
WBOR NEWS
YOU NEED TO LOSE SOME WEIGHT
WIGGLE WIGGLE WIGGLE
JIM DAVIS 2-4
SIGH
© 1996 PAWS, INC./Distributed by Universal Press Syndicate

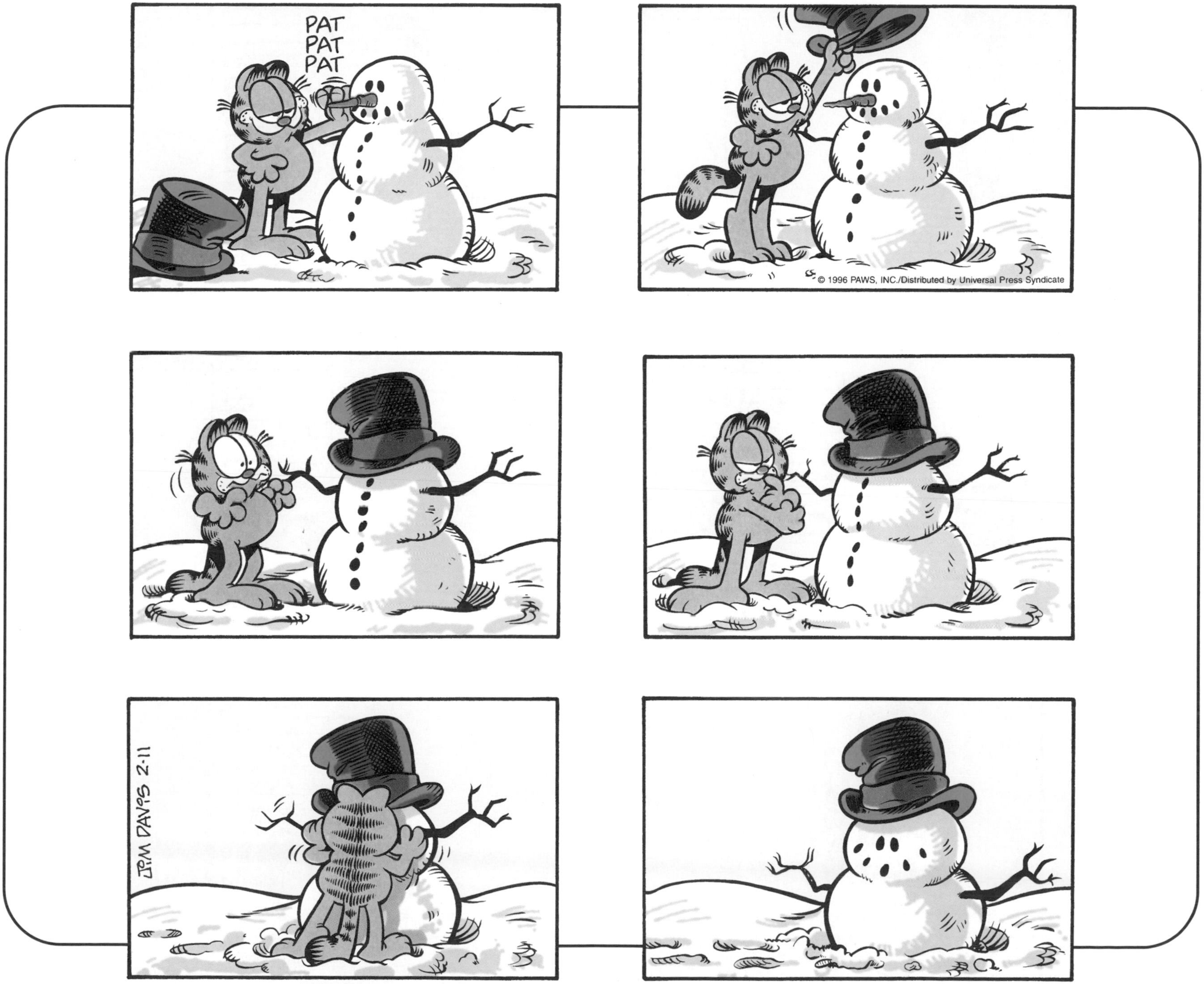
PAT
PAT
PAT
© 1996 PAWS, INC./Distributed by Universal Press Syndicate
JIM DAVIS 2-11

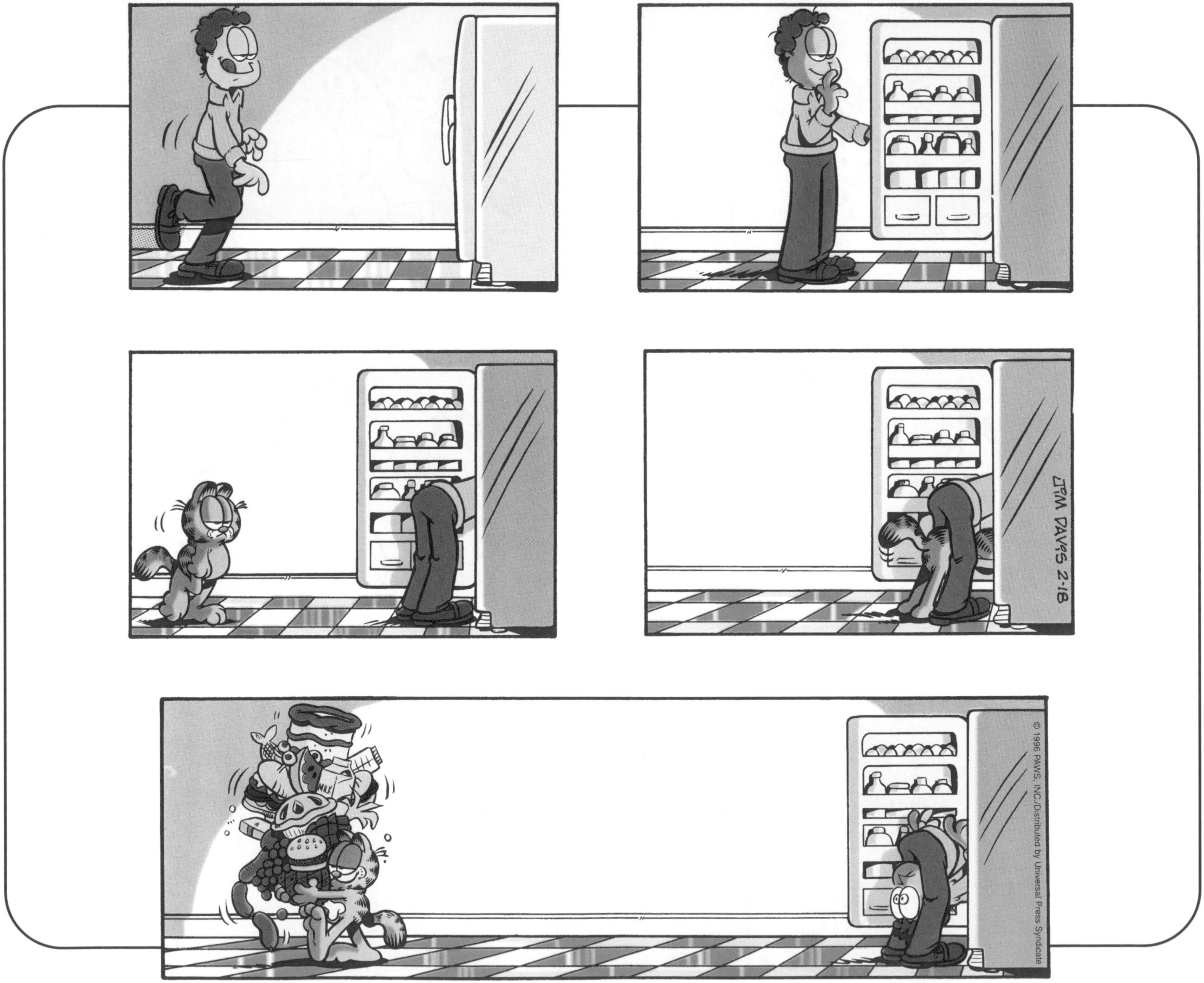
JIM DAVIS 2-18
MILK
© 1996 PAWS, INC./Distributed by Universal Press Syndicate

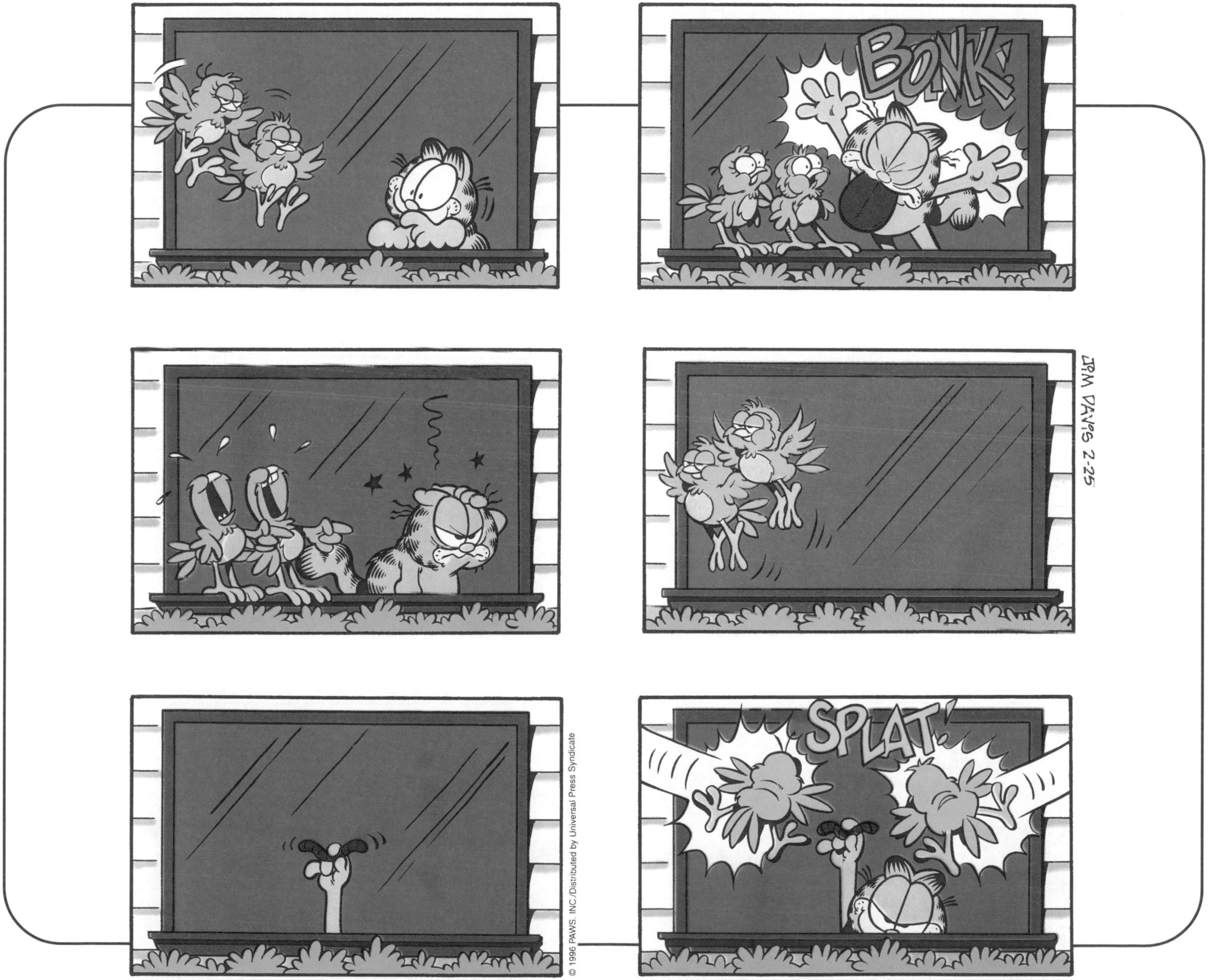
BONK!
JPM DAVIS 2-25
SPLAT!

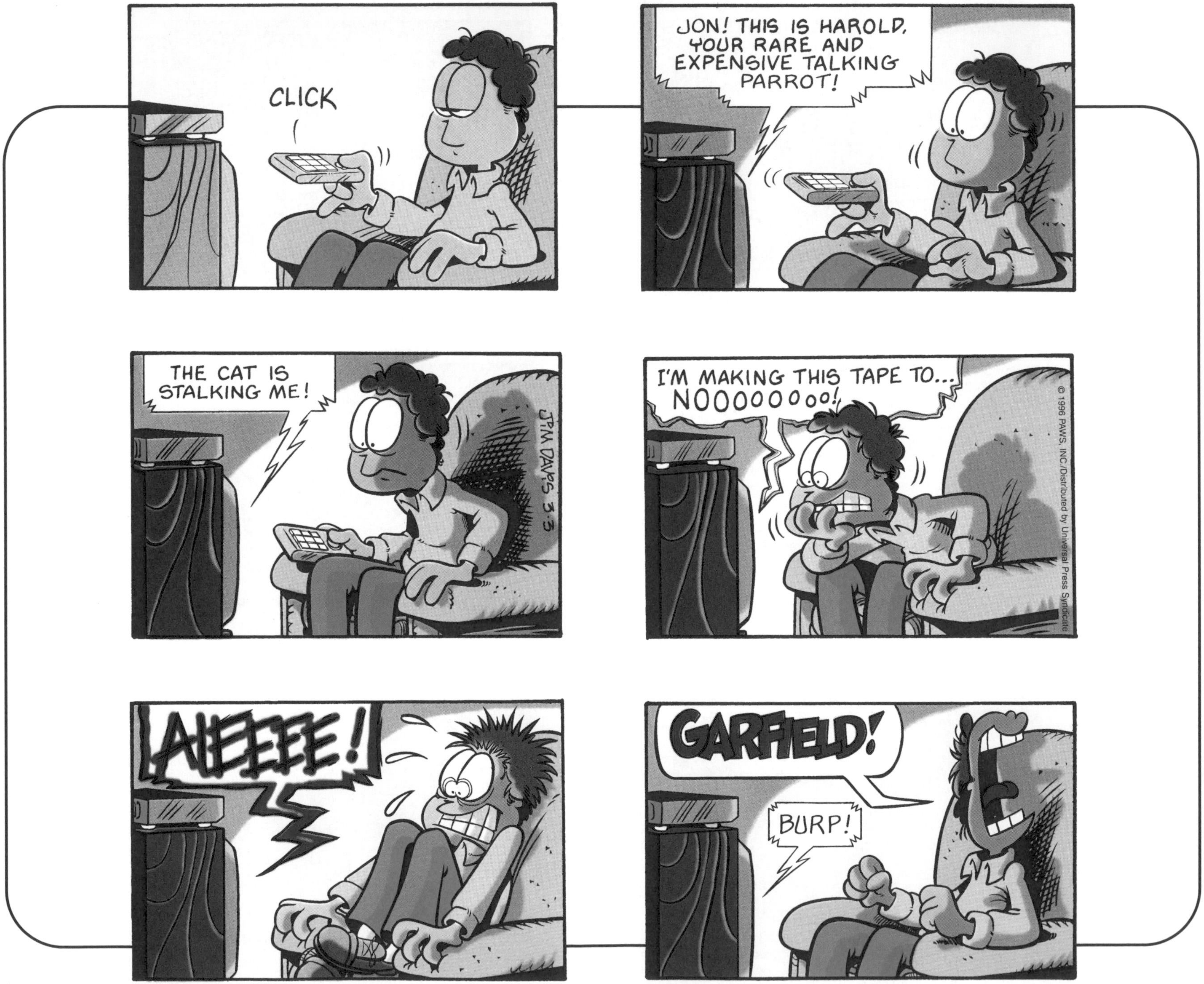
CLICK
JON! THIS IS HAROLD, YOUR RARE AND EXPENSIVE TALKING PARROT!
THE CAT IS STALKING ME!
JPM DAVIS 3-3
I'M MAKING THIS TAPE TO... NOOOOOOoo!
© 1996 PAWS, INC./Distributed by Universal Press Syndicate
AIEEEE!
GARFIELD!
BURP!

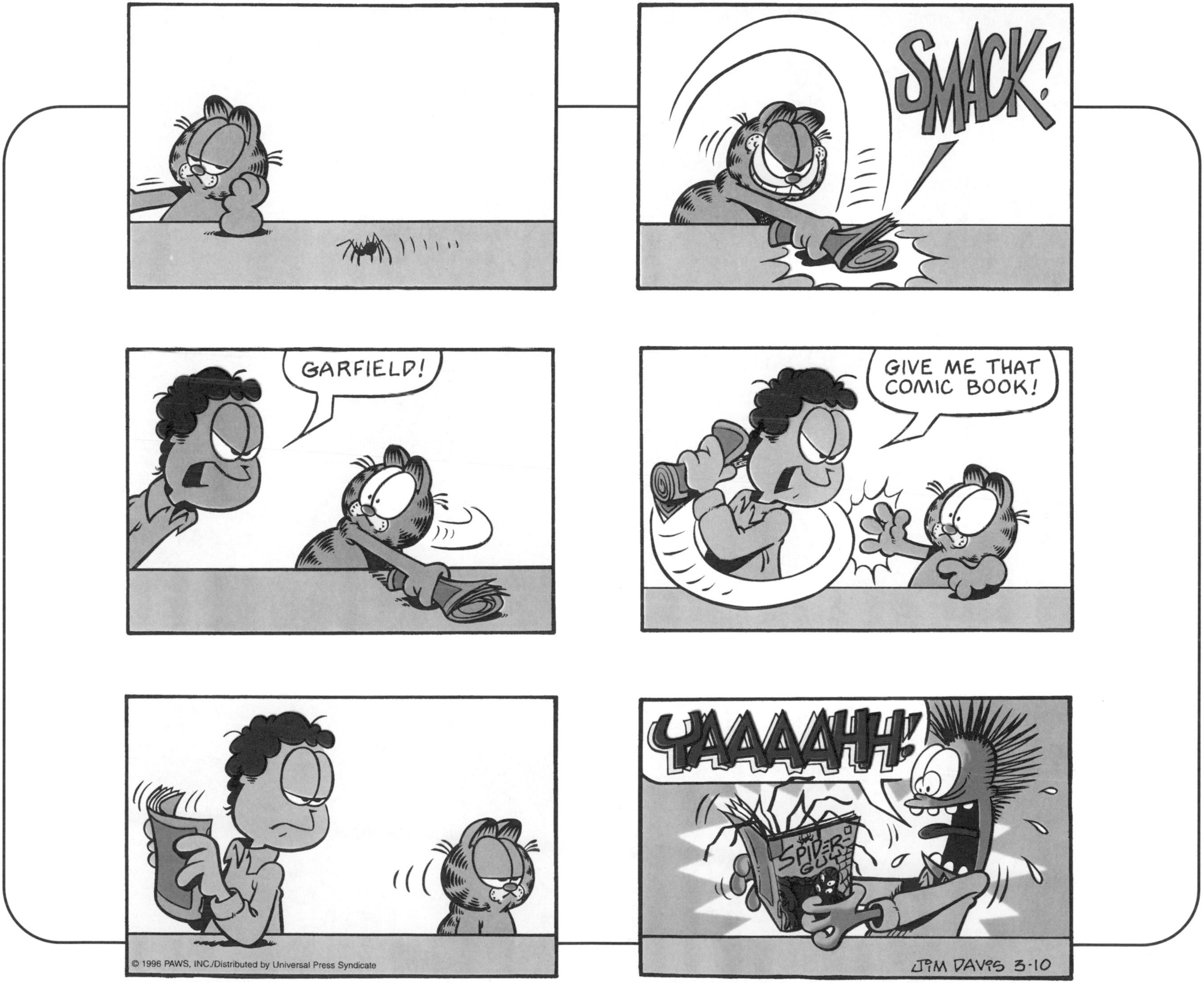
SMACK!
GARFIELD!
GIVE ME THAT COMIC BOOK!
YAAAAHH!
SPIDER-GUY
© 1996 PAWS, INC./Distributed by Universal Press Syndicate
JIM DAVIS 3-10

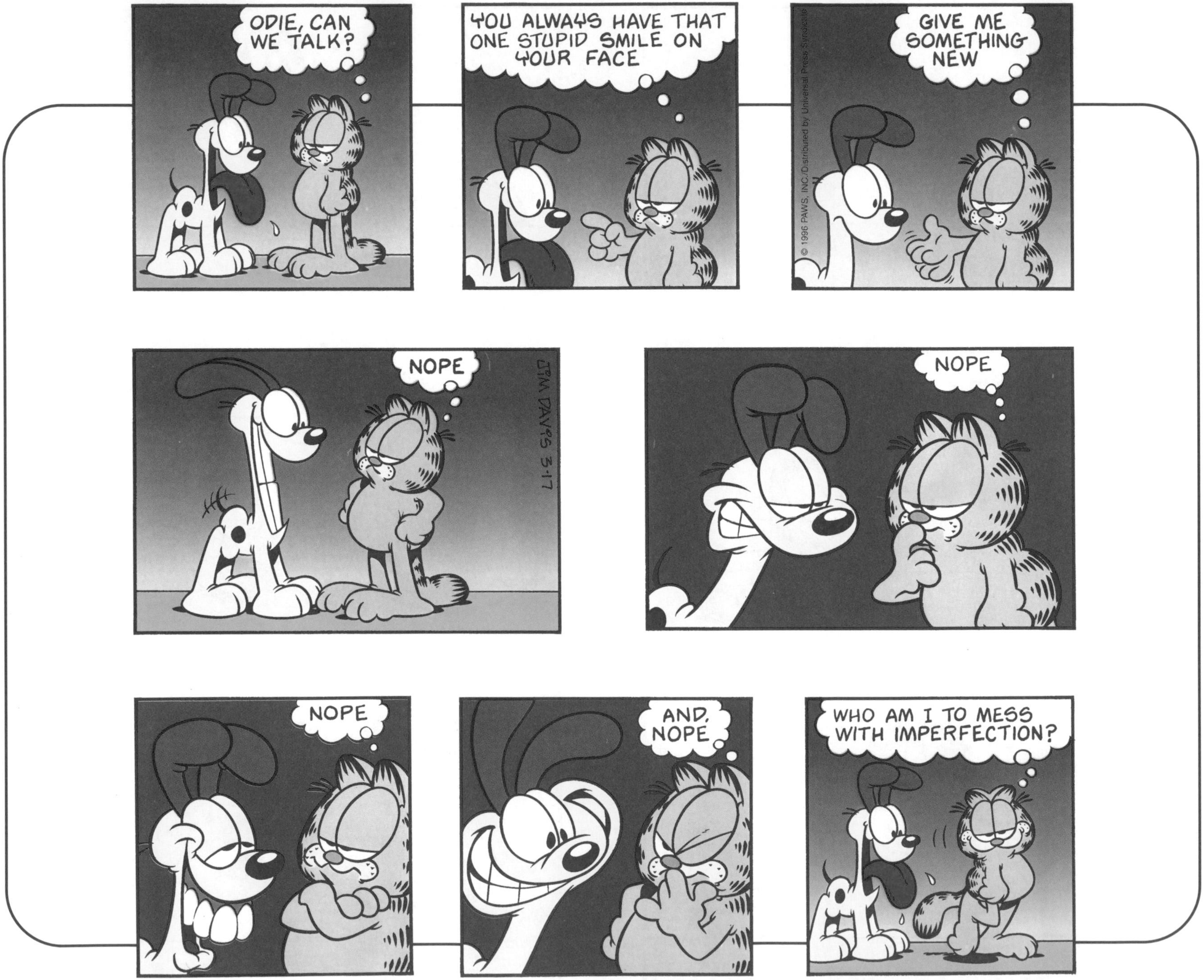
ODIE, CAN WE TALK?
YOU ALWAYS HAVE THAT ONE STUPID SMILE ON YOUR FACE
GIVE ME SOMETHING NEW
© 1996 PAWS, INC./Distributed by Universal Press Syndicate
NOPE
JIM DAVIS 3-17
NOPE
NOPE
AND, NOPE
WHO AM I TO MESS WITH IMPERFECTION?

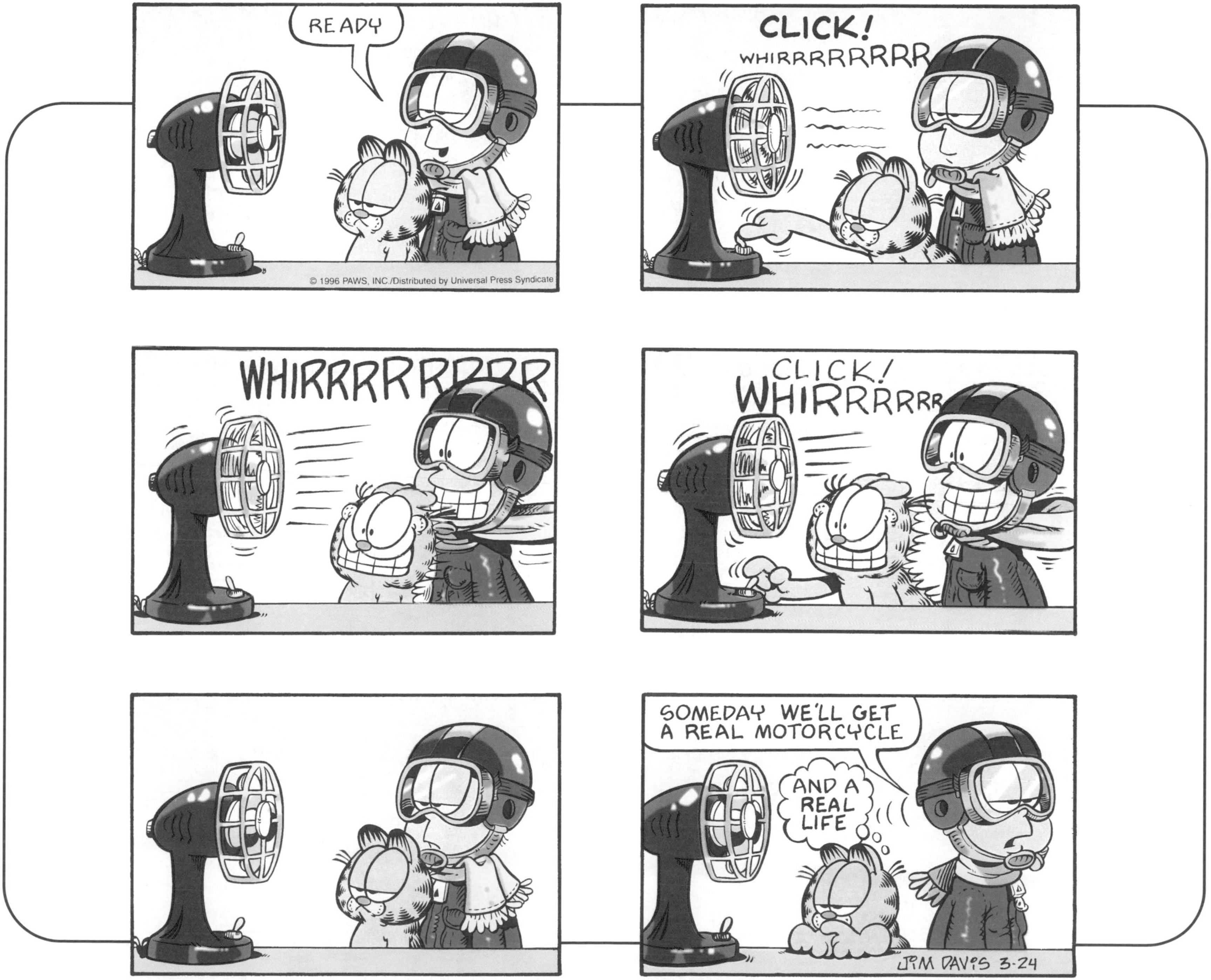
READY
© 1996 PAWS, INC./Distributed by Universal Press Syndicate
CLICK!
WHIRRRRRRRR
WHIRRRRRRRR
CLICK!
WHIRRRRRR
SOMEDAY WE'LL GET A REAL MOTORCYCLE
AND A REAL LIFE
JIM DAVIS 3-24

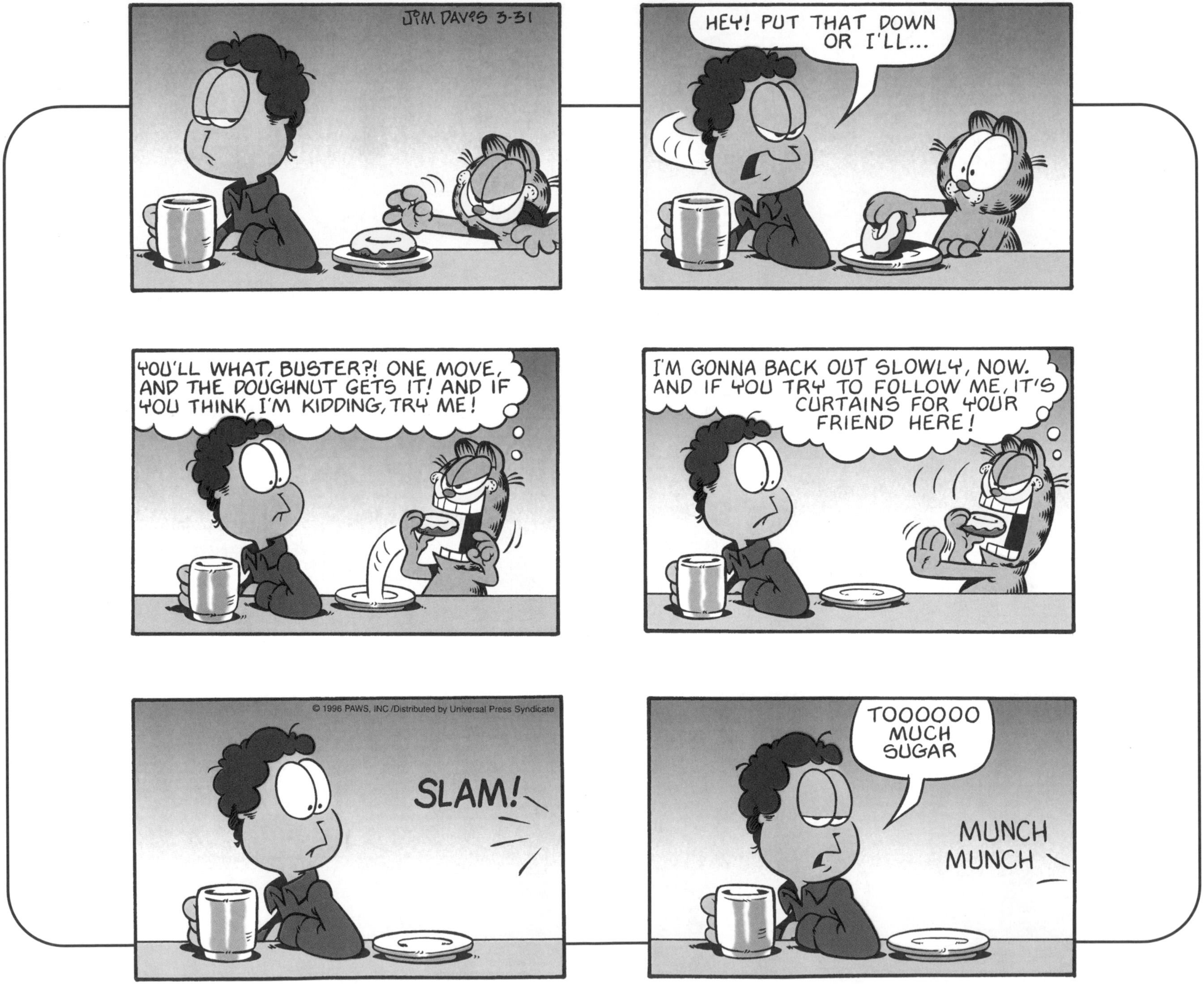
JIM DAVIS 3-31
HEY! PUT THAT DOWN OR I'LL...
YOU'LL WHAT, BUSTER?! ONE MOVE, AND THE DOUGHNUT GETS IT! AND IF YOU THINK I'M KIDDING, TRY ME!
I'M GONNA BACK OUT SLOWLY, NOW. AND IF YOU TRY TO FOLLOW ME, IT'S CURTAINS FOR YOUR FRIEND HERE!
© 1996 PAWS, INC./Distributed by Universal Press Syndicate
SLAM!
TOOOOOO MUCH SUGAR
MUNCH MUNCH

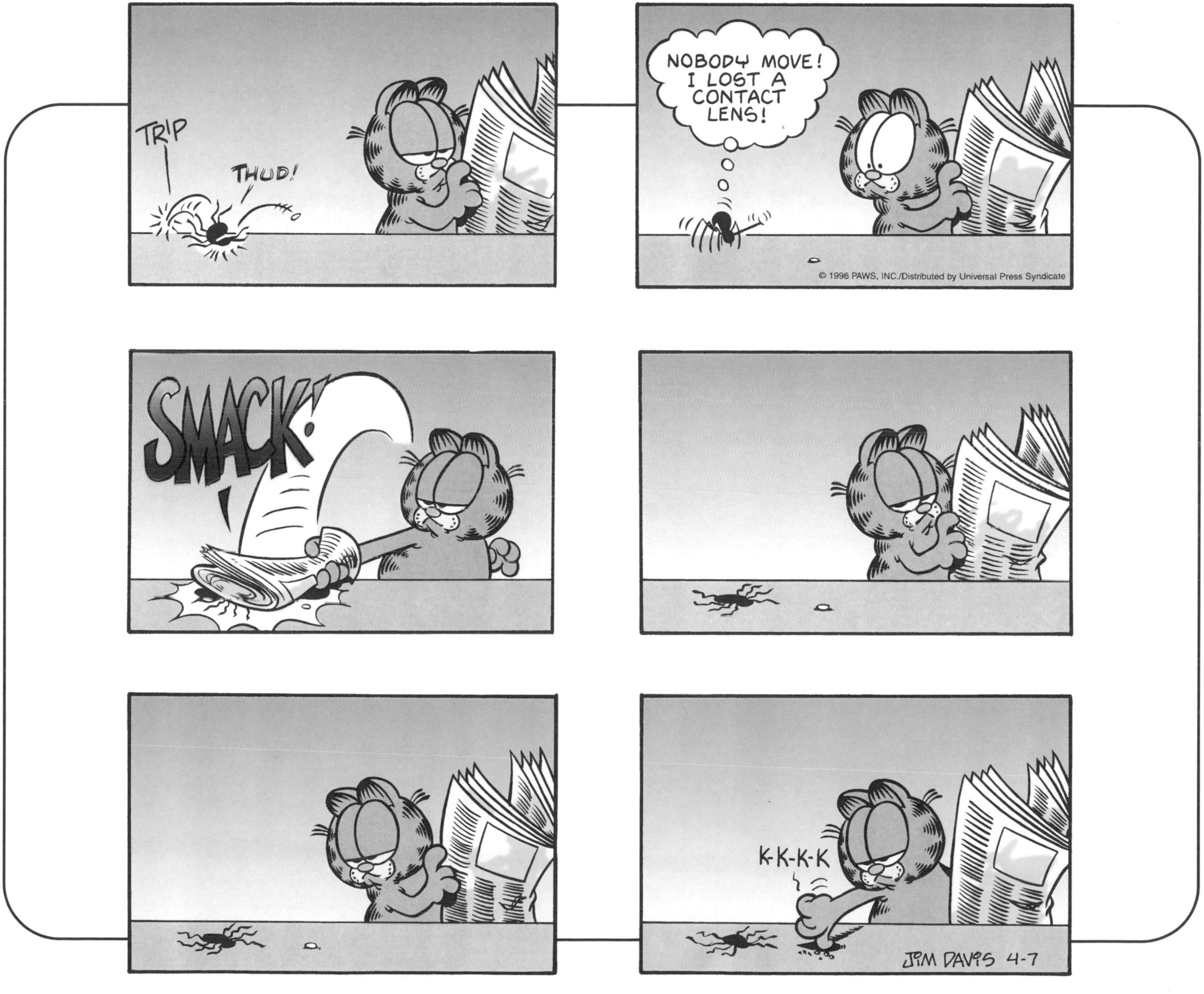
TRIP
THUD!
NOBODY MOVE! I LOST A CONTACT LENS!
© 1996 PAWS, INC./Distributed by Universal Press Syndicate
SMACK!
K-K-K-K
JIM DAVIS 4-7

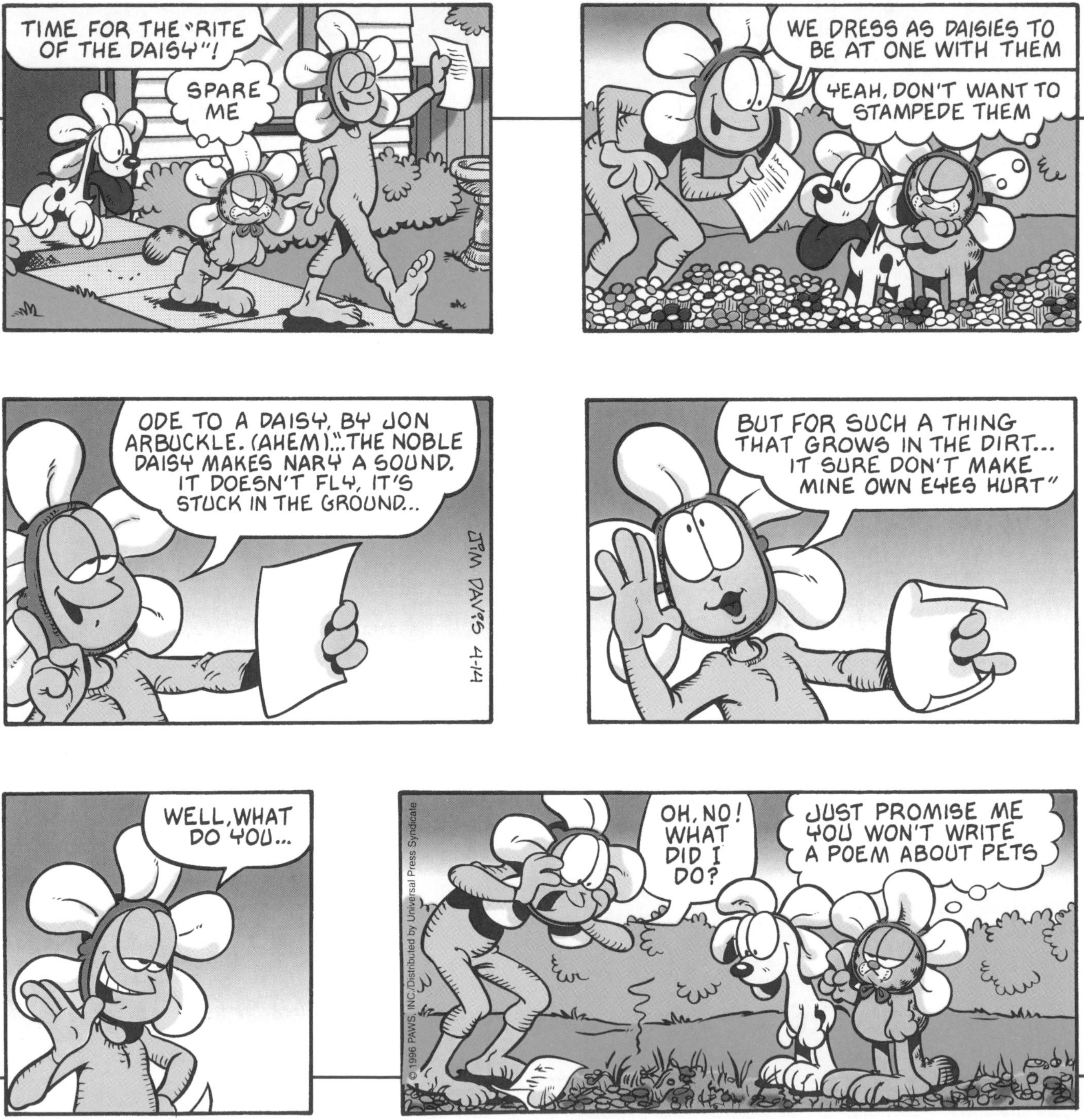
TIME FOR THE "RITE OF THE DAISY"!
SPARE ME
WE DRESS AS DAISIES TO BE AT ONE WITH THEM
YEAH, DON'T WANT TO STAMPEDE THEM
ODE TO A DAISY, BY JON ARBUCKLE. (AHEM) "...THE NOBLE DAISY MAKES NARY A SOUND. IT DOESN'T FLY, IT'S STUCK IN THE GROUND...
JIM DAVIS 4-14
BUT FOR SUCH A THING THAT GROWS IN THE DIRT... IT SURE DON'T MAKE MINE OWN EYES HURT"
WELL, WHAT DO YOU...
OH, NO! WHAT DID I DO?
JUST PROMISE ME YOU WON'T WRITE A POEM ABOUT PETS
© 1996 PAWS, INC./Distributed by Universal Press Syndicate

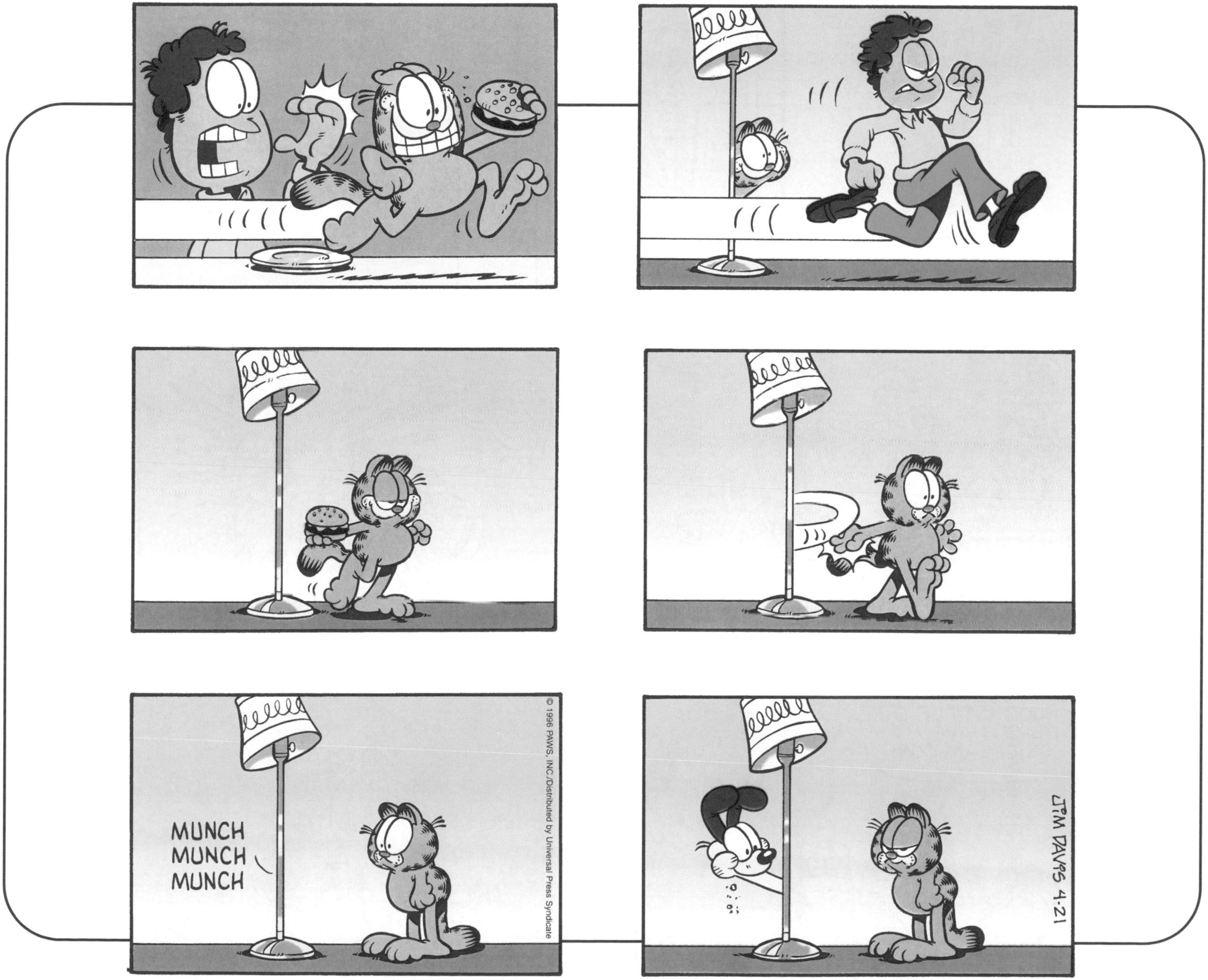
MUNCH
MUNCH
MUNCH
© 1996 PAWS, INC./Distributed by Universal Press Syndicate
JIM DAVIS 4-21

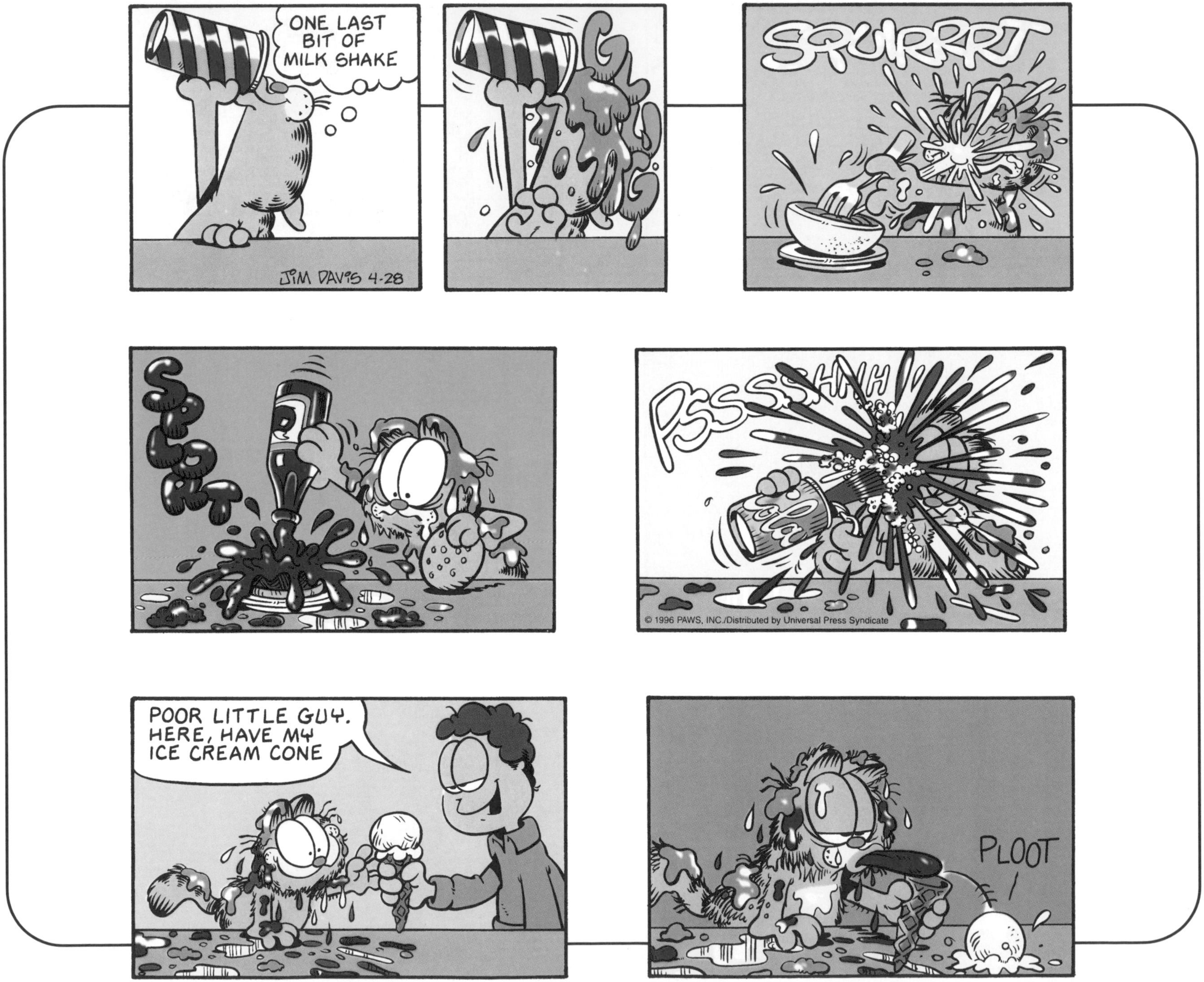
ONE LAST BIT OF MILK SHAKE
JIM DAVIS 4-28
SQUIRRRT
PSSSSHHH
© 1996 PAWS, INC./Distributed by Universal Press Syndicate
POOR LITTLE GUY. HERE, HAVE MY ICE CREAM CONE
PLOOT

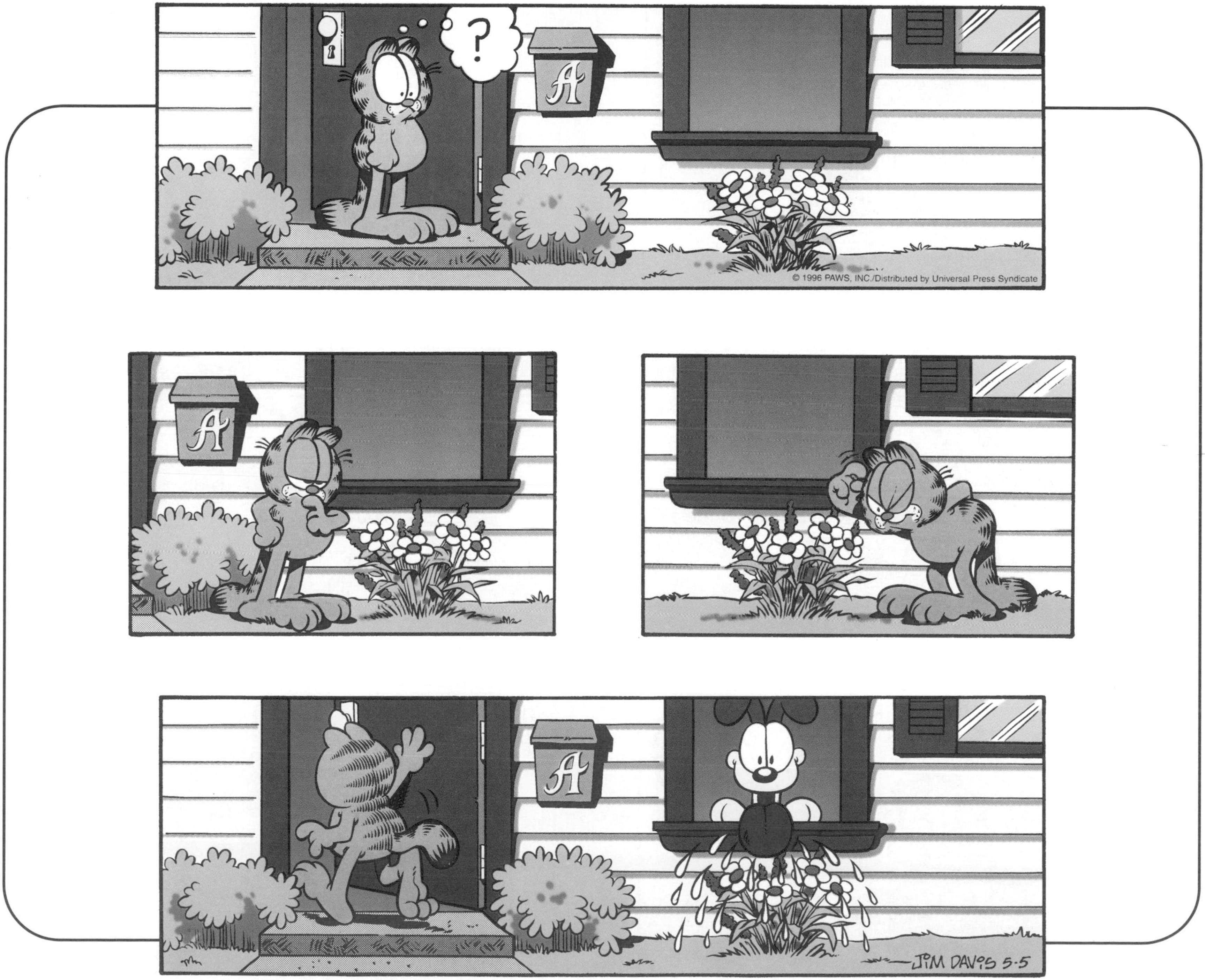
?
JIM DAVIS 5·5

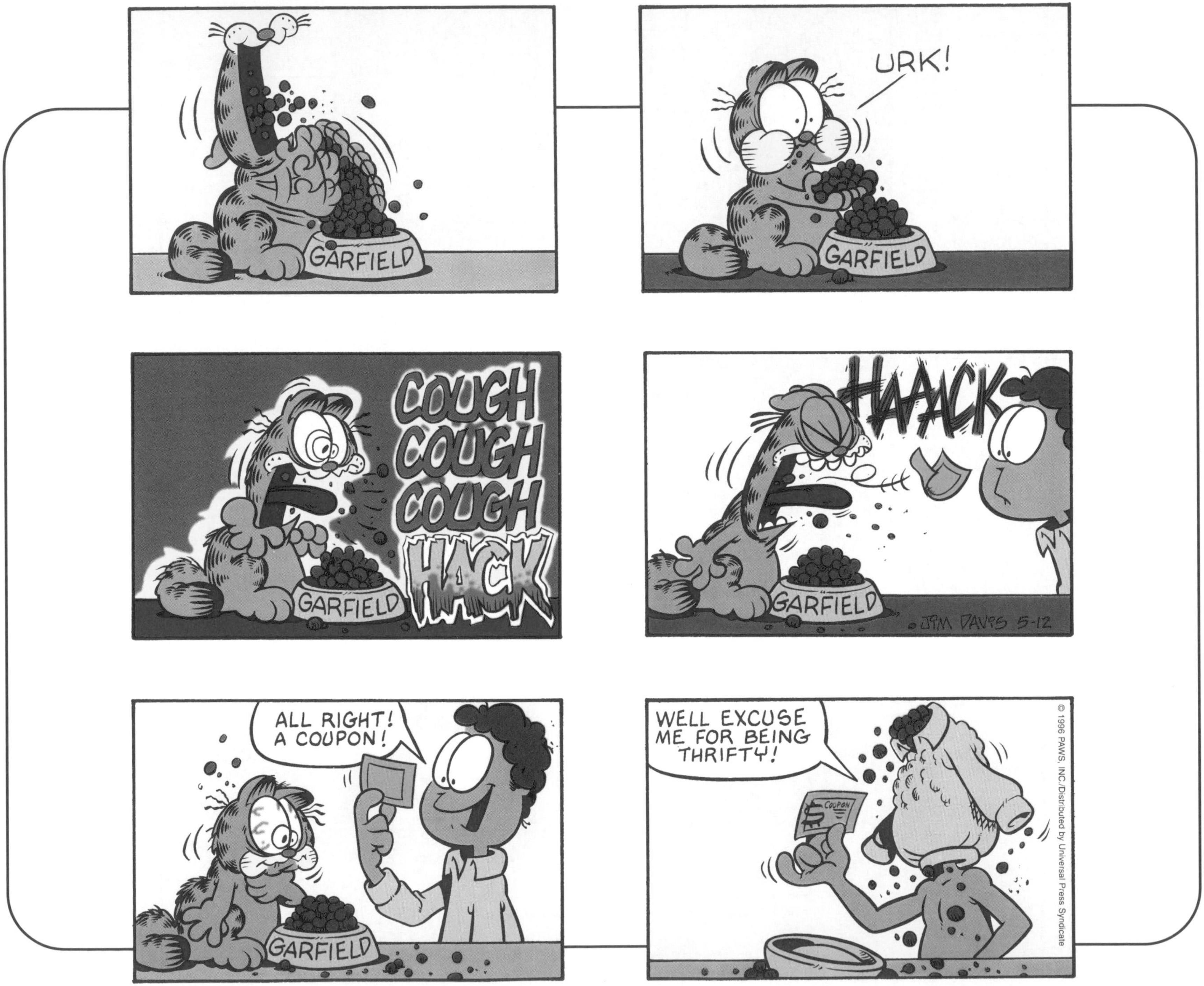
URK!
COUGH
COUGH
COUGH
HACK
HAAACK
JIM DAVIS 5-12
ALL RIGHT! A COUPON!
WELL EXCUSE ME FOR BEING THRIFTY!
COUPON
© 1996 PAWS, INC./Distributed by Universal Press Syndicate

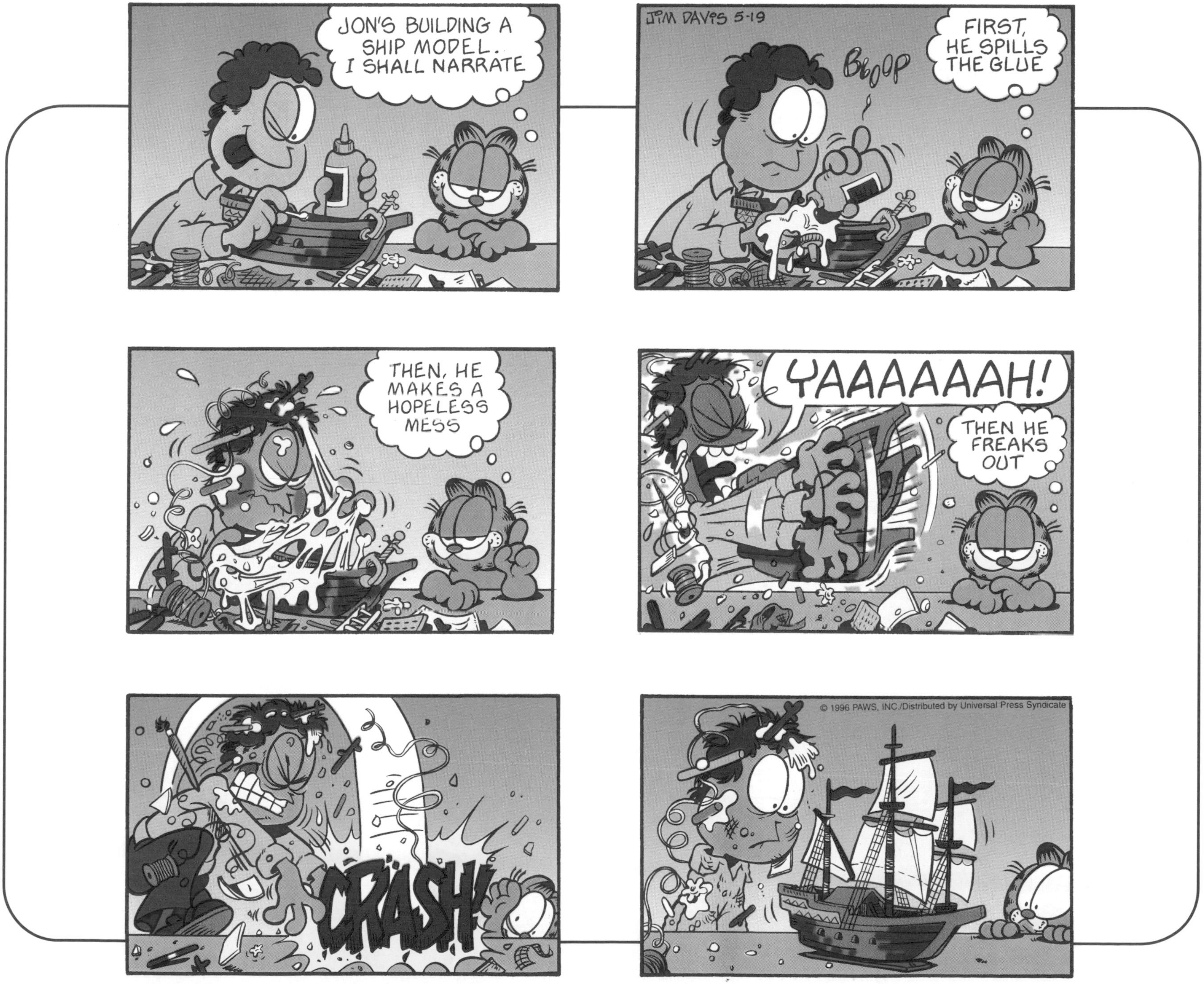
JON'S BUILDING A SHIP MODEL. I SHALL NARRATE
JIM DAVIS 5-19
BLOOP
FIRST, HE SPILLS THE GLUE
THEN, HE MAKES A HOPELESS MESS
YAAAAAAH!
THEN HE FREAKS OUT
CRASH!

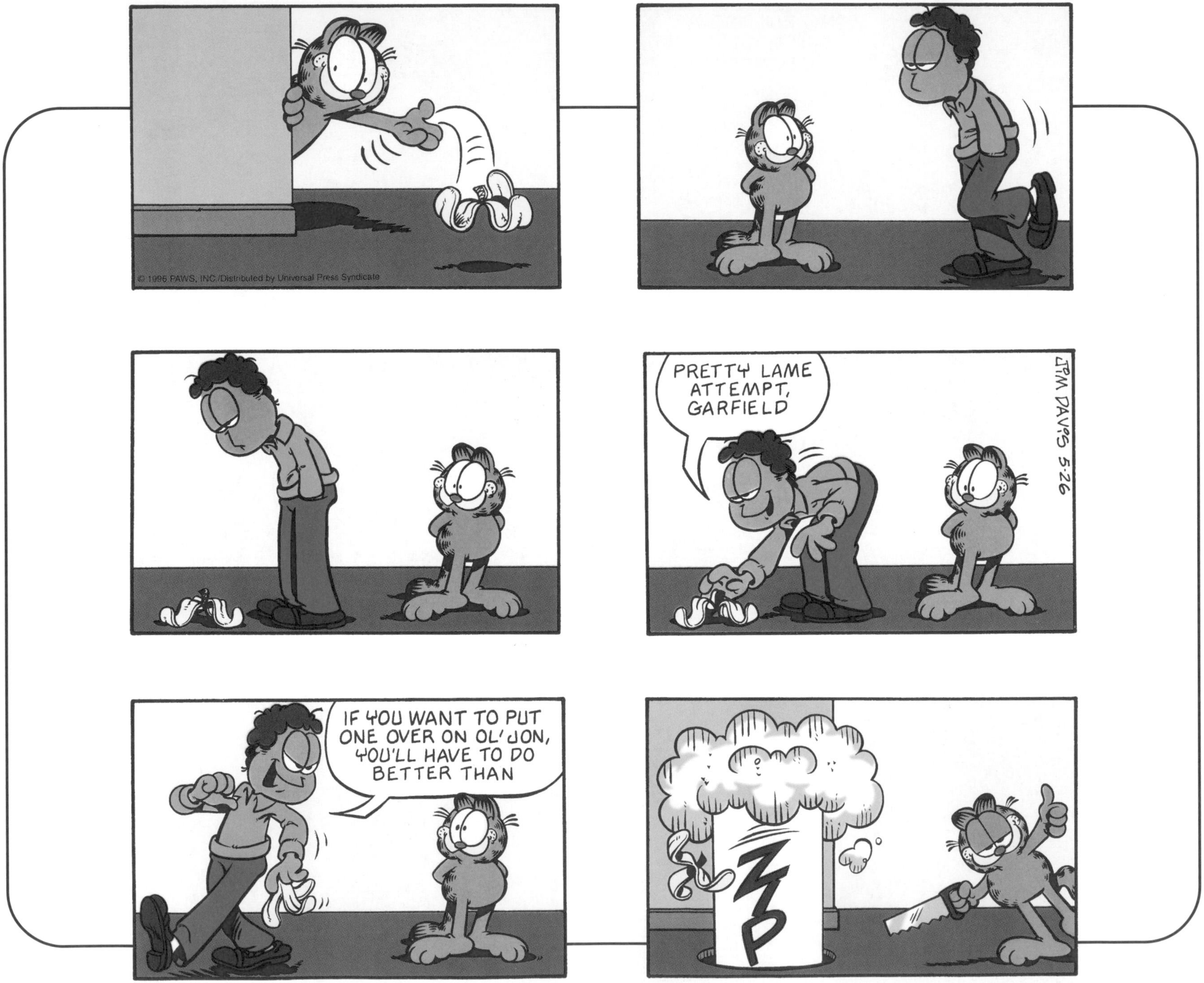
© 1996 PAWS, INC./Distributed by Universal Press Syndicate
PRETTY LAME ATTEMPT, GARFIELD
JPM DAVIS 5-26
IF YOU WANT TO PUT ONE OVER ON OL' JON, YOU'LL HAVE TO DO BETTER THAN
ZIP

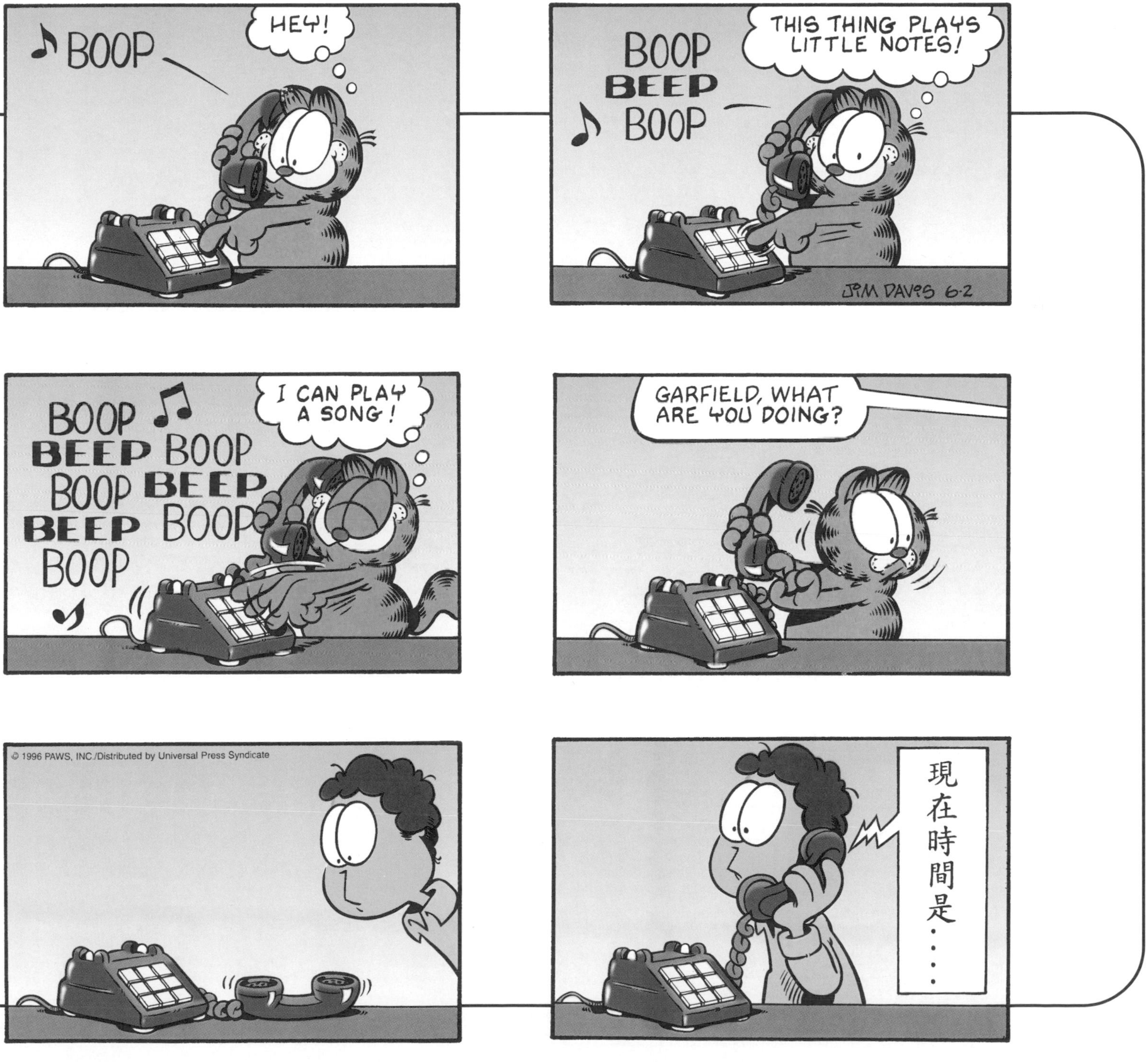
BOOP
HEY!
BOOP BEEP BOOP
THIS THING PLAYS LITTLE NOTES!
JIM DAVIS 6-2
BOOP BEEP BOOP BEEP BOOP BOOP BEEP BOOP
I CAN PLAY A SONG!
GARFIELD, WHAT ARE YOU DOING?
© 1996 PAWS, INC./Distributed by Universal Press Syndicate
現在時間是⋯⋯

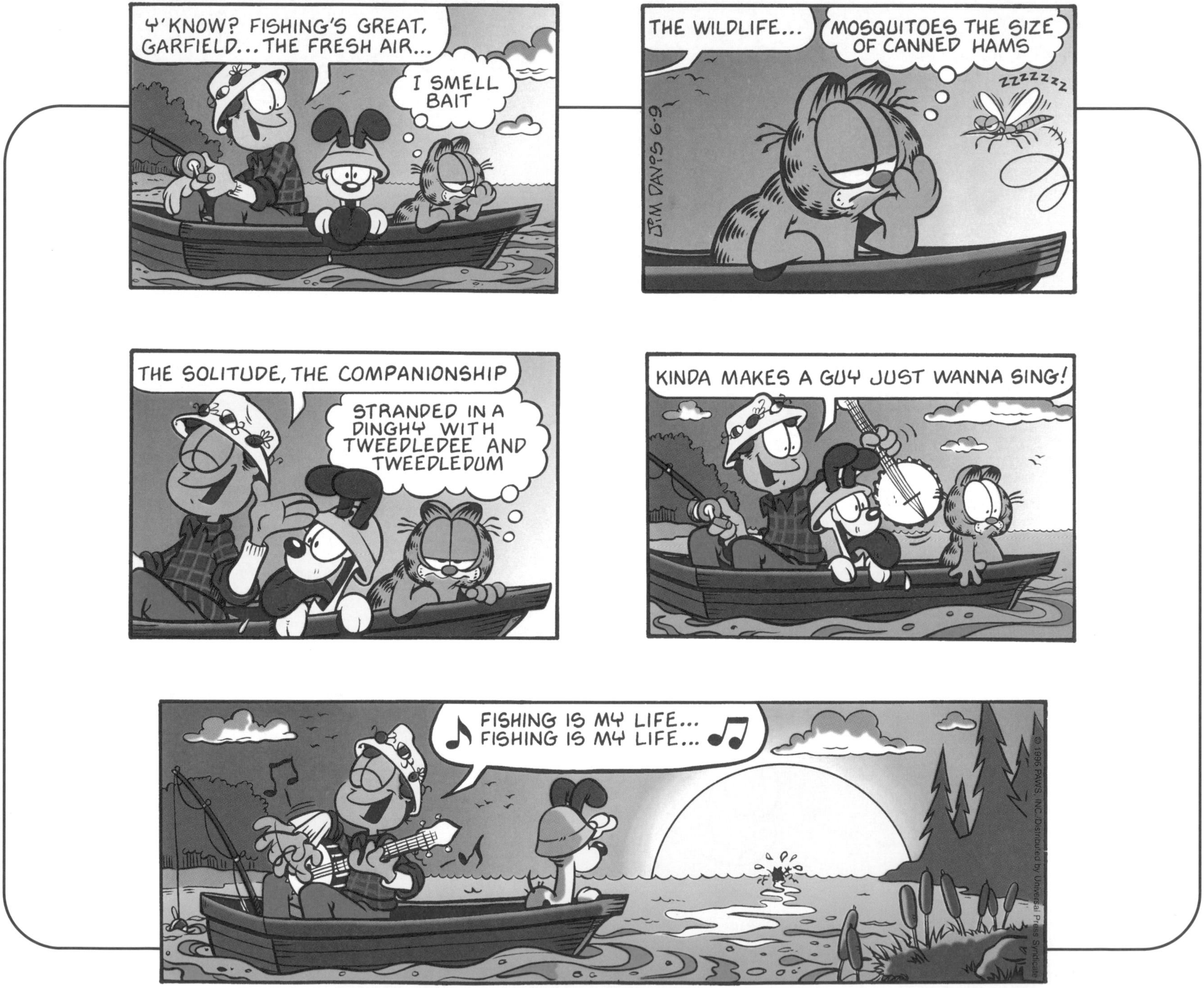
Y'KNOW? FISHING'S GREAT, GARFIELD... THE FRESH AIR...
I SMELL BAIT
THE WILDLIFE...
MOSQUITOES THE SIZE OF CANNED HAMS
ZZZZZZZ
JIM DAVIS 6-9
THE SOLITUDE, THE COMPANIONSHIP
STRANDED IN A DINGHY WITH TWEEDLEDEE AND TWEEDLEDUM
KINDA MAKES A GUY JUST WANNA SING!
FISHING IS MY LIFE... FISHING IS MY LIFE...
© 1996 PAWS, INC./Distributed by Universal Press Syndicate

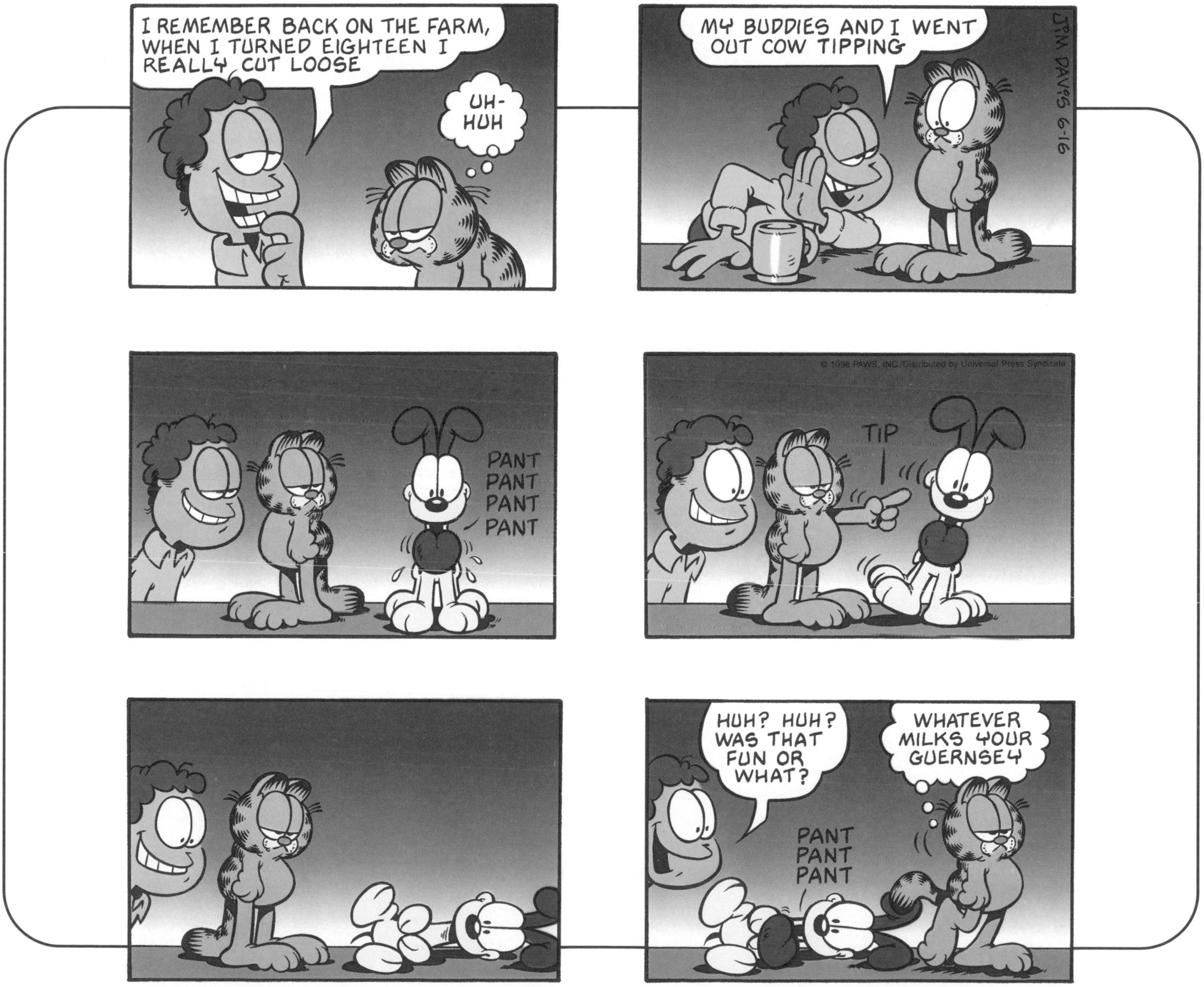
I REMEMBER BACK ON THE FARM, WHEN I TURNED EIGHTEEN I REALLY CUT LOOSE
UH-HUH
MY BUDDIES AND I WENT OUT COW TIPPING
JPM DAVPS 6-16
© 1996 PAWS, INC./Distributed by Universal Press Syndicate
PANT PANT PANT PANT
TIP
HUH? HUH? WAS THAT FUN OR WHAT?
WHATEVER MILKS YOUR GUERNSEY
PANT PANT PANT

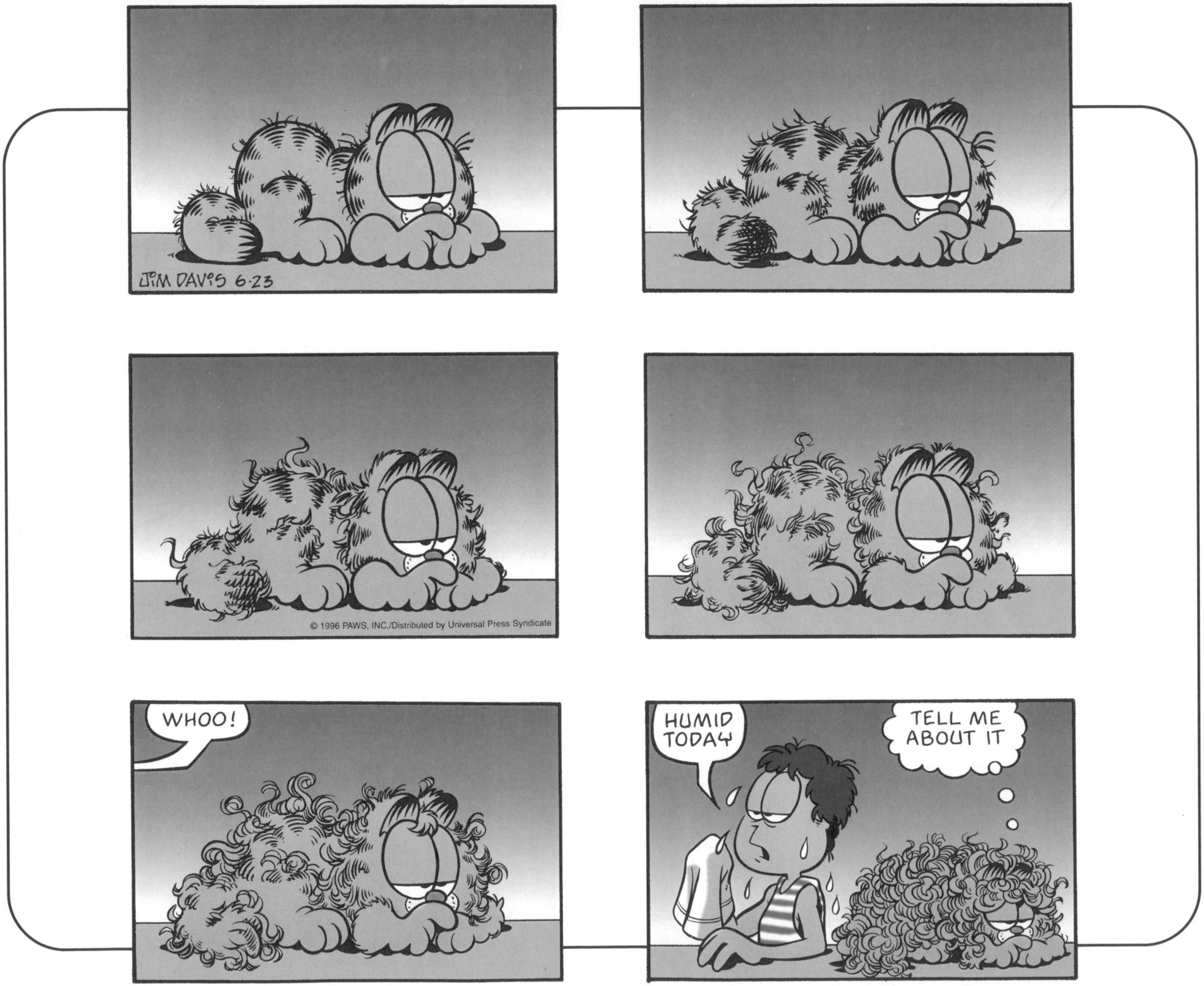
JIM DAVIS 6-23
© 1996 PAWS, INC./Distributed by Universal Press Syndicate
WHOO!
HUMID TODAY
TELL ME ABOUT IT

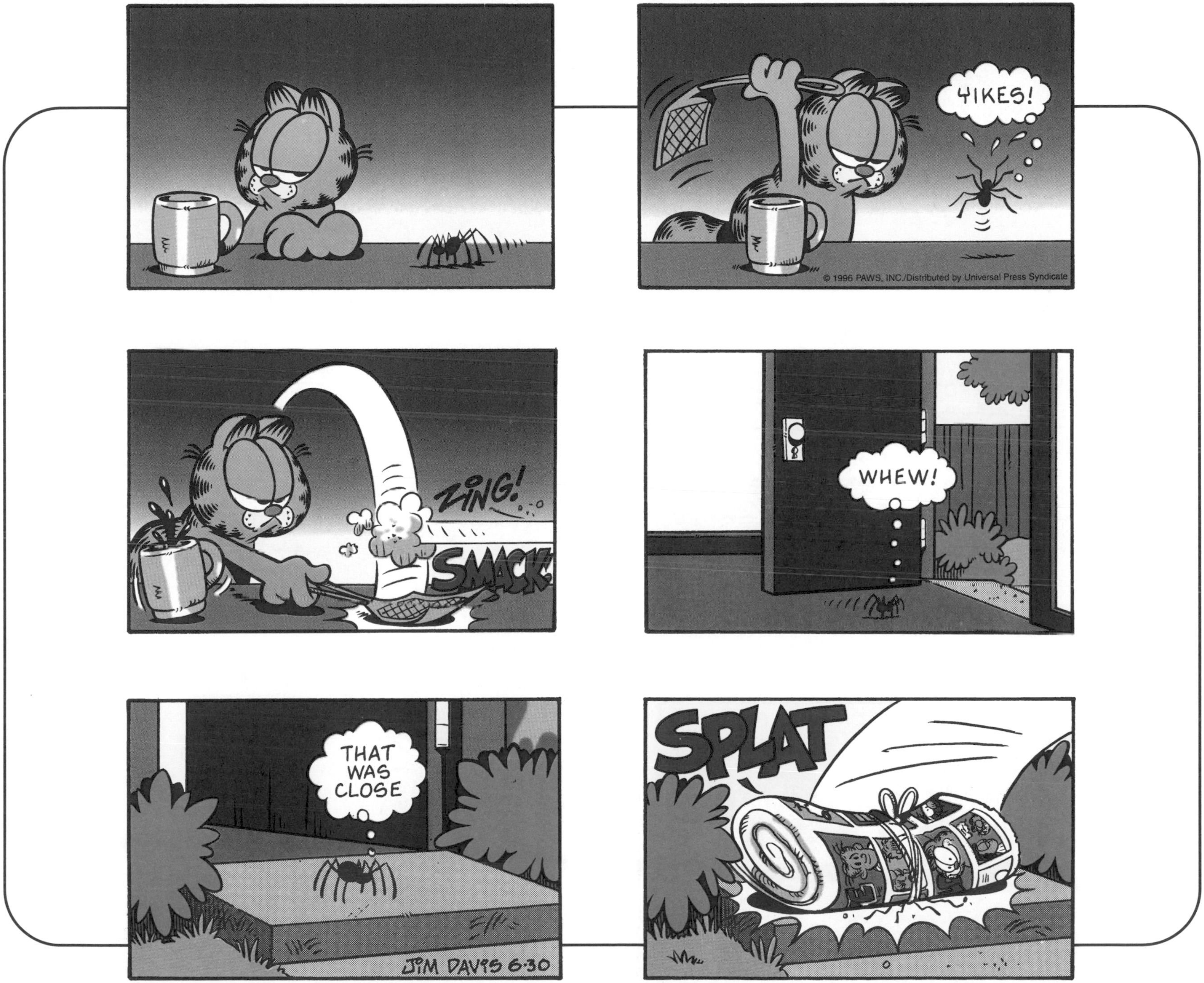
YIKES!
© 1996 PAWS, INC./Distributed by Universal Press Syndicate
ZING!
SMACK
WHEW!
THAT WAS CLOSE
JIM DAVIS 6-30
SPLAT

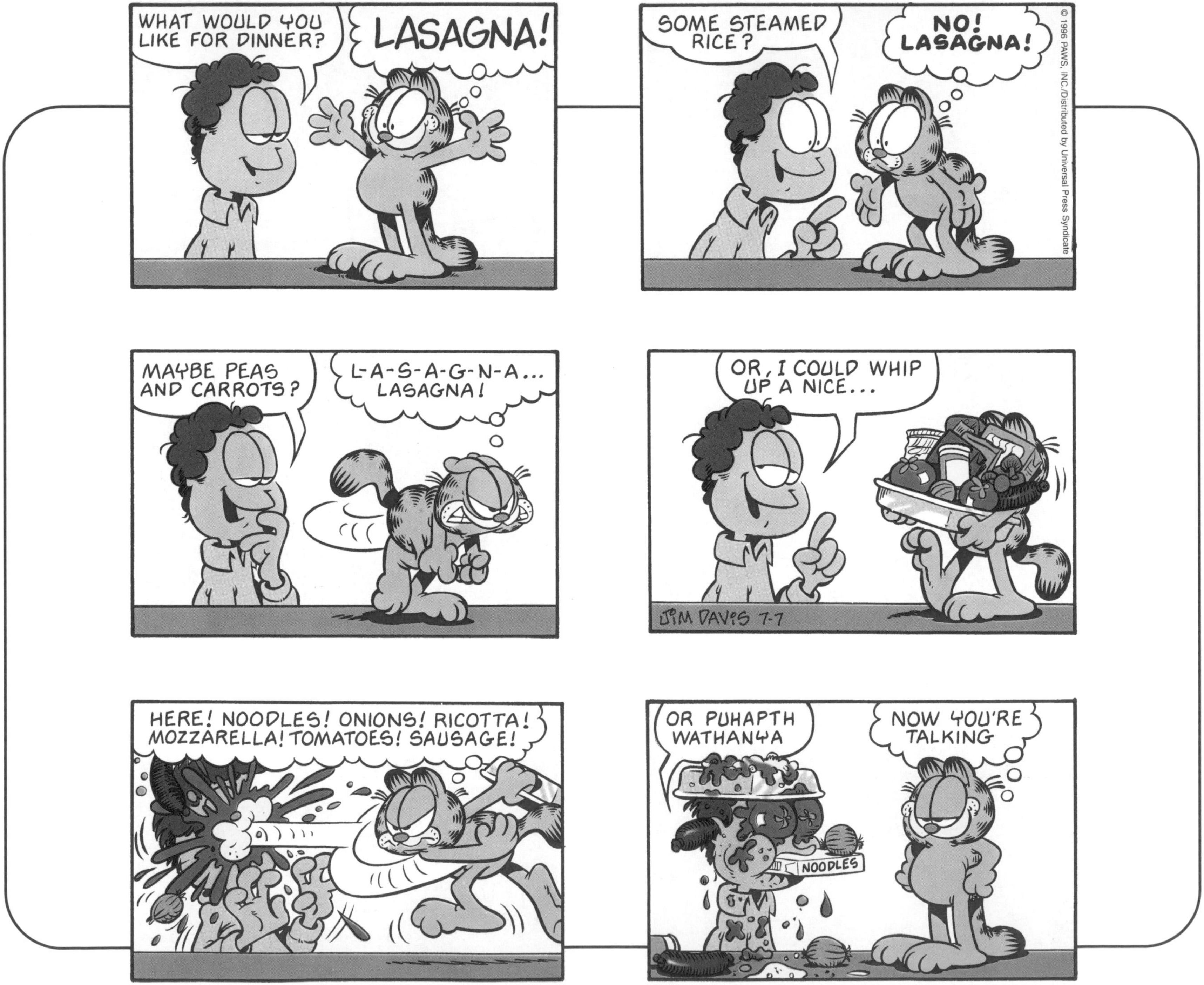
WHAT WOULD YOU LIKE FOR DINNER?
LASAGNA!
SOME STEAMED RICE?
NO! LASAGNA!
© 1996 PAWS, INC./Distributed by Universal Press Syndicate
MAYBE PEAS AND CARROTS?
L-A-S-A-G-N-A... LASAGNA!
OR, I COULD WHIP UP A NICE...
JIM DAVIS 7-7
HERE! NOODLES! ONIONS! RICOTTA! MOZZARELLA! TOMATOES! SAUSAGE!
OR PUHAPTH WATHANYA
NOODLES
NOW YOU'RE TALKING

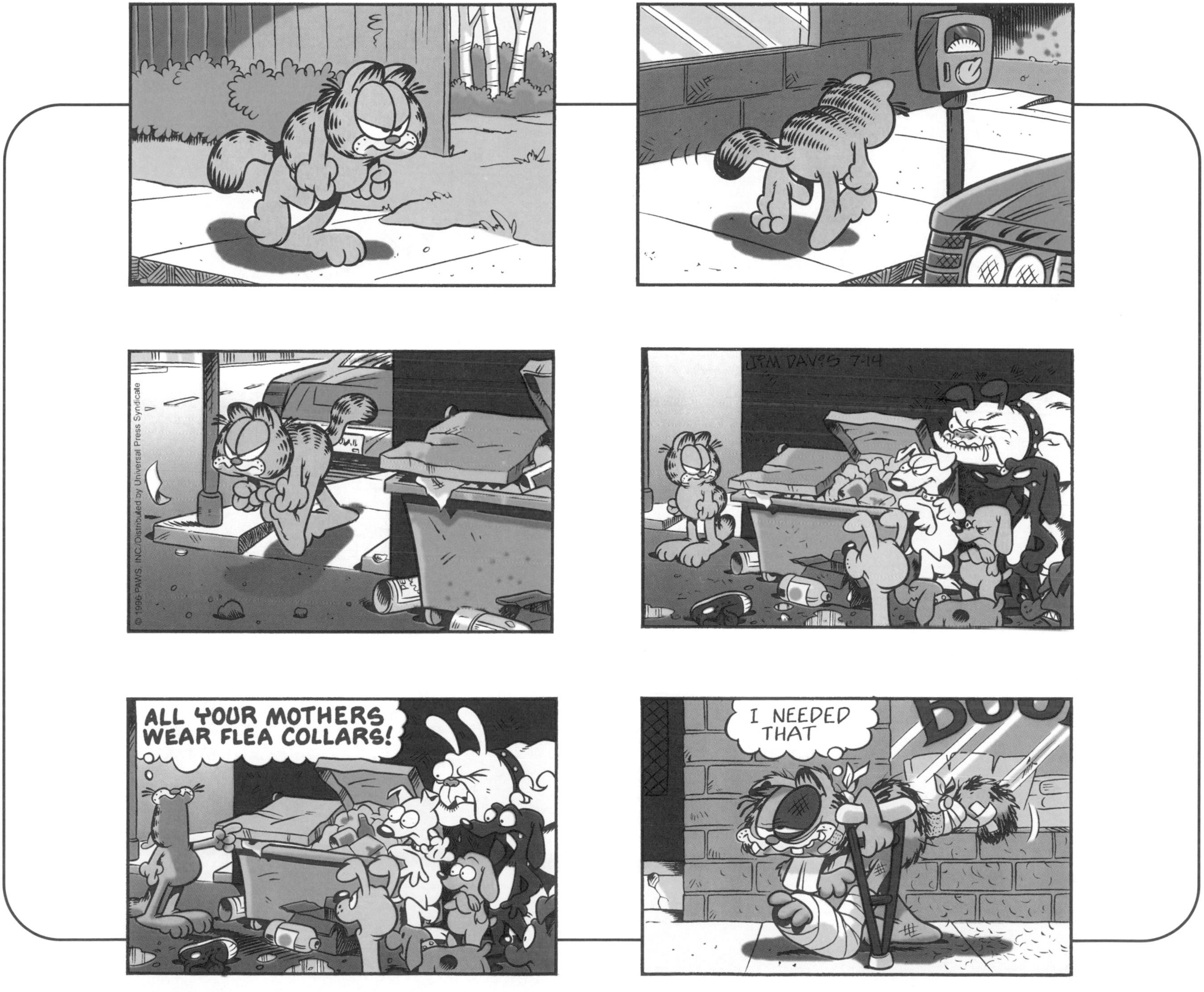
© 1996 PAWS, INC./Distributed by Universal Press Syndicate
JIM DAVIS 7-14
ALL YOUR MOTHERS WEAR FLEA COLLARS!
I NEEDED THAT

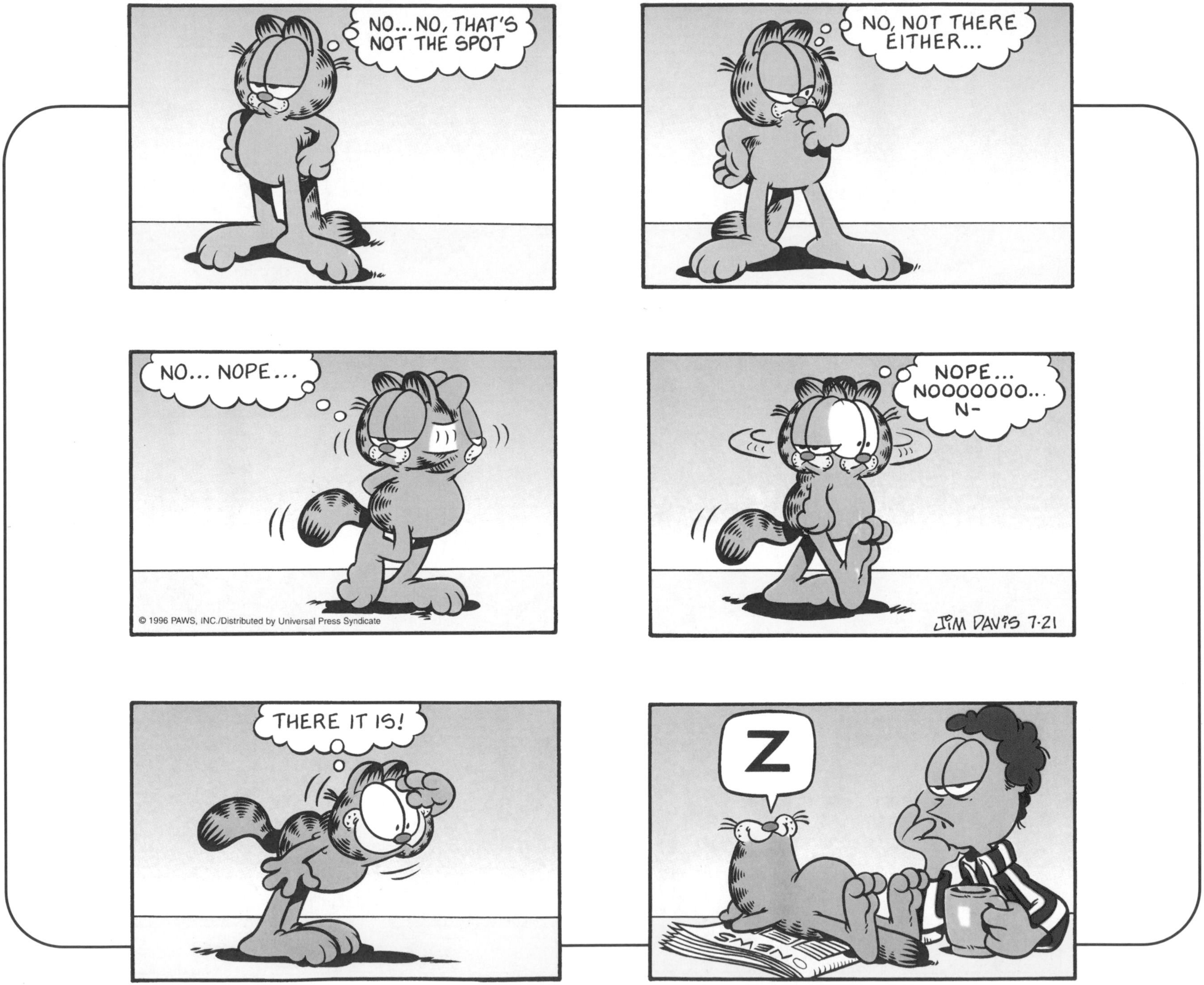

NO... NO, THAT'S NOT THE SPOT
NO, NOT THERE EITHER...
NO... NOPE...
NOPE... NOOOOOOO... N-
© 1996 PAWS, INC./Distributed by Universal Press Syndicate
JIM DAVIS 7-21
THERE IT IS!
Z
NEWS

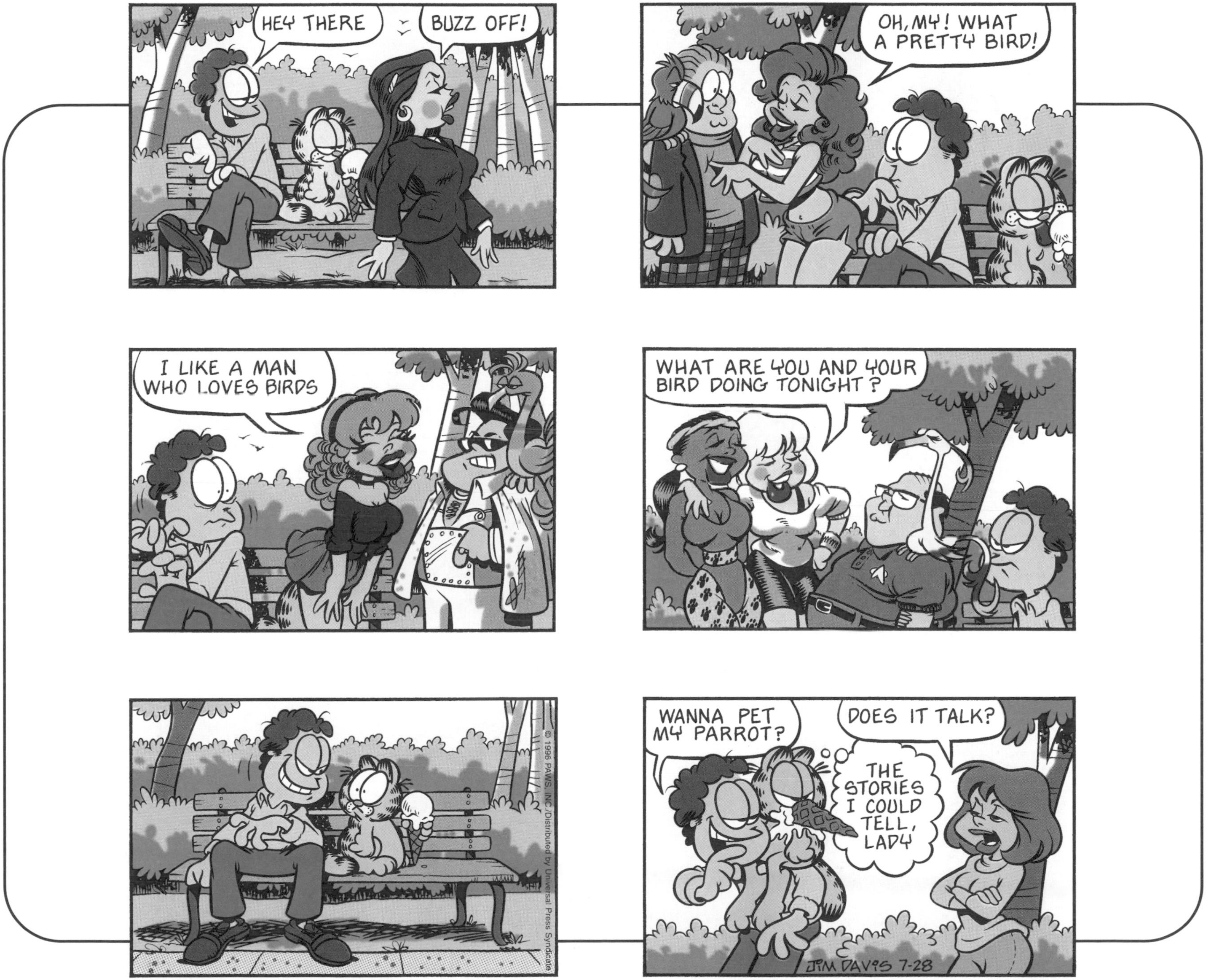
HEY THERE
BUZZ OFF!
OH, MY! WHAT A PRETTY BIRD!
I LIKE A MAN WHO LOVES BIRDS
WHAT ARE YOU AND YOUR BIRD DOING TONIGHT?
© 1996 PAWS, INC./Distributed by Universal Press Syndicate
WANNA PET MY PARROT?
DOES IT TALK?
THE STORIES I COULD TELL, LADY
JIM DAVIS 7-28

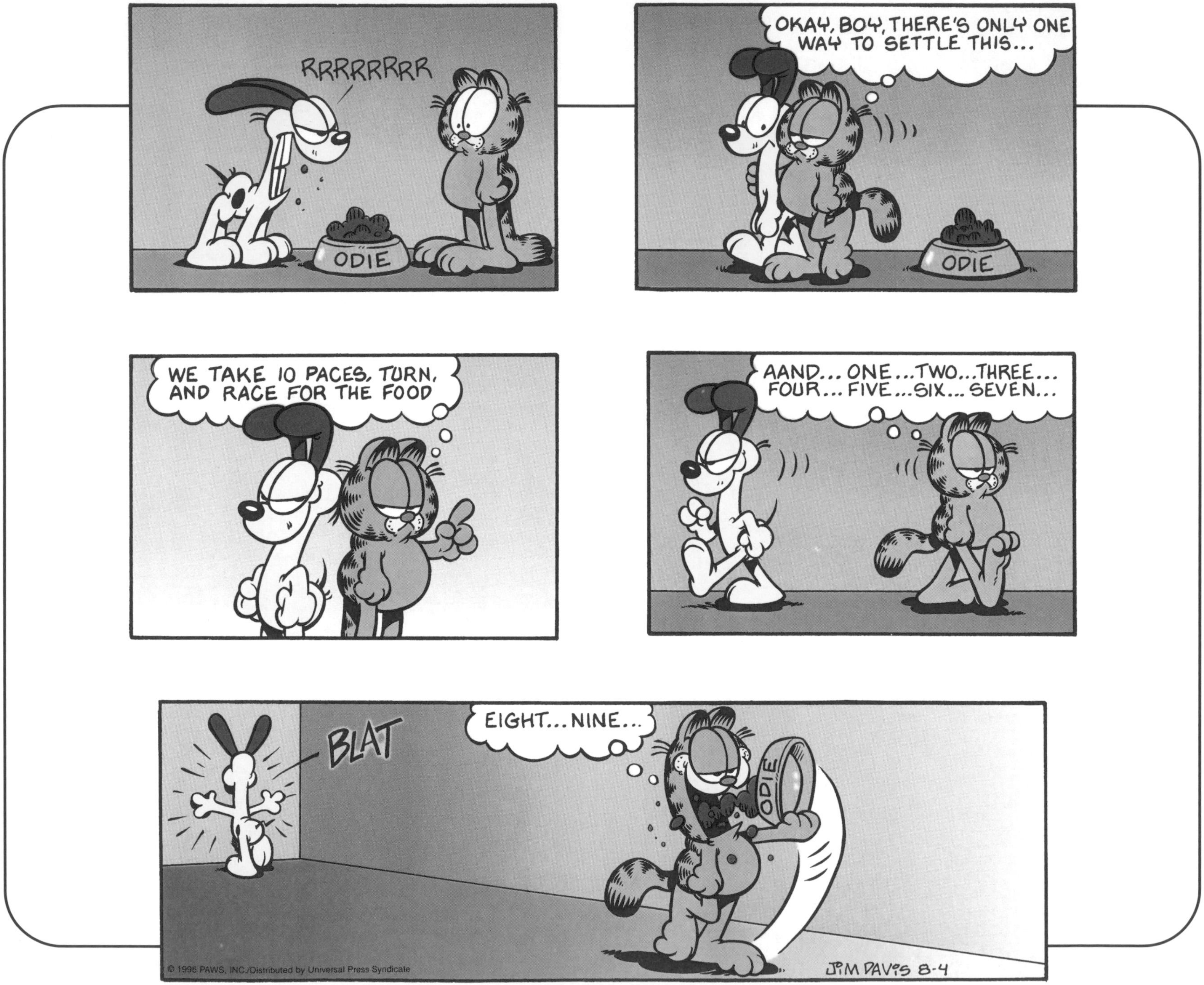
RRRRRRRR
ODIE
OKAY, BOY, THERE'S ONLY ONE WAY TO SETTLE THIS...
ODIE
WE TAKE 10 PACES, TURN, AND RACE FOR THE FOOD
AAND... ONE...TWO...THREE... FOUR... FIVE...SIX... SEVEN...
BLAT
EIGHT... NINE...
ODIE
© 1996 PAWS, INC./Distributed by Universal Press Syndicate
JIM DAVIS 8-4

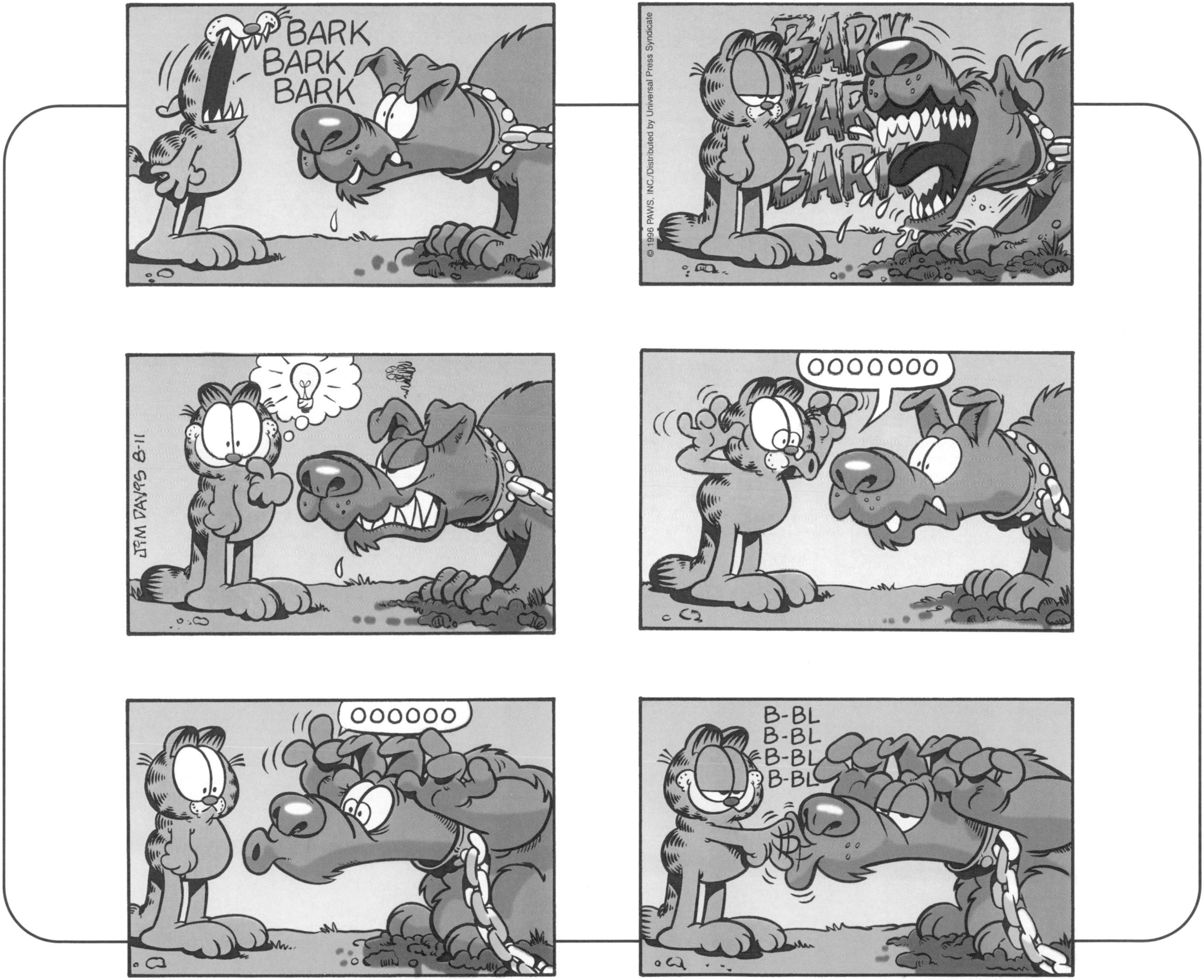
BARK
BARK
BARK
© 1996 PAWS, INC./Distributed by Universal Press Syndicate
JIM DAVIS 8-11
OOOOOOO
OOOOOO
B-BL
B-BL
B-BL
B-BL

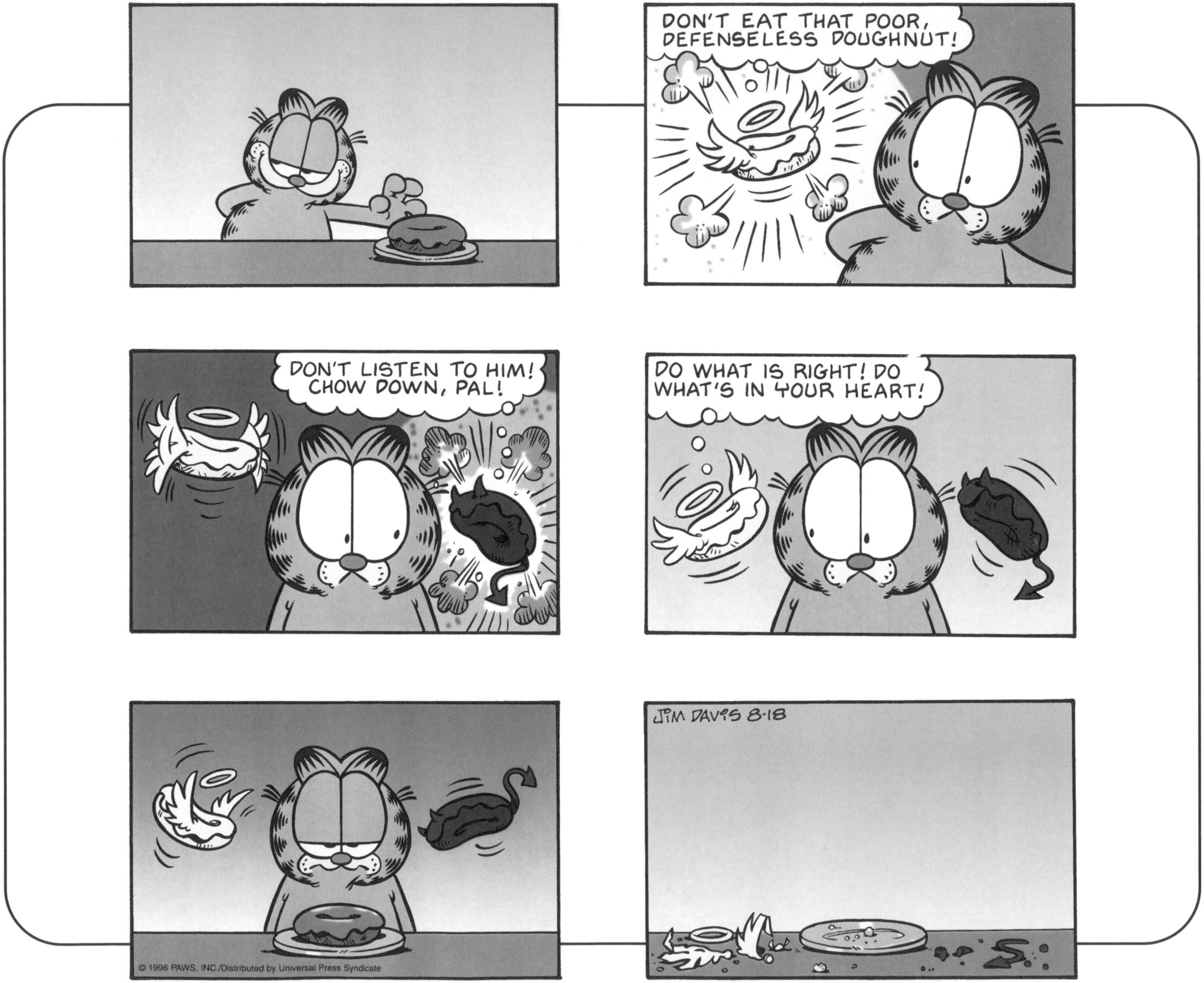
DON'T EAT THAT POOR, DEFENSELESS DOUGHNUT!
DON'T LISTEN TO HIM! CHOW DOWN, PAL!
DO WHAT IS RIGHT! DO WHAT'S IN YOUR HEART!
JIM DAVIS 8-18
© 1996 PAWS, INC./Distributed by Universal Press Syndicate

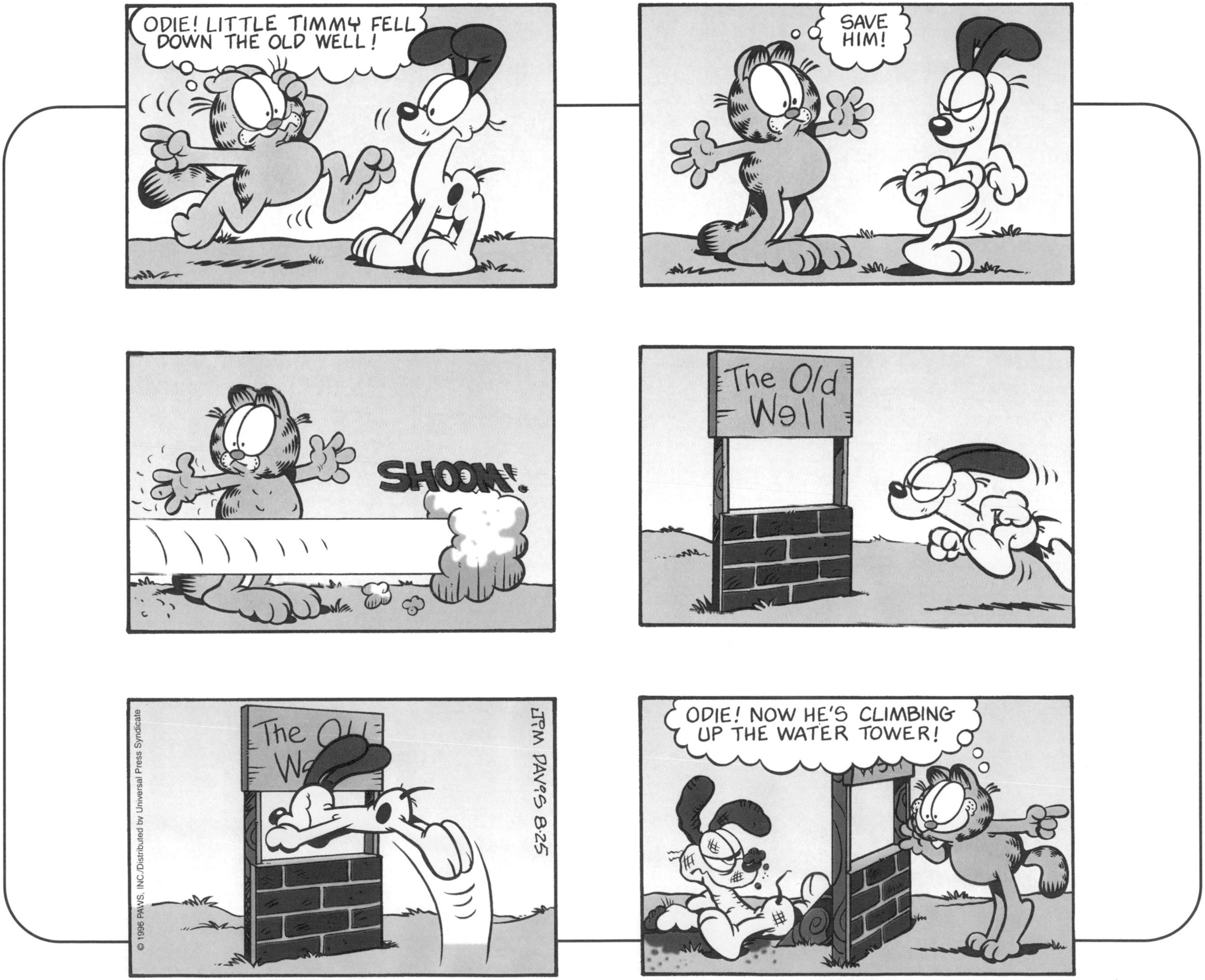
ODIE! LITTLE TIMMY FELL DOWN THE OLD WELL!
SAVE HIM!
SHOOM!
The Old Well
JPM DAVIS 8-25
© 1996 PAWS, INC./Distributed by Universal Press Syndicate
ODIE! NOW HE'S CLIMBING UP THE WATER TOWER!

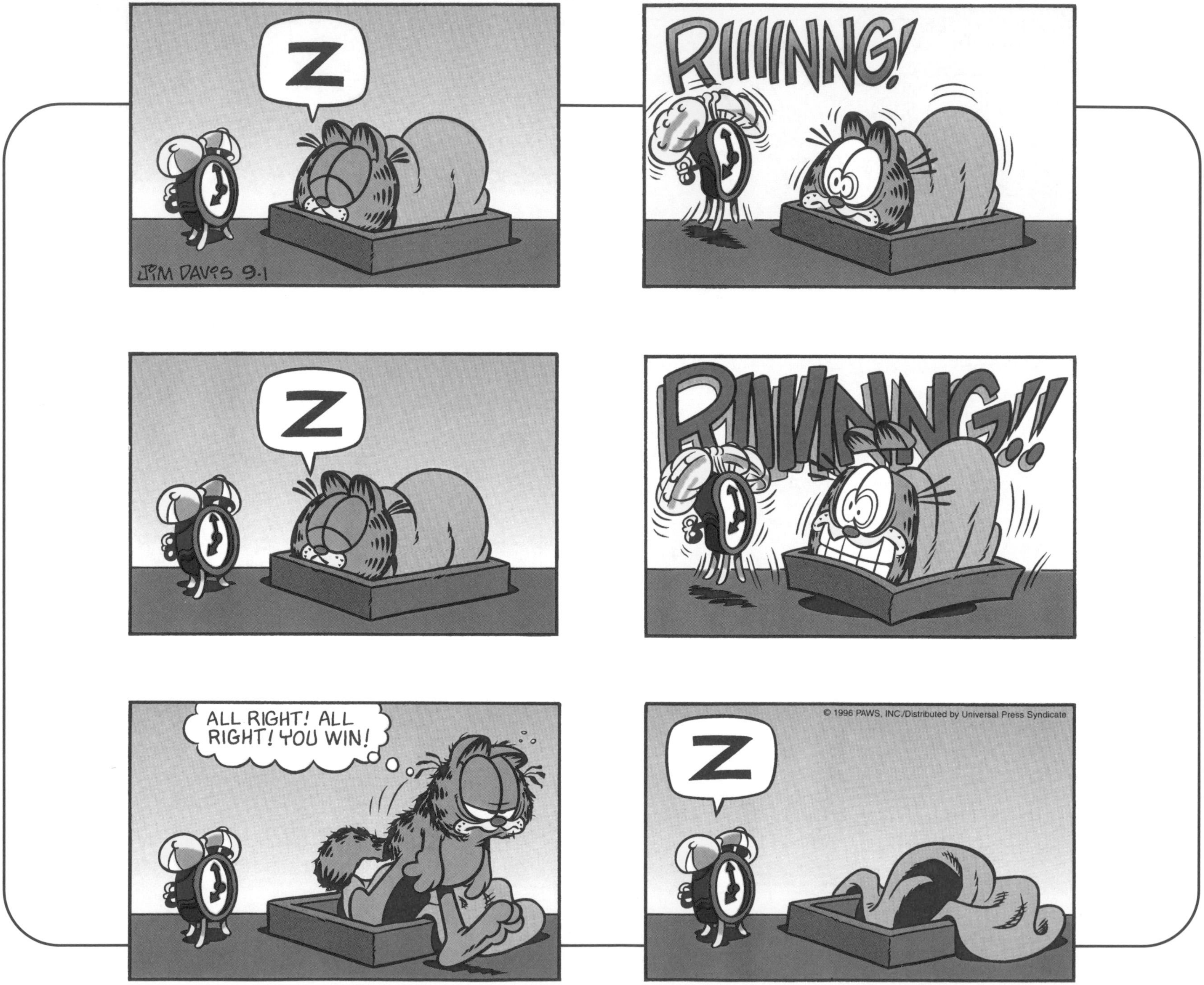
Z
JIM DAVIS 9-1
RIIIINNG!
Z
RIIIINNG!!
ALL RIGHT! ALL RIGHT! YOU WIN!
© 1996 PAWS, INC./Distributed by Universal Press Syndicate
Z

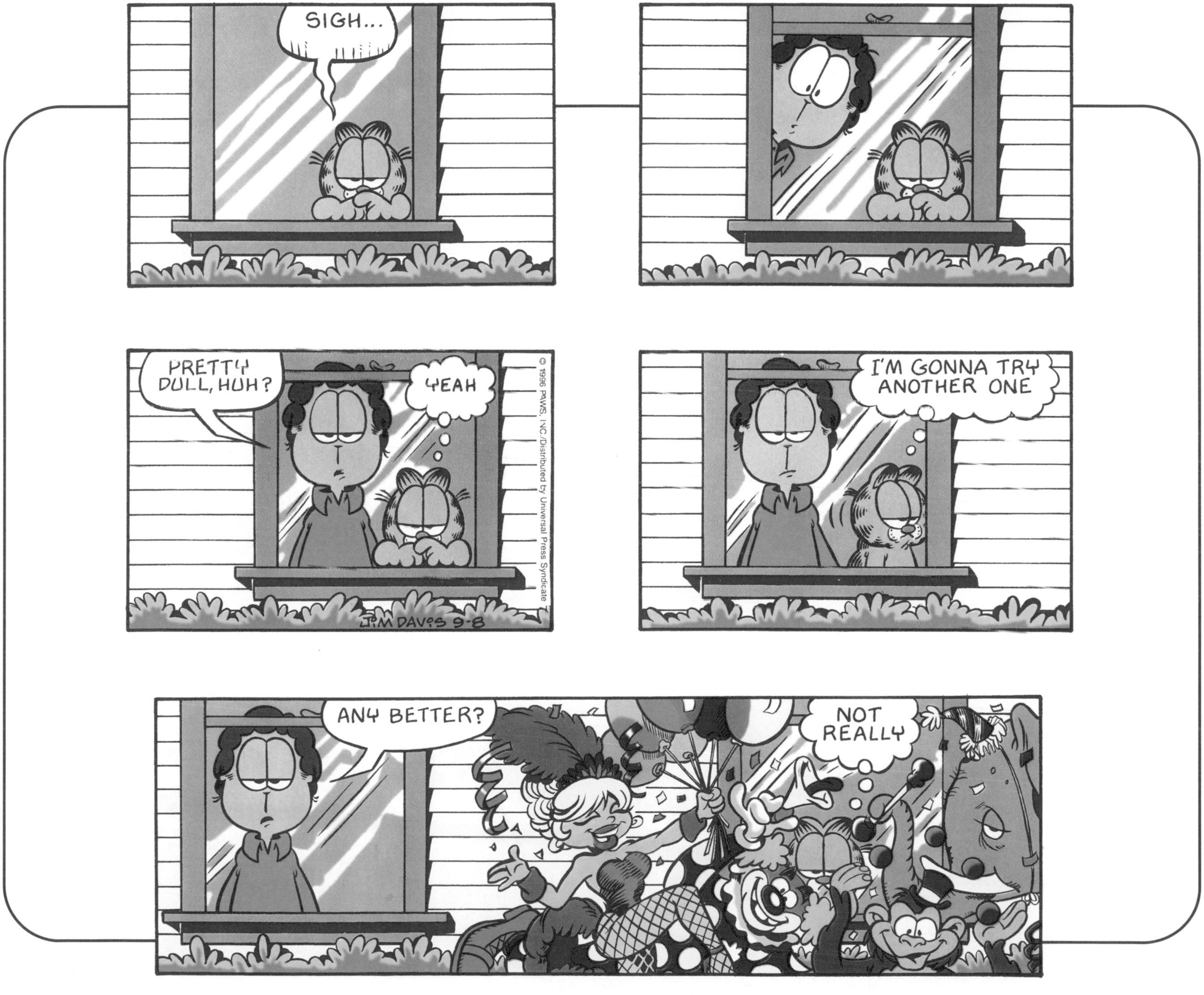
SIGH...
PRETTY DULL, HUH?
YEAH
© 1996 PAWS, INC./Distributed by Universal Press Syndicate
JIM DAVIS 9-8
I'M GONNA TRY ANOTHER ONE
ANY BETTER?
NOT REALLY

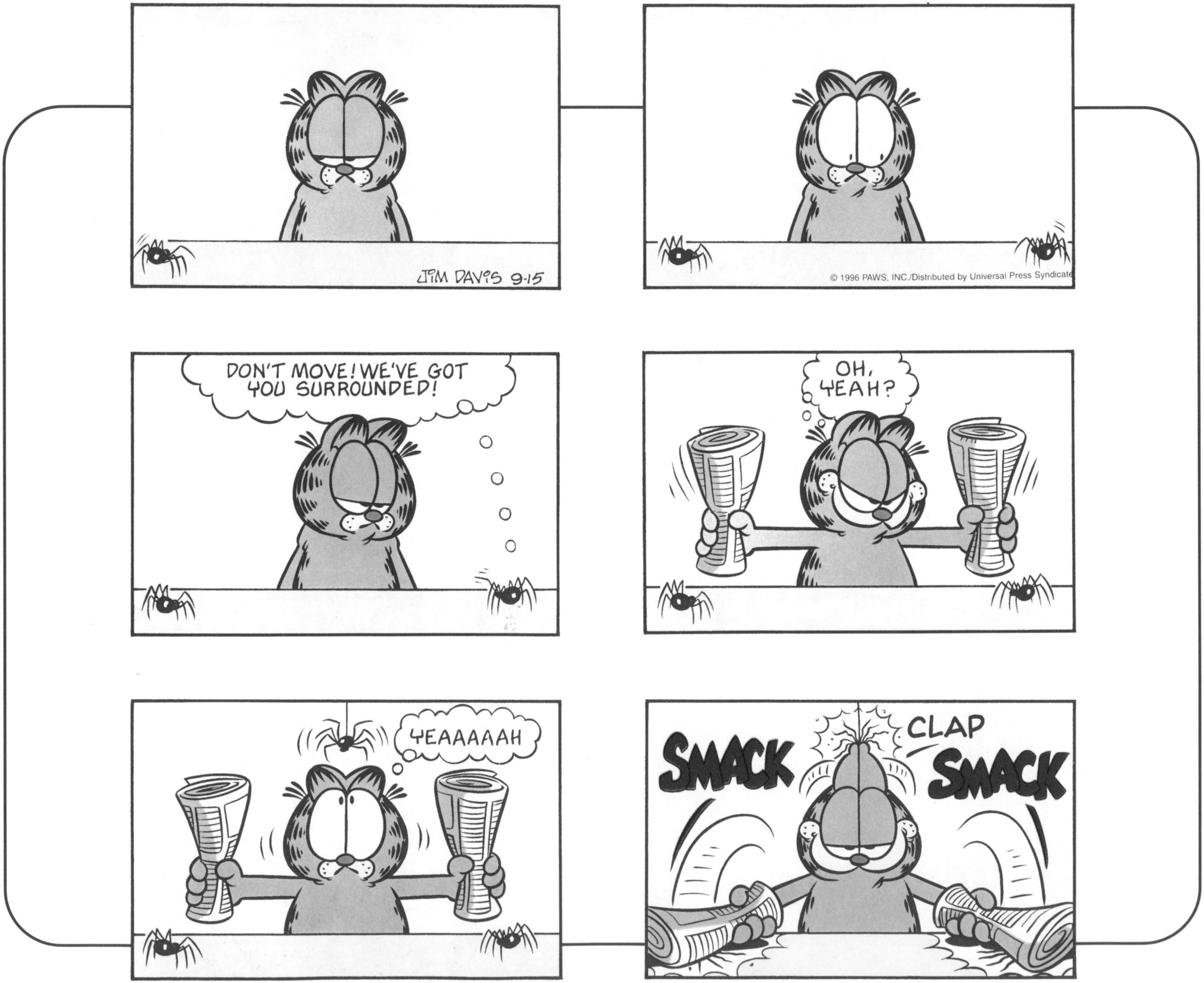
JIM DAVIS 9-15
© 1996 PAWS, INC./Distributed by Universal Press Syndicate
DON'T MOVE! WE'VE GOT YOU SURROUNDED!
OH, YEAH?
YEAAAAAAH
SMACK
CLAP
SMACK

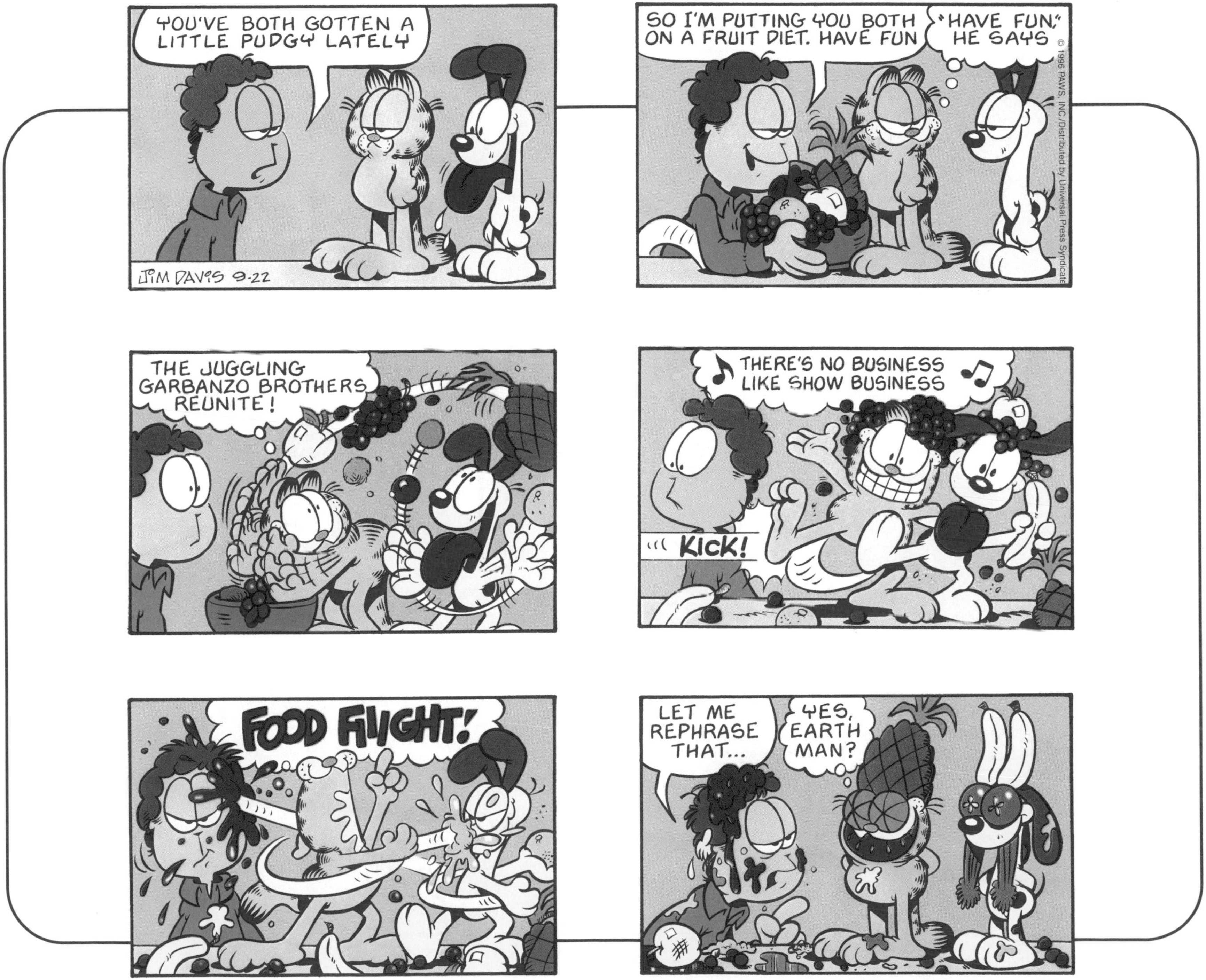
YOU'VE BOTH GOTTEN A LITTLE PUDGY LATELY
JIM DAVIS 9-22
SO I'M PUTTING YOU BOTH ON A FRUIT DIET. HAVE FUN
"HAVE FUN," HE SAYS
© 1996 PAWS, INC./Distributed by Universal Press Syndicate
THE JUGGLING GARBANZO BROTHERS REUNITE!
THERE'S NO BUSINESS LIKE SHOW BUSINESS
KICK!
FOOD FIGHT!
LET ME REPHRASE THAT...
YES, EARTH MAN?

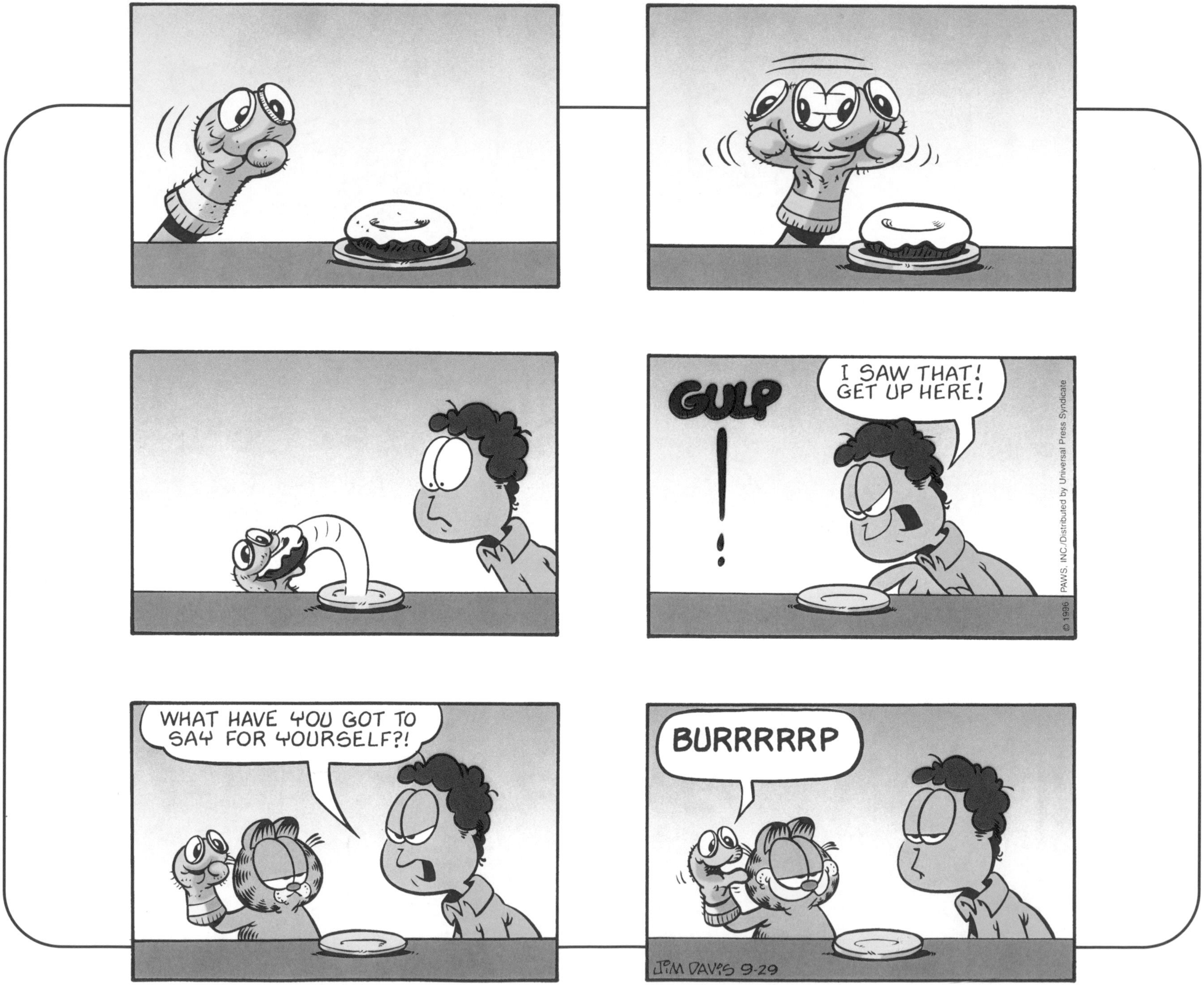
GULP
I SAW THAT! GET UP HERE!
© 1996 PAWS, INC./Distributed by Universal Press Syndicate
WHAT HAVE YOU GOT TO SAY FOR YOURSELF?!
BURRRRRP
JIM DAVIS 9-29

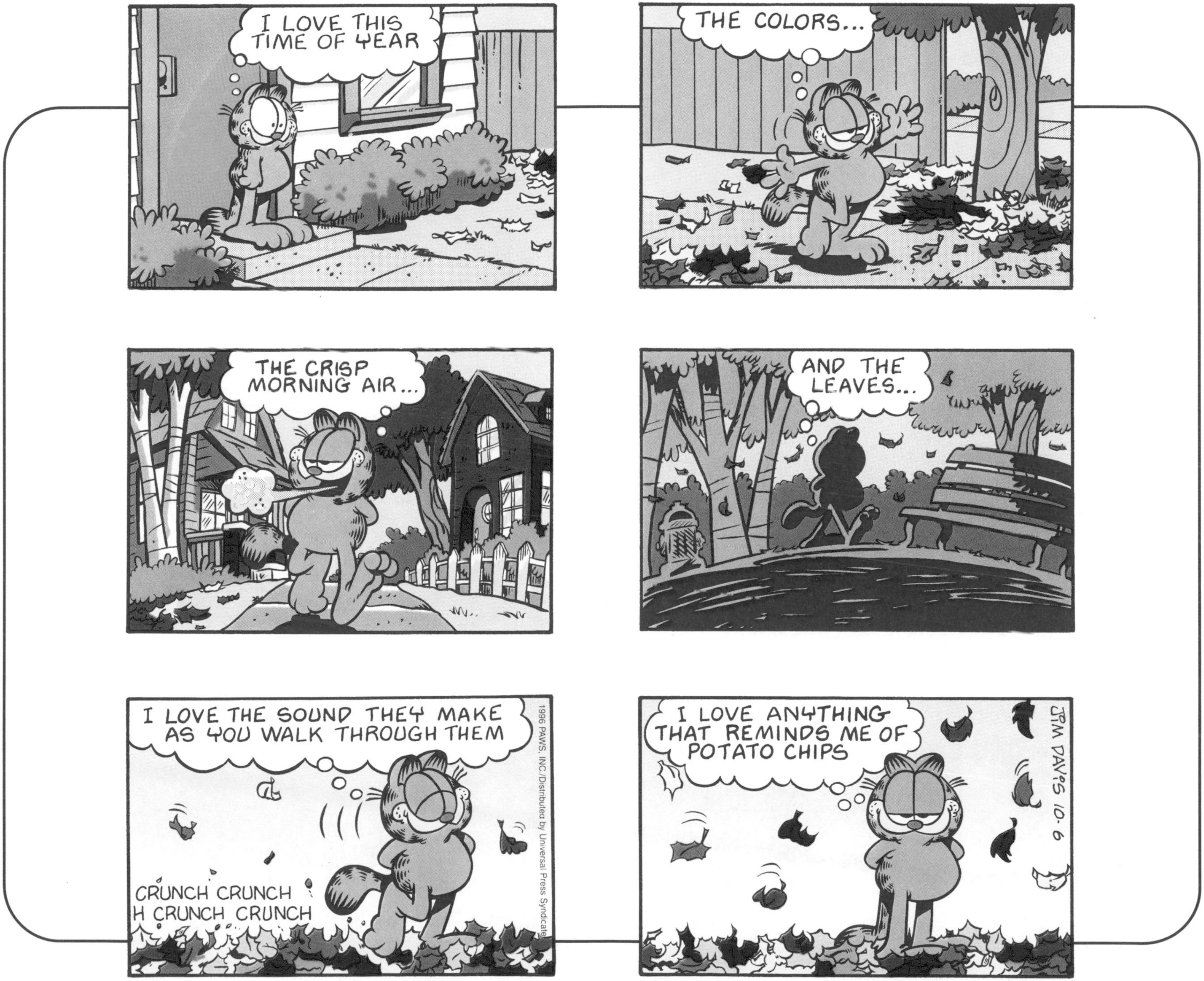
I LOVE THIS TIME OF YEAR
THE COLORS...
THE CRISP MORNING AIR...
AND THE LEAVES...
I LOVE THE SOUND THEY MAKE AS YOU WALK THROUGH THEM
CRUNCH CRUNCH
H CRUNCH CRUNCH
1996 PAWS, INC./Distributed by Universal Press Syndicate
I LOVE ANYTHING THAT REMINDS ME OF POTATO CHIPS
JIM DAVIS 10-6

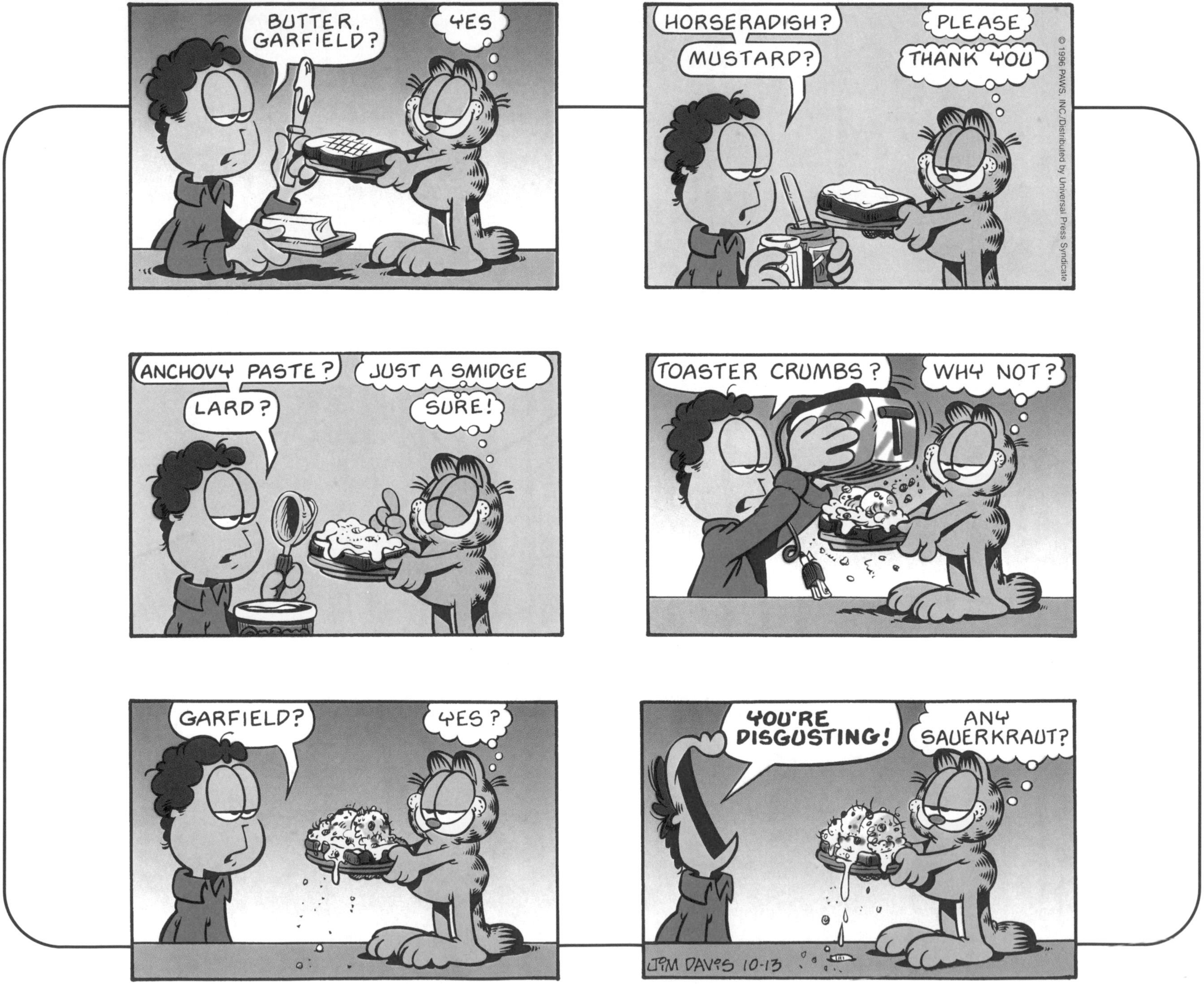
BUTTER, GARFIELD?
YES
HORSERADISH?
PLEASE
MUSTARD?
THANK YOU
© 1996 PAWS, INC./Distributed by Universal Press Syndicate
ANCHOVY PASTE?
JUST A SMIDGE
LARD?
SURE!
TOASTER CRUMBS?
WHY NOT?
GARFIELD?
YES?
YOU'RE DISGUSTING!
ANY SAUERKRAUT?
JIM DAVIS 10-13

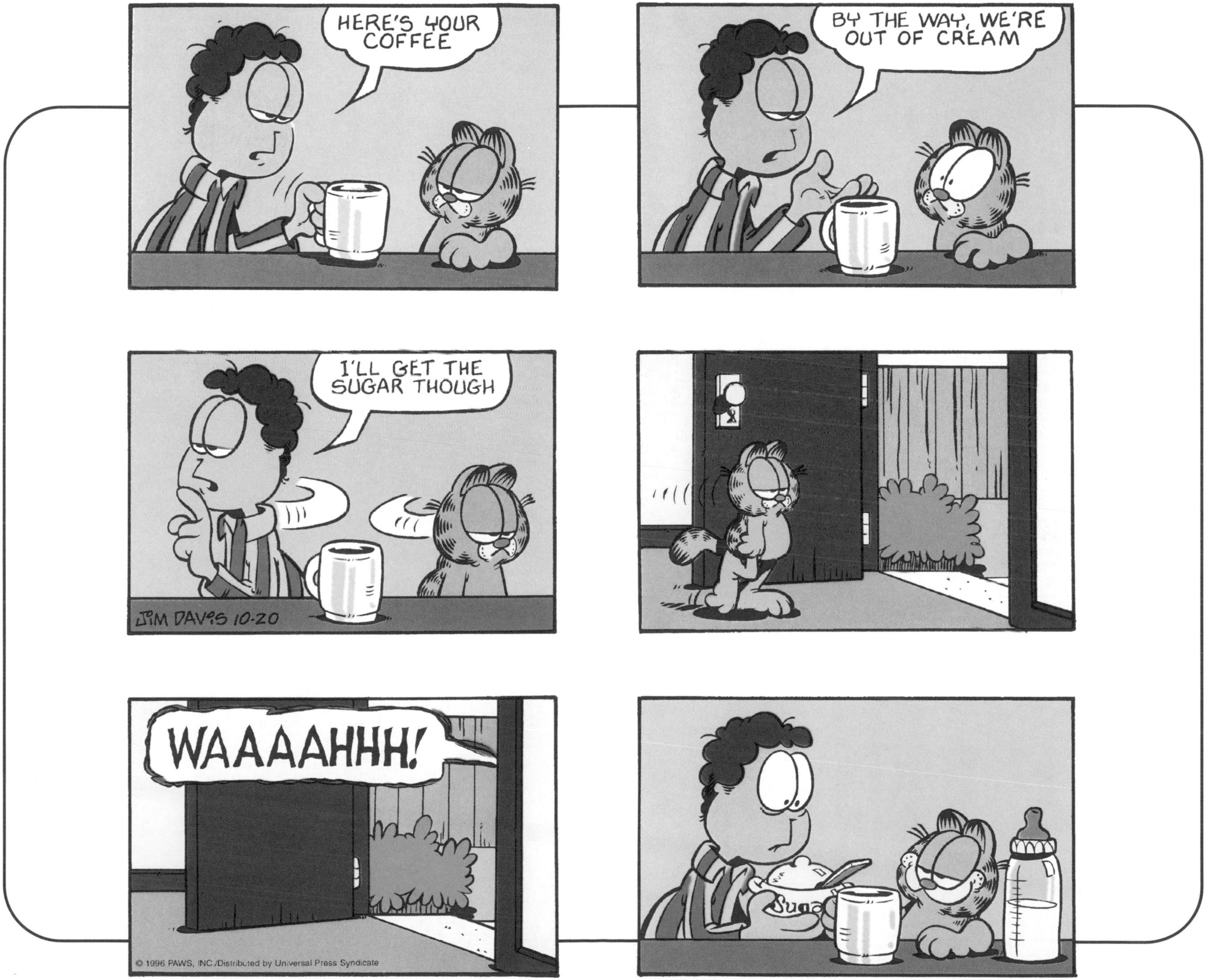
HERE'S YOUR COFFEE
BY THE WAY, WE'RE OUT OF CREAM
I'LL GET THE SUGAR THOUGH
JIM DAVIS 10-20
WAAAAHHH!
© 1996 PAWS, INC./Distributed by Universal Press Syndicate

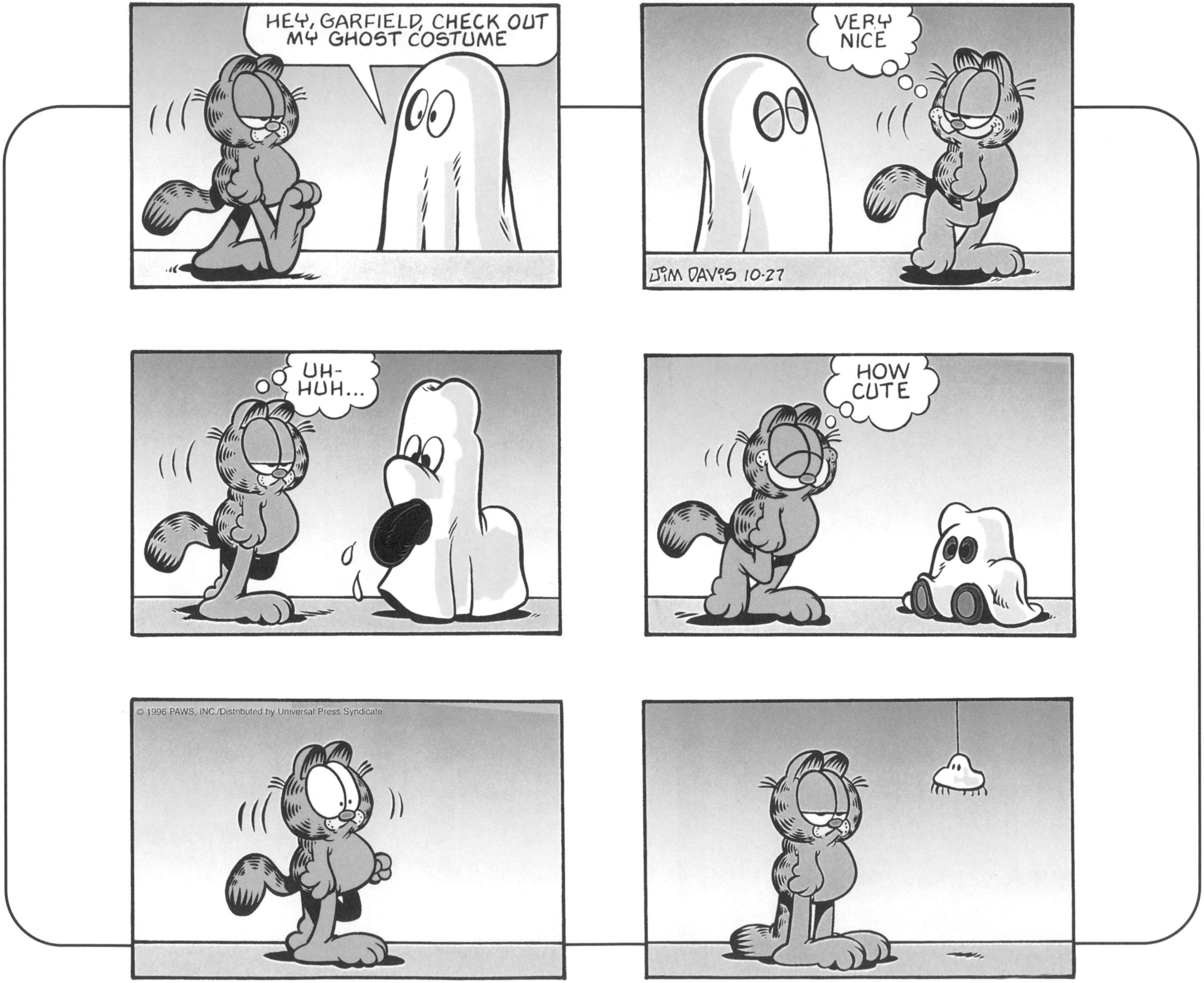
HEY, GARFIELD, CHECK OUT MY GHOST COSTUME
VERY NICE
JIM DAVIS 10-27
UH-HUH...
HOW CUTE
© 1996 PAWS, INC./Distributed by Universal Press Syndicate

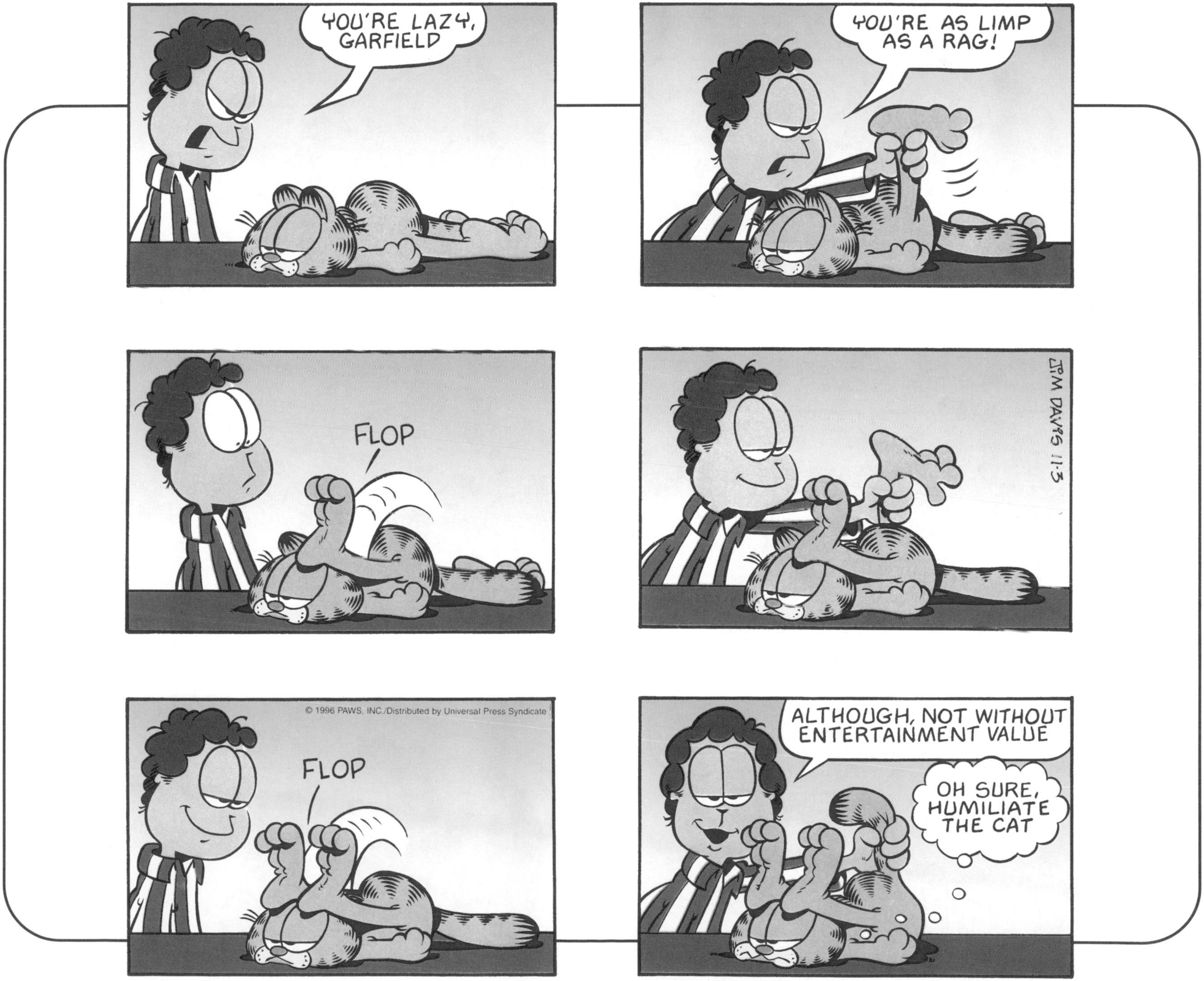
YOU'RE LAZY, GARFIELD
YOU'RE AS LIMP AS A RAG!
FLOP
JIM DAVIS 11-3
© 1996 PAWS, INC./Distributed by Universal Press Syndicate
FLOP
ALTHOUGH, NOT WITHOUT ENTERTAINMENT VALUE
OH SURE, HUMILIATE THE CAT

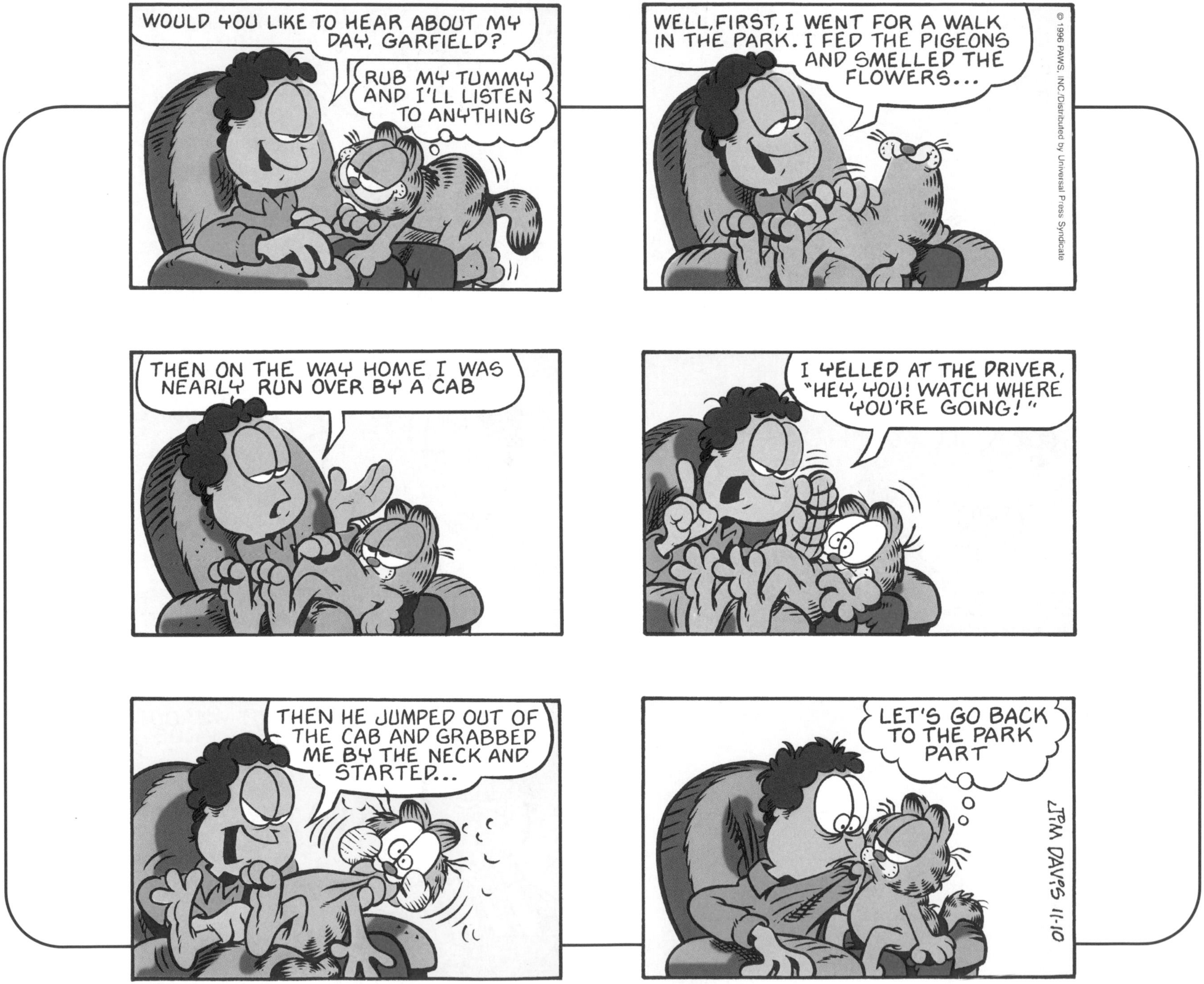
WOULD YOU LIKE TO HEAR ABOUT MY DAY, GARFIELD?
RUB MY TUMMY AND I'LL LISTEN TO ANYTHING
WELL, FIRST, I WENT FOR A WALK IN THE PARK. I FED THE PIGEONS AND SMELLED THE FLOWERS...
© 1996 PAWS, INC./Distributed by Universal Press Syndicate
THEN ON THE WAY HOME I WAS NEARLY RUN OVER BY A CAB
I YELLED AT THE DRIVER, "HEY, YOU! WATCH WHERE YOU'RE GOING!"
THEN HE JUMPED OUT OF THE CAB AND GRABBED ME BY THE NECK AND STARTED...
LET'S GO BACK TO THE PARK PART
JIM DAVIS 11-10

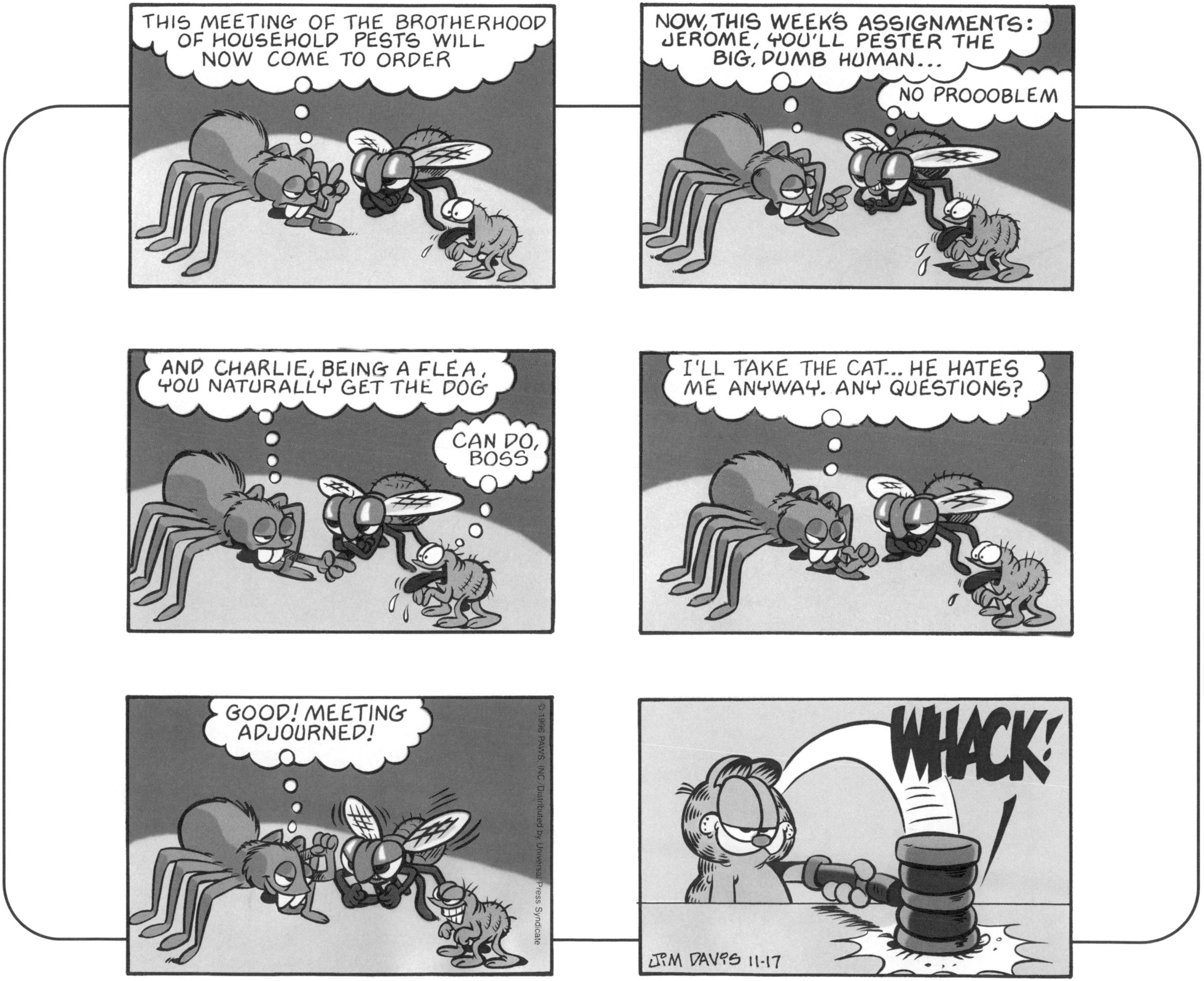
THIS MEETING OF THE BROTHERHOOD OF HOUSEHOLD PESTS WILL NOW COME TO ORDER
NOW, THIS WEEK'S ASSIGNMENTS: JEROME, YOU'LL PESTER THE BIG, DUMB HUMAN...
NO PROOOBLEM
AND CHARLIE, BEING A FLEA, YOU NATURALLY GET THE DOG
CAN DO, BOSS
I'LL TAKE THE CAT... HE HATES ME ANYWAY. ANY QUESTIONS?
GOOD! MEETING ADJOURNED!
© 1996 PAWS, INC. Distributed by Universal Press Syndicate
WHACK!
JIM DAVIS 11-17

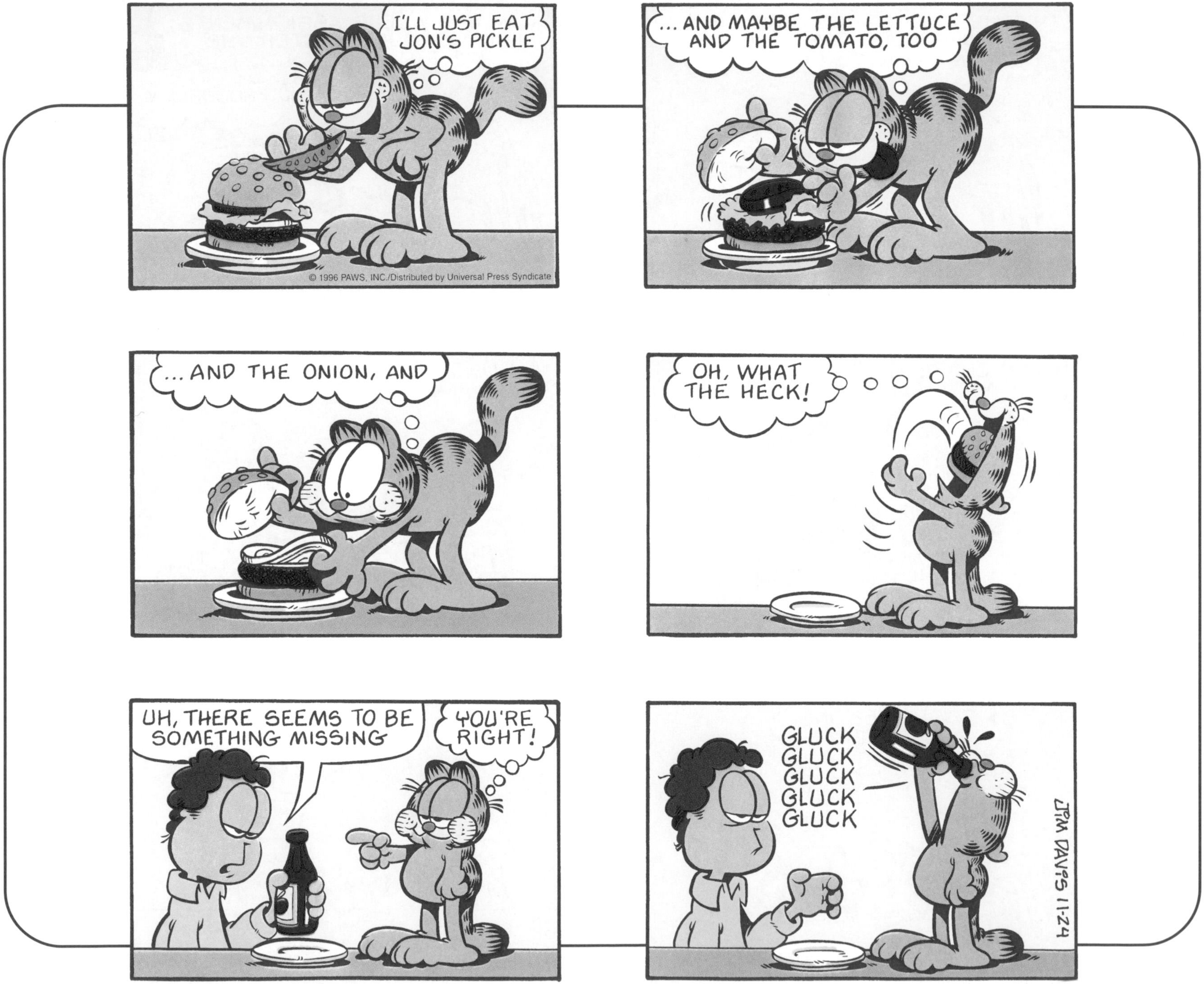
I'LL JUST EAT JON'S PICKLE
© 1996 PAWS, INC./Distributed by Universal Press Syndicate
... AND MAYBE THE LETTUCE AND THE TOMATO, TOO
... AND THE ONION, AND
OH, WHAT THE HECK!
UH, THERE SEEMS TO BE SOMETHING MISSING
YOU'RE RIGHT!
GLUCK GLUCK GLUCK GLUCK GLUCK
JIM DAVIS 11-24

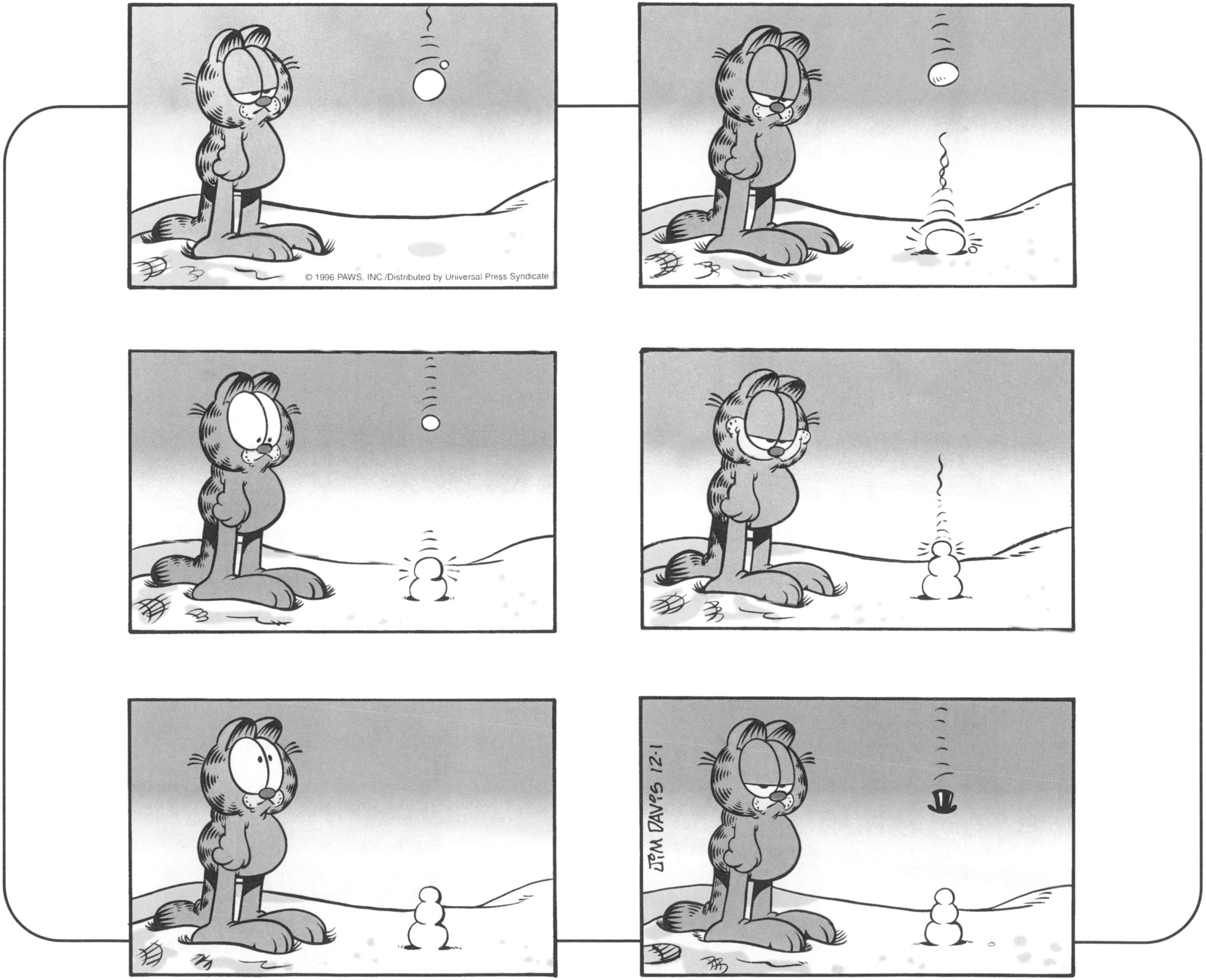
© 1996 PAWS, INC./Distributed by Universal Press Syndicate
JIM DAVIS 12·1

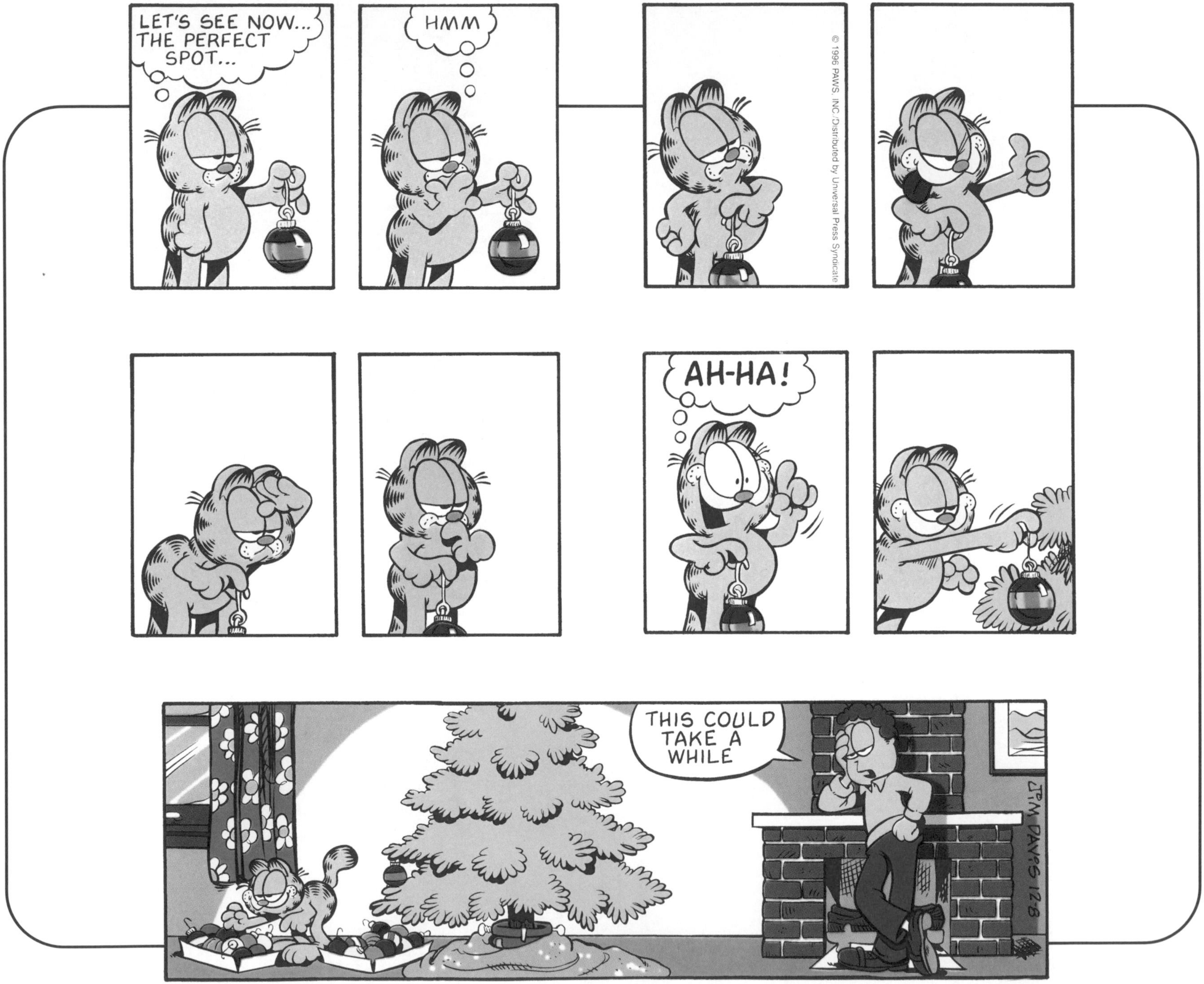
LET'S SEE NOW... THE PERFECT SPOT...
HMM
© 1996 PAWS, INC./Distributed by Universal Press Syndicate
AH-HA!
THIS COULD TAKE A WHILE
JIM DAVIS 12-8

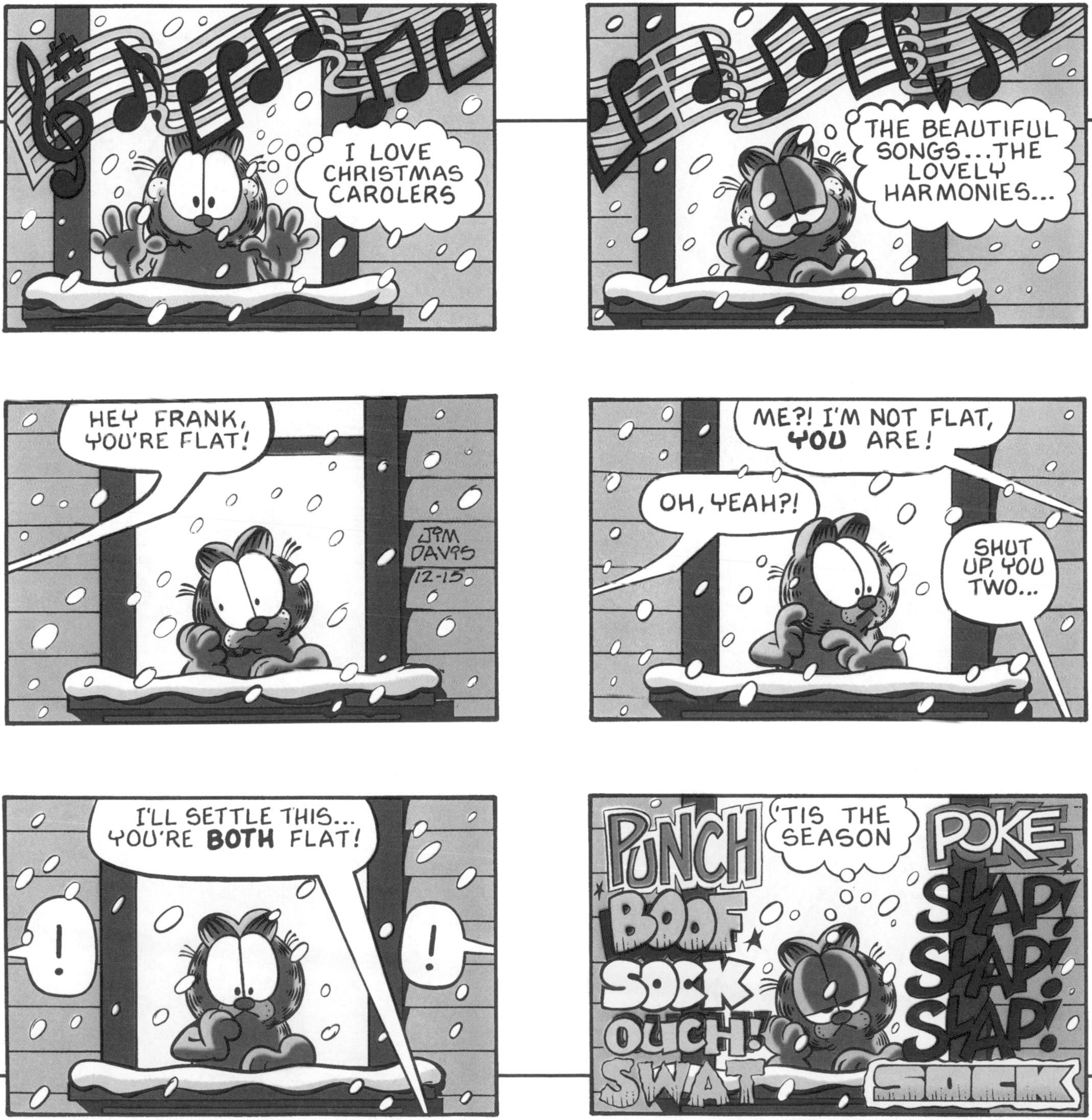
I LOVE CHRISTMAS CAROLERS
THE BEAUTIFUL SONGS...THE LOVELY HARMONIES...
HEY FRANK, YOU'RE FLAT!
JIM DAVIS 12-15
ME?! I'M NOT FLAT, YOU ARE!
OH, YEAH?!
SHUT UP, YOU TWO...
I'LL SETTLE THIS... YOU'RE BOTH FLAT!
!
!
PUNCH
'TIS THE SEASON
POKE
BOOF
SOCK
OUCH!
SWAT
SLAP! SLAP! SLAP!
SOCK

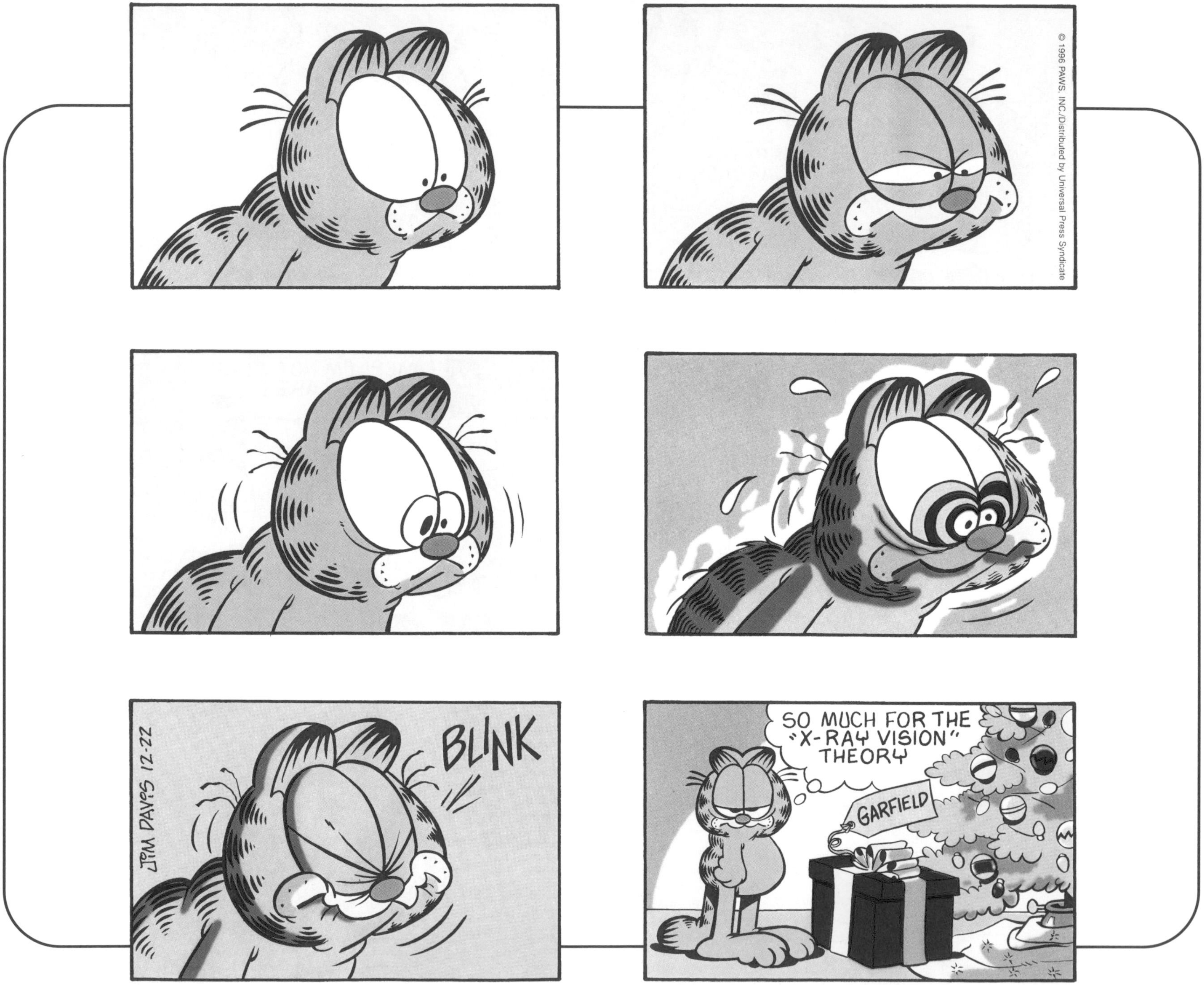
JIM DAVIS 12-22
BLINK
SO MUCH FOR THE "X-RAY VISION" THEORY
GARFIELD

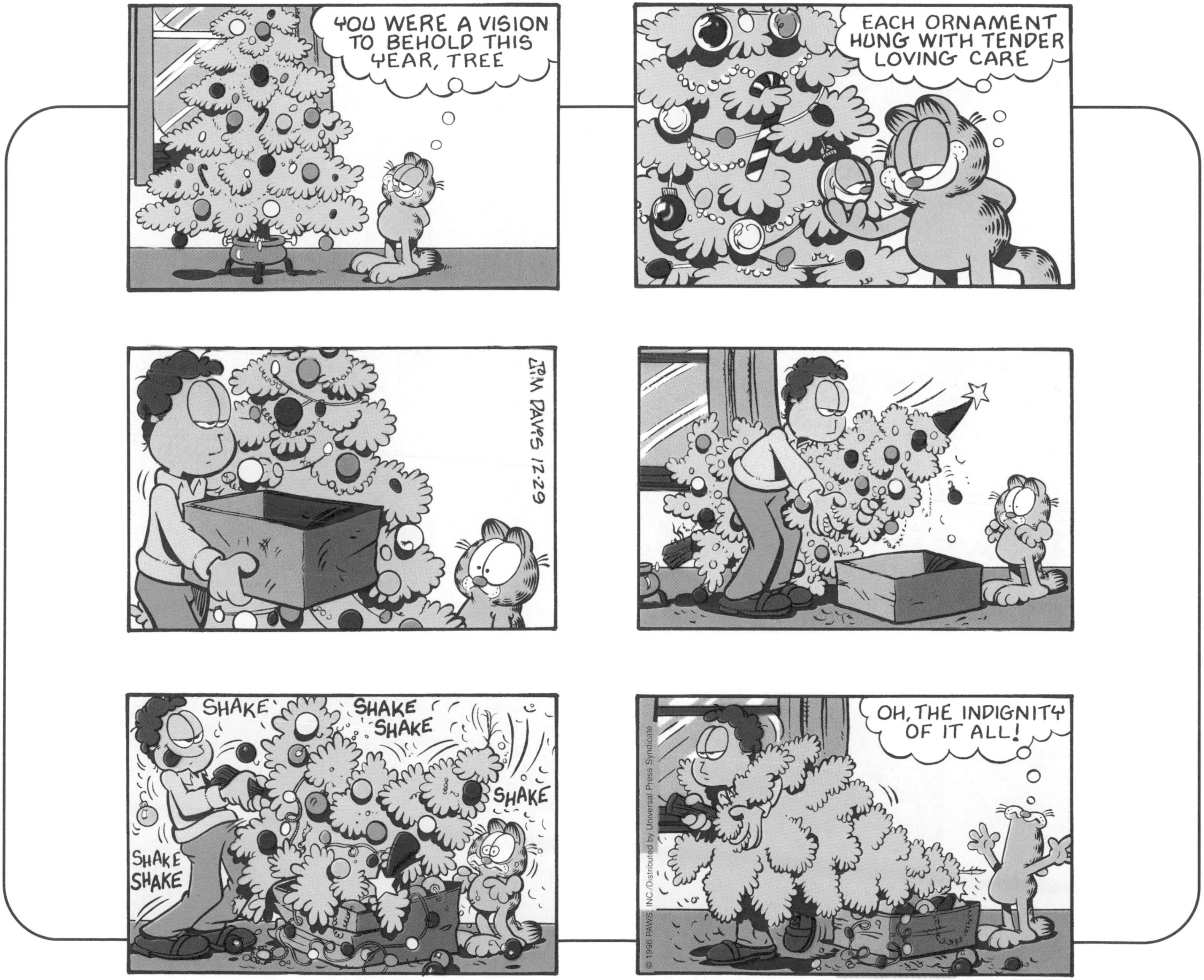
YOU WERE A VISION TO BEHOLD THIS YEAR, TREE
EACH ORNAMENT HUNG WITH TENDER LOVING CARE
JIM DAVIS 12-29
SHAKE
SHAKE SHAKE
SHAKE
SHAKE SHAKE
OH, THE INDIGNITY OF IT ALL!
© 1996 PAWS, INC./Distributed by Universal Press Syndicate

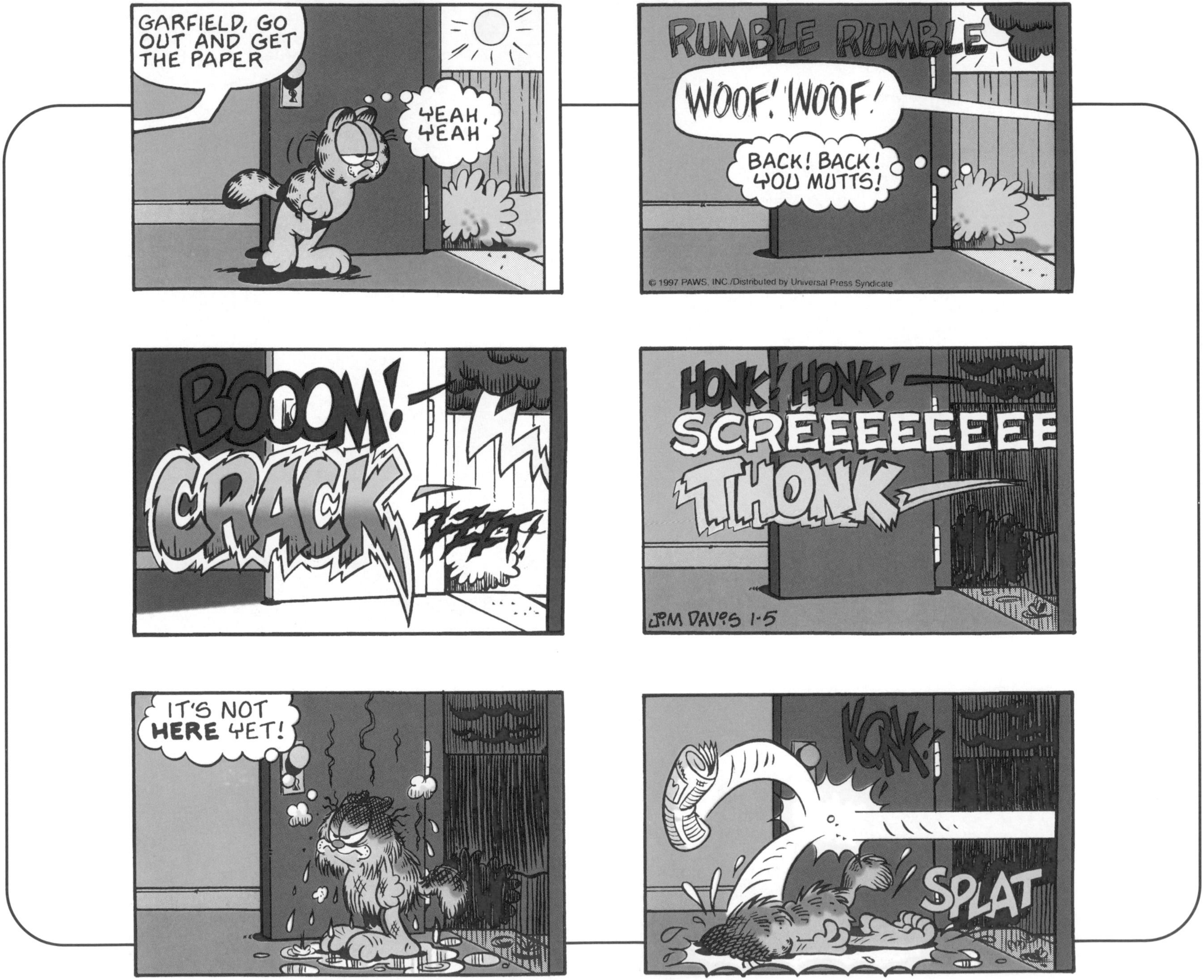
GARFIELD, GO OUT AND GET THE PAPER
YEAH, YEAH
RUMBLE RUMBLE
WOOF! WOOF!
BACK! BACK! YOU MUTTS!
© 1997 PAWS, INC./Distributed by Universal Press Syndicate
BOOOM!
CRACK
HONK! HONK!
SCREEEEEEEEE
THONK
JIM DAVIS 1-5
IT'S NOT **HERE** YET!
KONK!
SPLAT

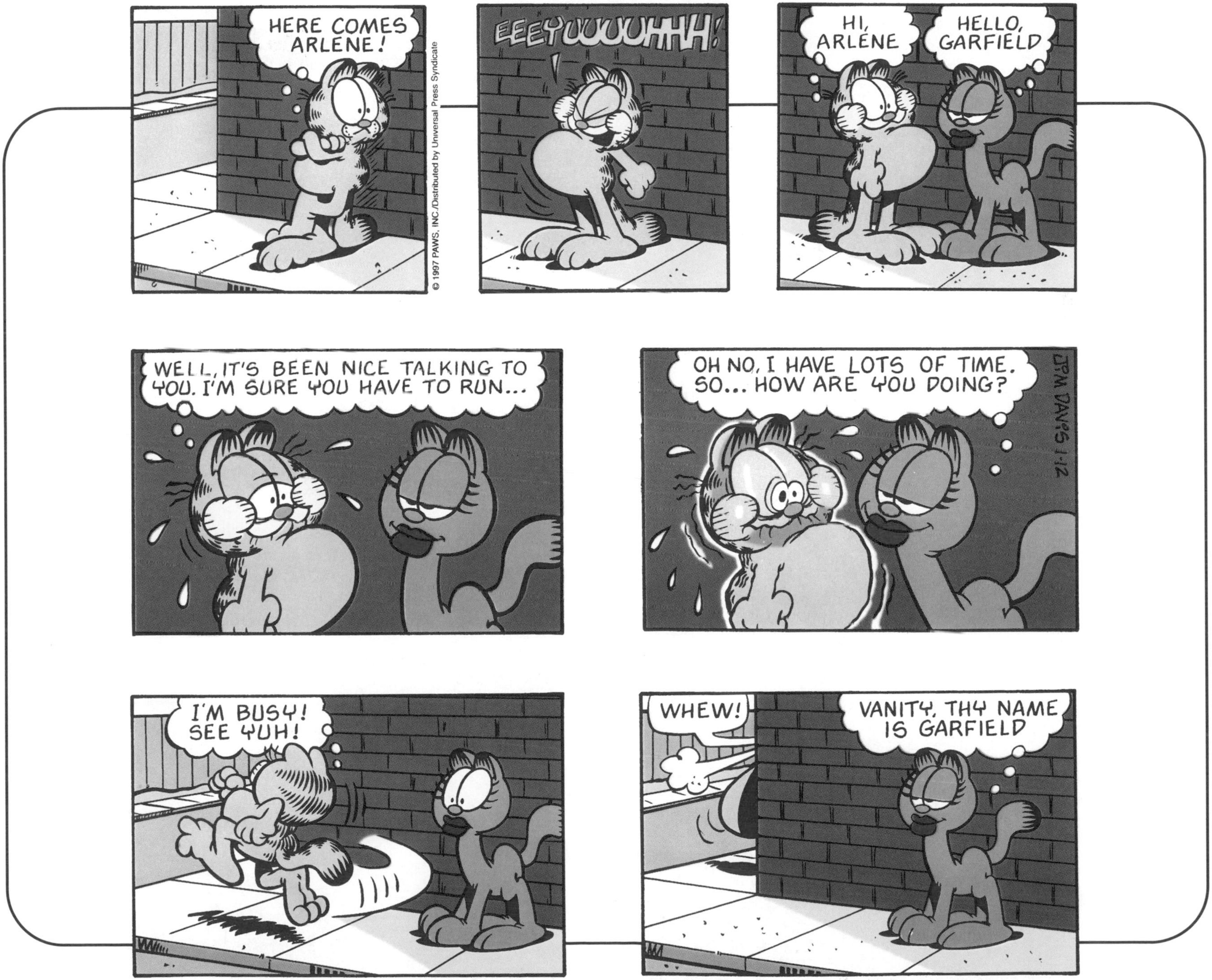
HERE COMES ARLENE!
EEEYUUUUHHH!
HI, ARLENE
HELLO, GARFIELD
WELL, IT'S BEEN NICE TALKING TO YOU. I'M SURE YOU HAVE TO RUN...
OH NO, I HAVE LOTS OF TIME. SO... HOW ARE YOU DOING?
JPM DAVIS 1-12
I'M BUSY! SEE YUH!
WHEW!
VANITY, THY NAME IS GARFIELD

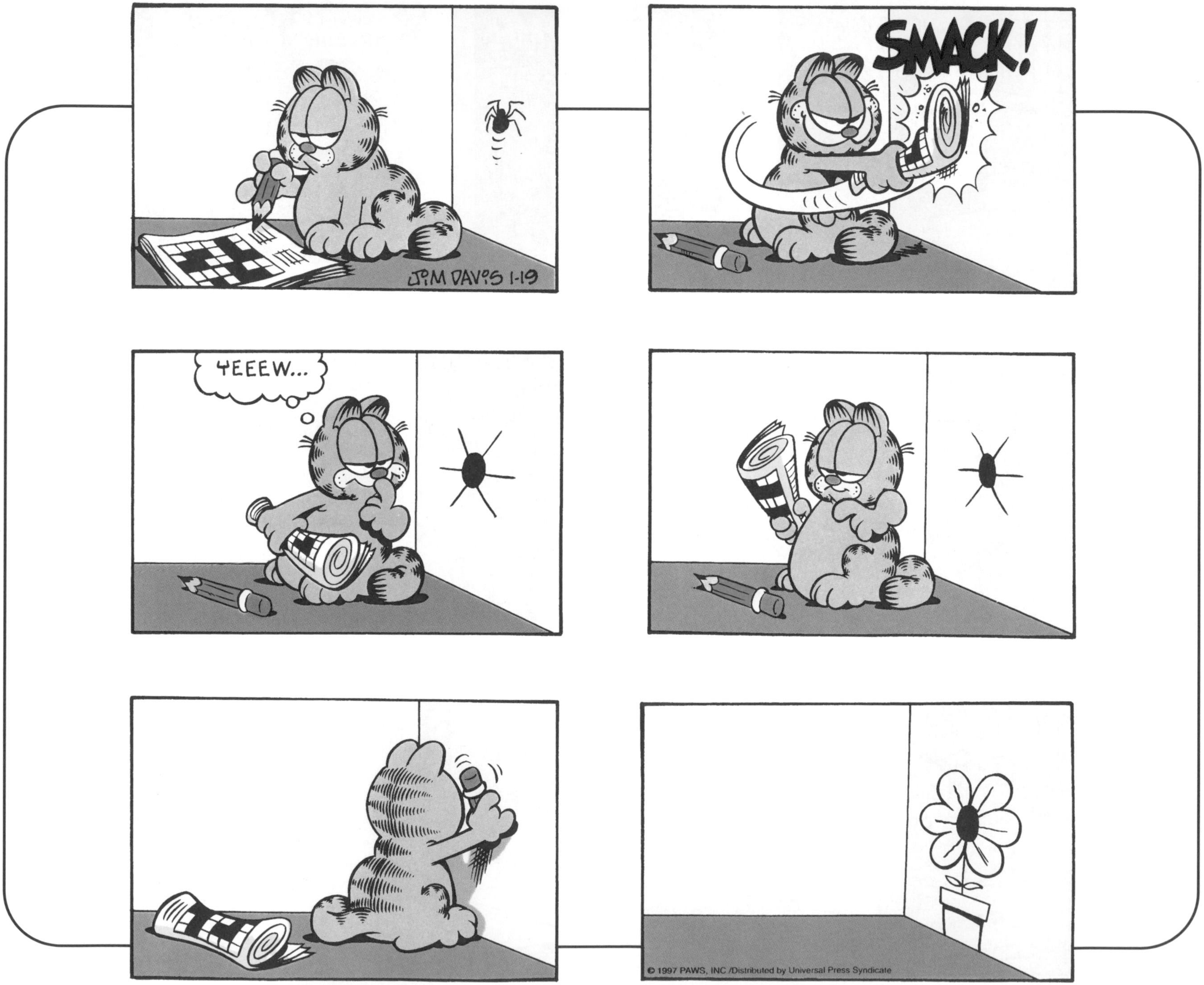
JIM DAVIS 1-19
SMACK!
YEEEW...
© 1997 PAWS, INC /Distributed by Universal Press Syndicate

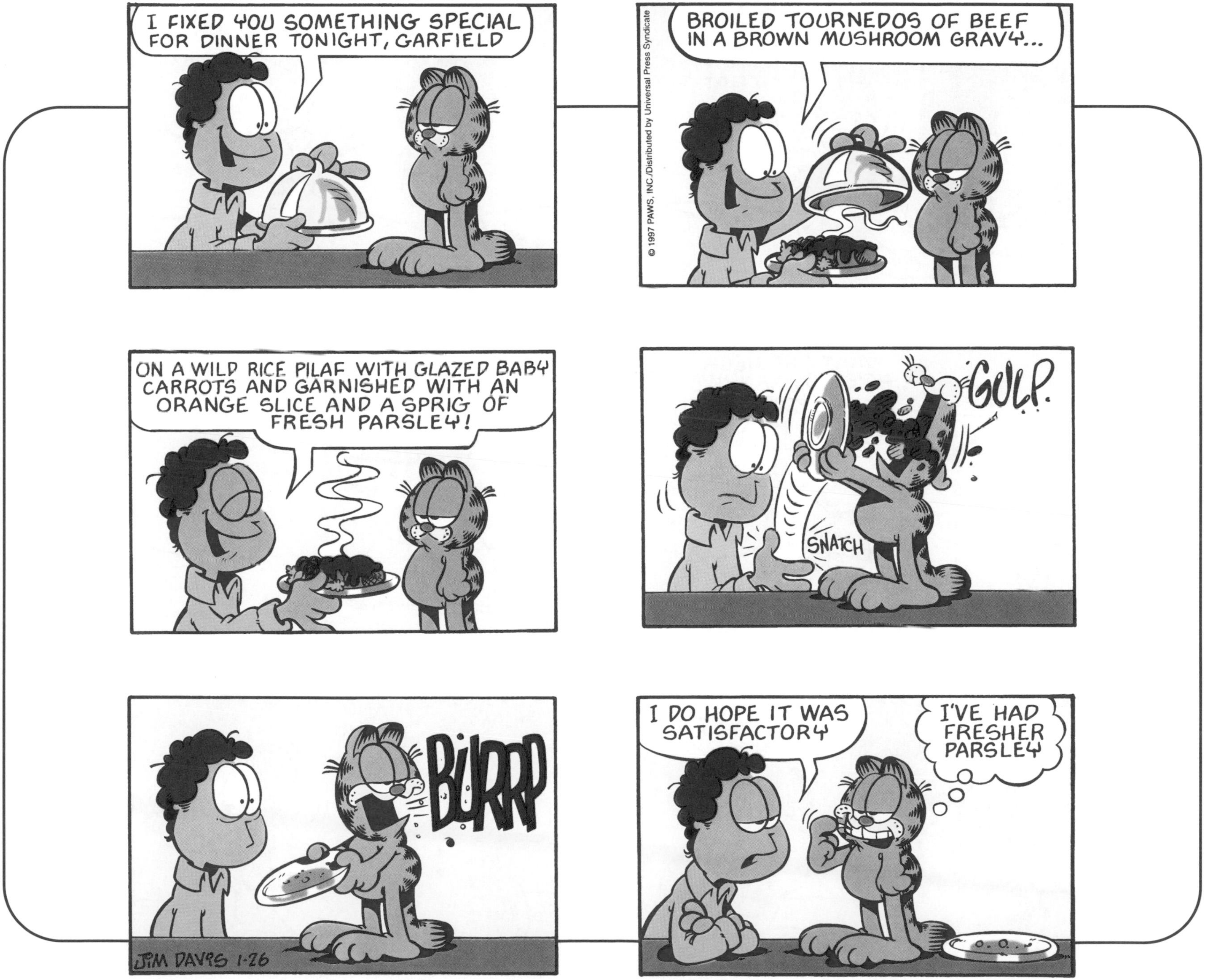
I FIXED YOU SOMETHING SPECIAL FOR DINNER TONIGHT, GARFIELD
© 1997 PAWS, INC./Distributed by Universal Press Syndicate
BROILED TOURNEDOS OF BEEF IN A BROWN MUSHROOM GRAVY...
ON A WILD RICE PILAF WITH GLAZED BABY CARROTS AND GARNISHED WITH AN ORANGE SLICE AND A SPRIG OF FRESH PARSLEY!
SNATCH
GULP
BURRP
JIM DAVIS 1-26
I DO HOPE IT WAS SATISFACTORY
I'VE HAD FRESHER PARSLEY

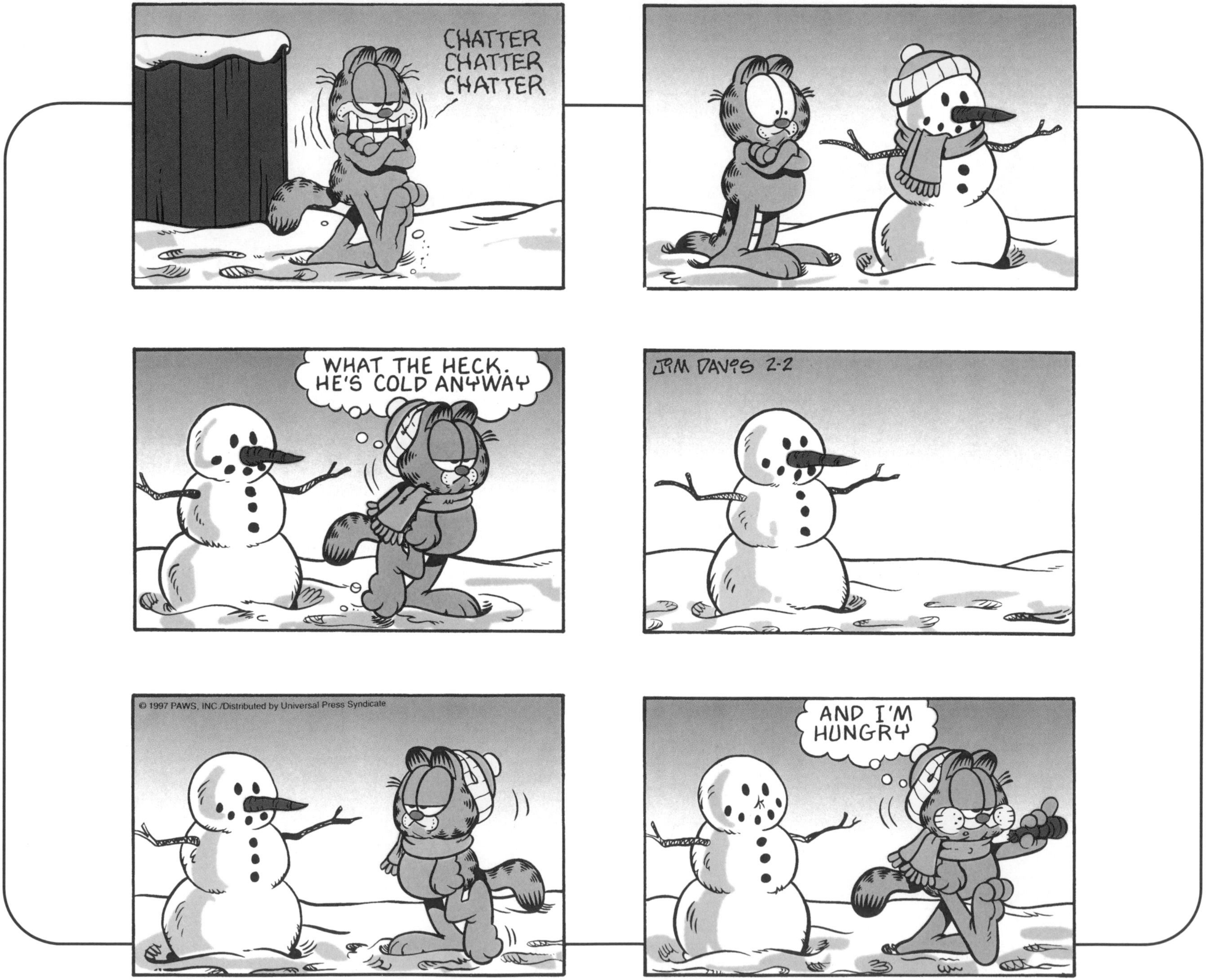
CHATTER
CHATTER
CHATTER
WHAT THE HECK.
HE'S COLD ANYWAY
JIM DAVIS 2-2
© 1997 PAWS, INC./Distributed by Universal Press Syndicate
AND I'M
HUNGRY

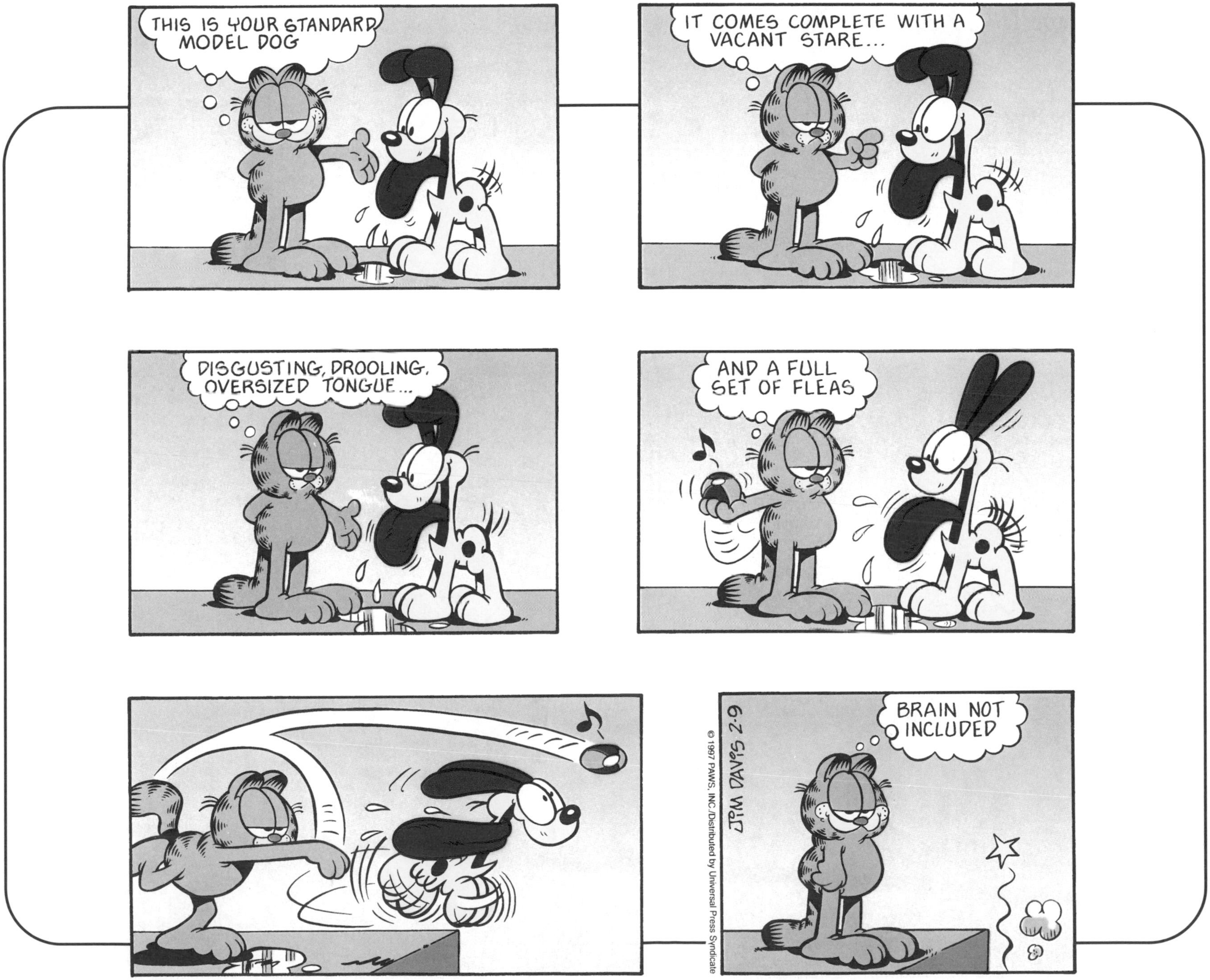
THIS IS YOUR STANDARD MODEL DOG
IT COMES COMPLETE WITH A VACANT STARE...
DISGUSTING, DROOLING, OVERSIZED TONGUE...
AND A FULL SET OF FLEAS
BRAIN NOT INCLUDED
JIM DAVIS 2-9

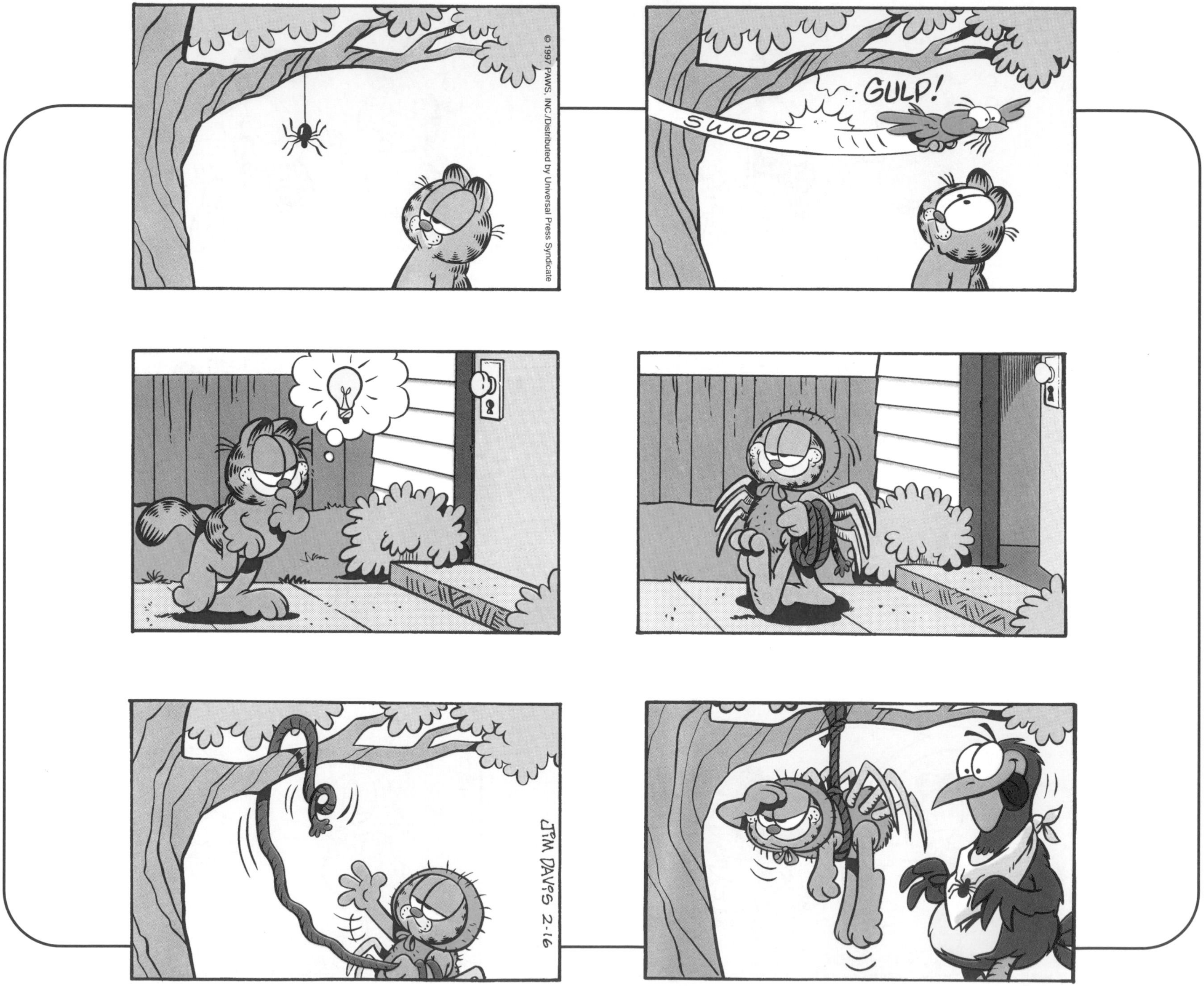
© 1997 PAWS, INC./Distributed by Universal Press Syndicate
SWOOP
GULP!
JIM DAVIS 2-16

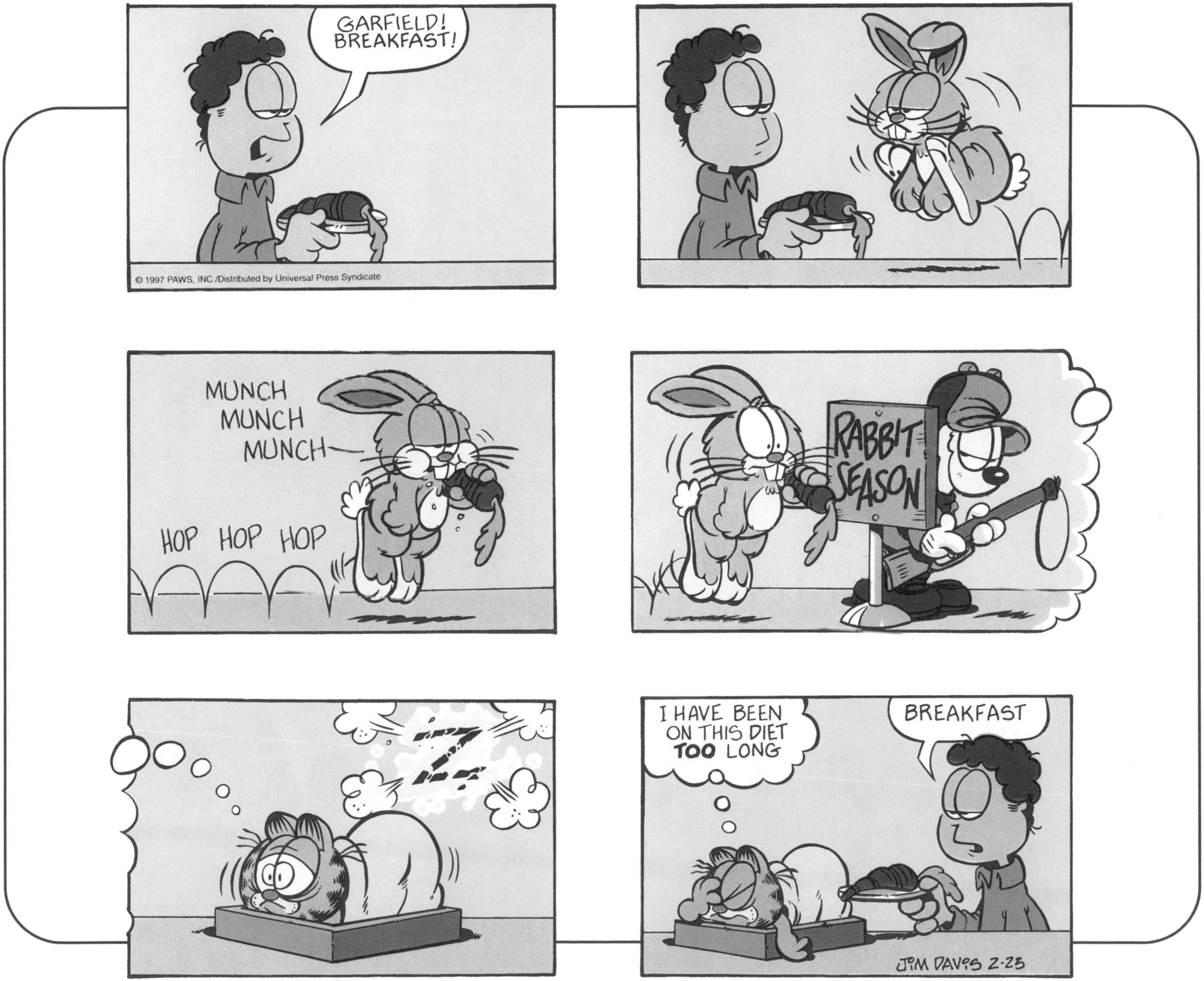
GARFIELD! BREAKFAST!
© 1997 PAWS, INC./Distributed by Universal Press Syndicate
MUNCH MUNCH MUNCH
HOP HOP HOP
RABBIT SEASON
I HAVE BEEN ON THIS DIET TOO LONG
BREAKFAST
JIM DAVIS 2-23

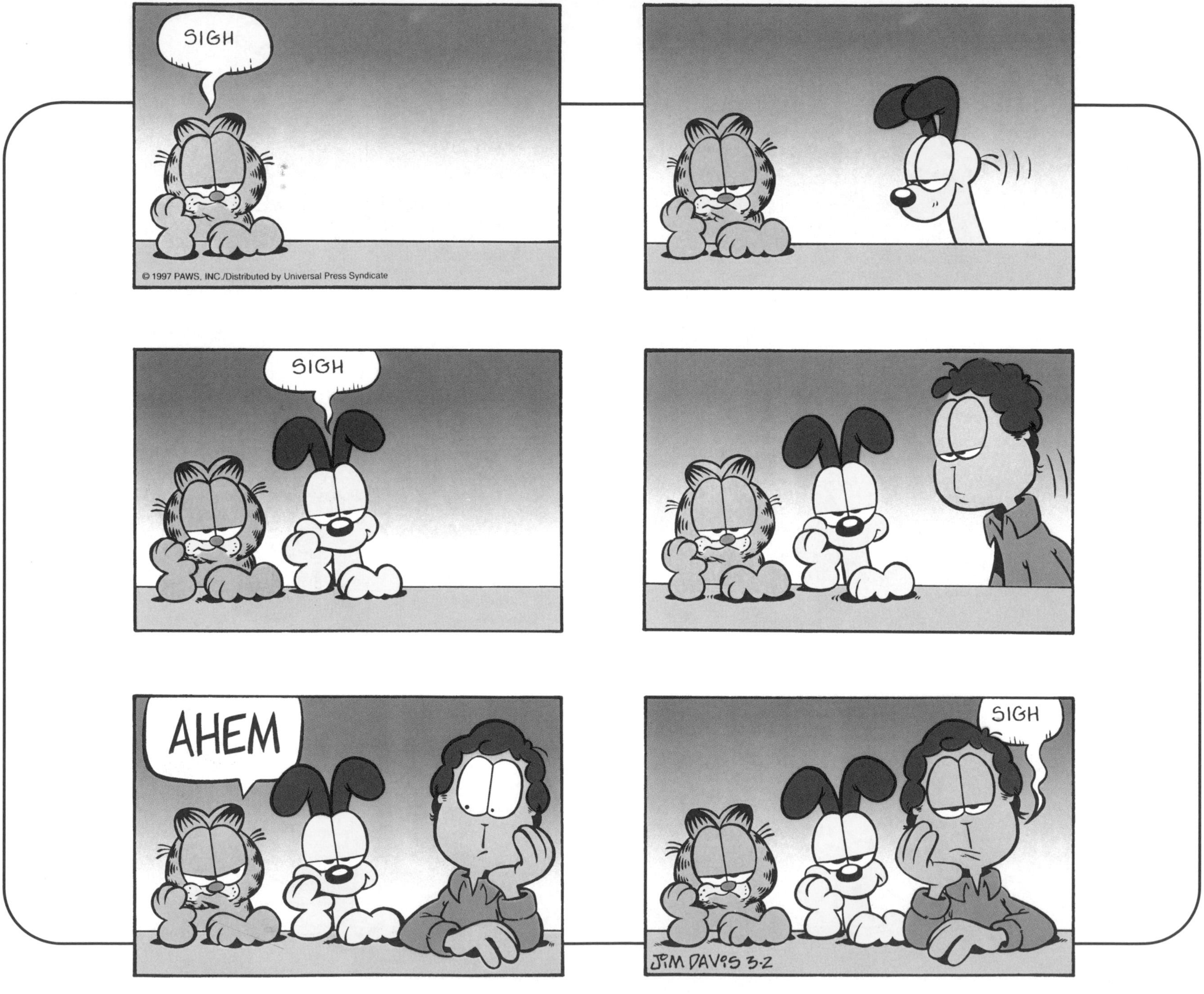
SIGH
© 1997 PAWS, INC./Distributed by Universal Press Syndicate
SIGH
AHEM
SIGH
JIM DAVIS 3-2

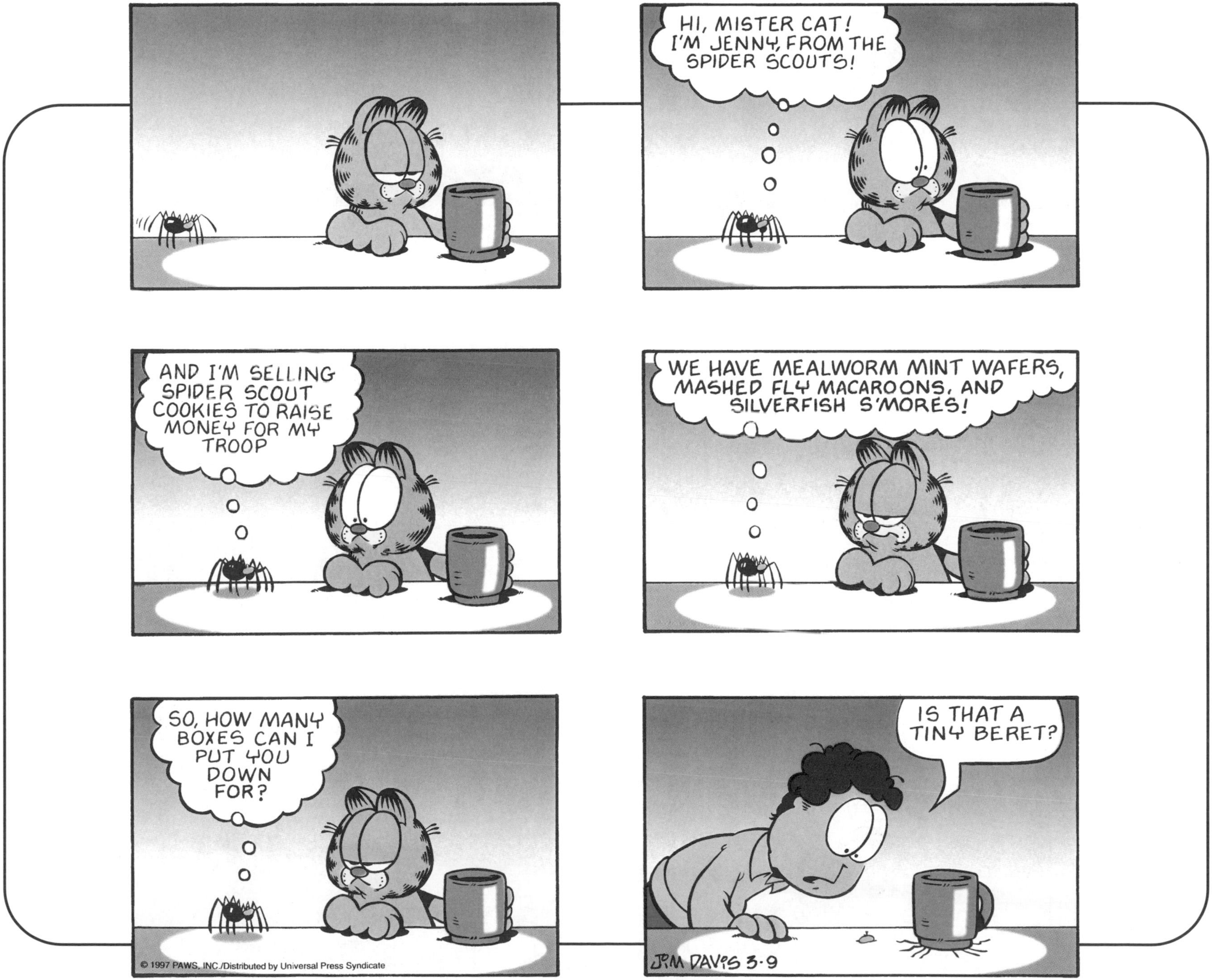
HI, MISTER CAT! I'M JENNY, FROM THE SPIDER SCOUTS!
AND I'M SELLING SPIDER SCOUT COOKIES TO RAISE MONEY FOR MY TROOP
WE HAVE MEALWORM MINT WAFERS, MASHED FLY MACAROONS, AND SILVERFISH S'MORES!
SO, HOW MANY BOXES CAN I PUT YOU DOWN FOR?
IS THAT A TINY BERET?
JIM DAVIS 3-9

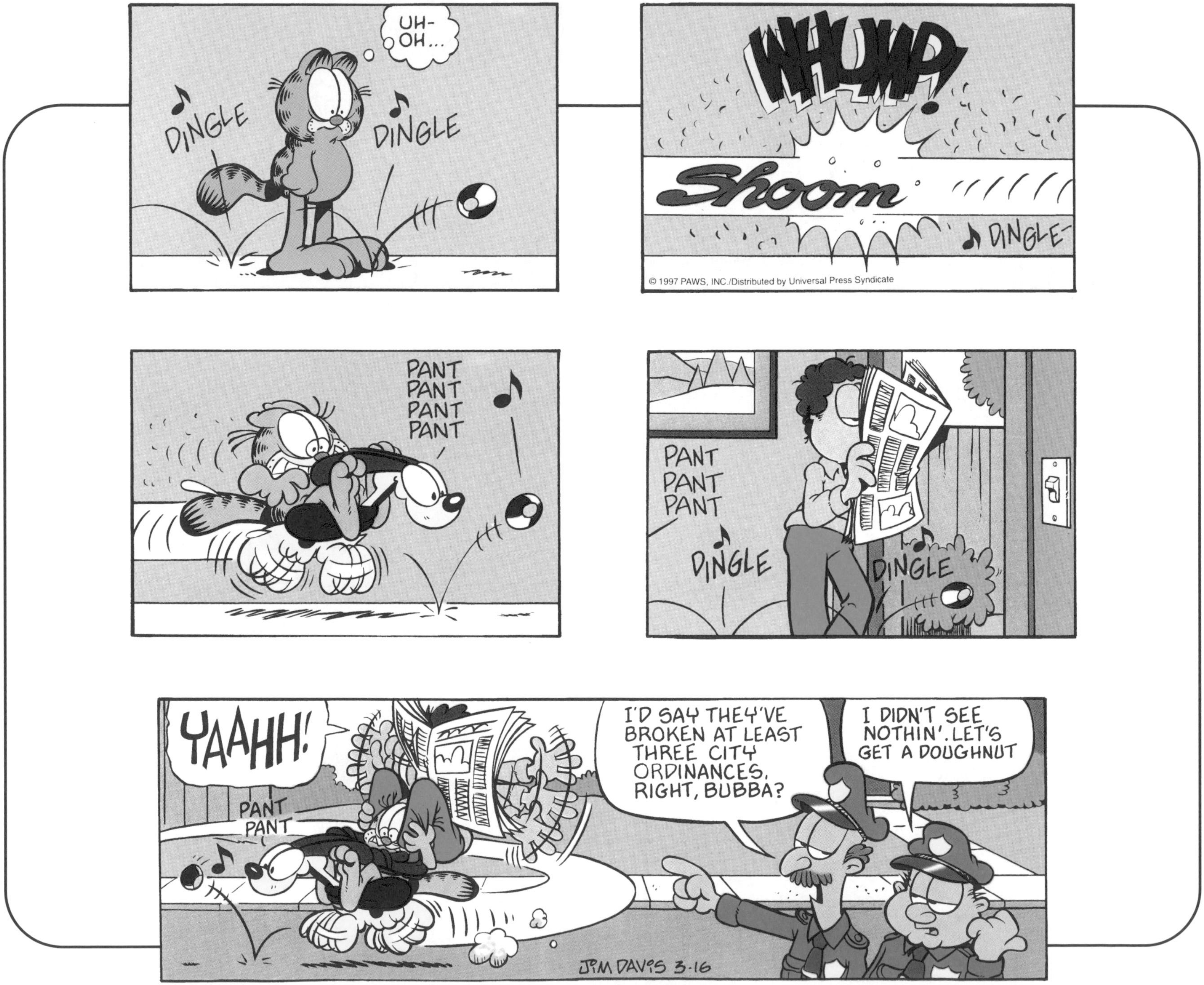
UH-OH...
DINGLE
DINGLE
WHUMP!
Shoom
DINGLE-
PANT PANT PANT PANT
PANT PANT PANT
DINGLE
DINGLE
YAAHH!
PANT PANT
I'D SAY THEY'VE BROKEN AT LEAST THREE CITY ORDINANCES, RIGHT, BUBBA?
I DIDN'T SEE NOTHIN'. LET'S GET A DOUGHNUT
JIM DAVIS 3-16

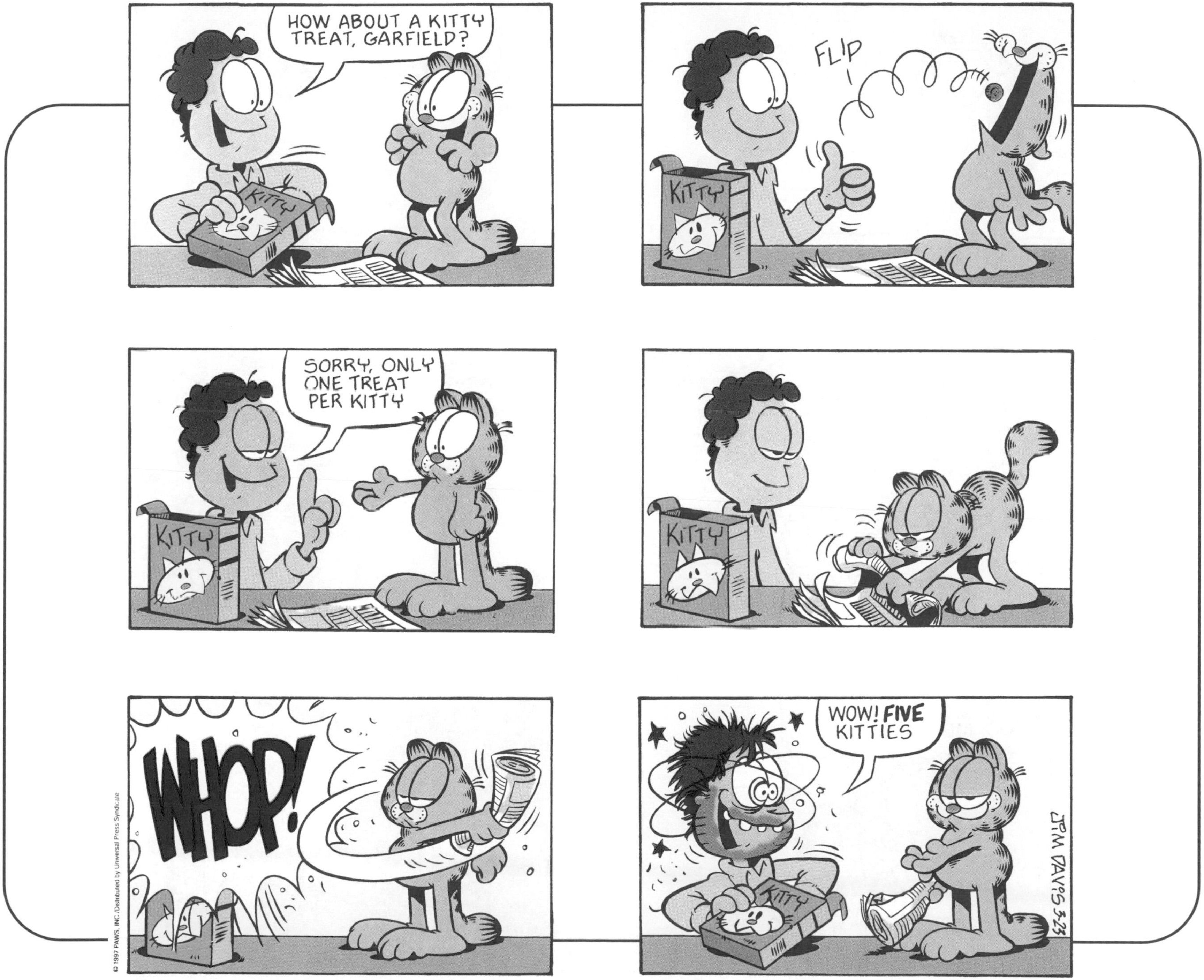
HOW ABOUT A KITTY TREAT, GARFIELD?
FLIP
SORRY, ONLY ONE TREAT PER KITTY
WHOP!
WOW! **FIVE** KITTIES
JIM DAVIS 3-23

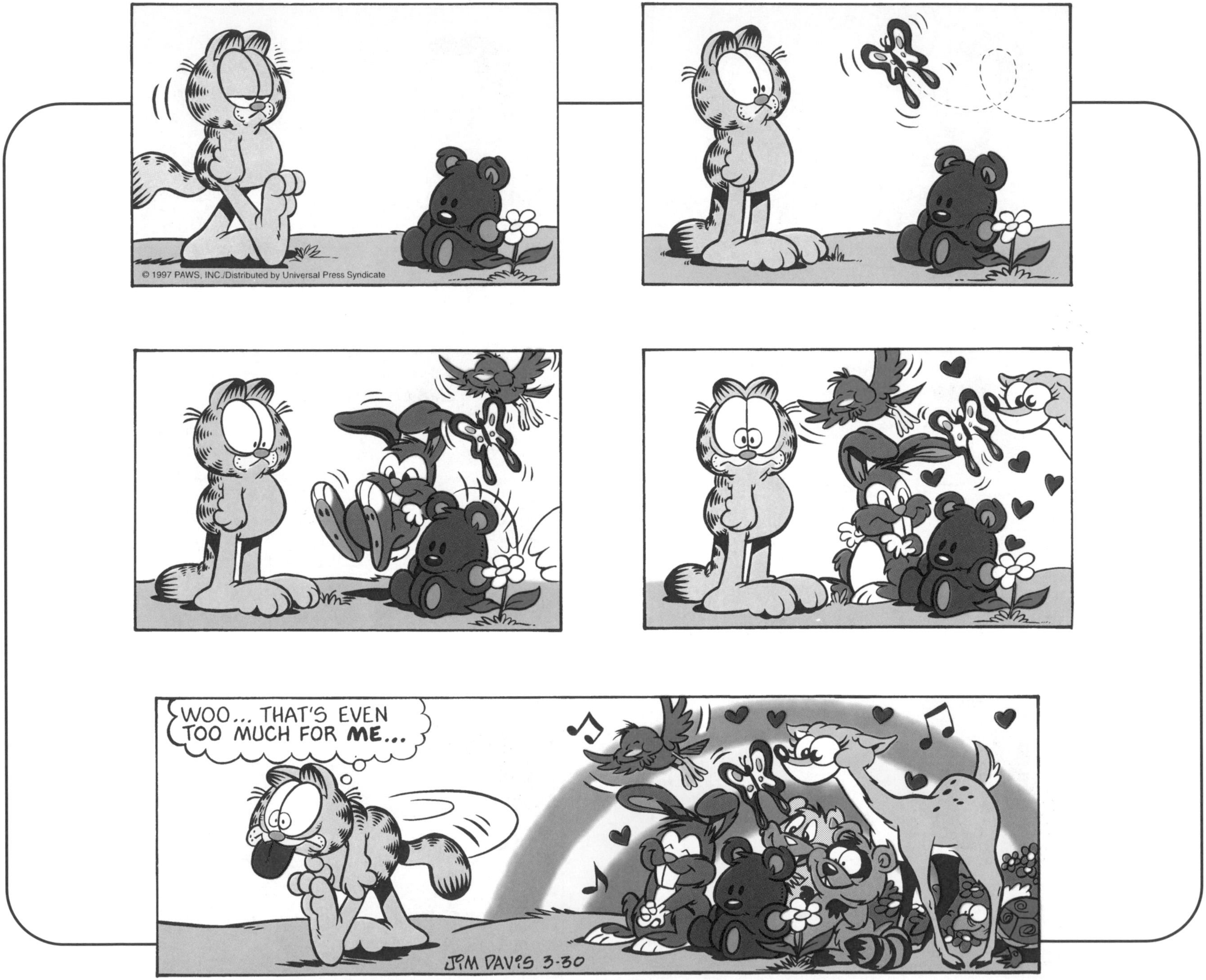

© 1997 PAWS, INC./Distributed by Universal Press Syndicate
WOO... THAT'S EVEN TOO MUCH FOR **ME**...
JIM DAVIS 3-30

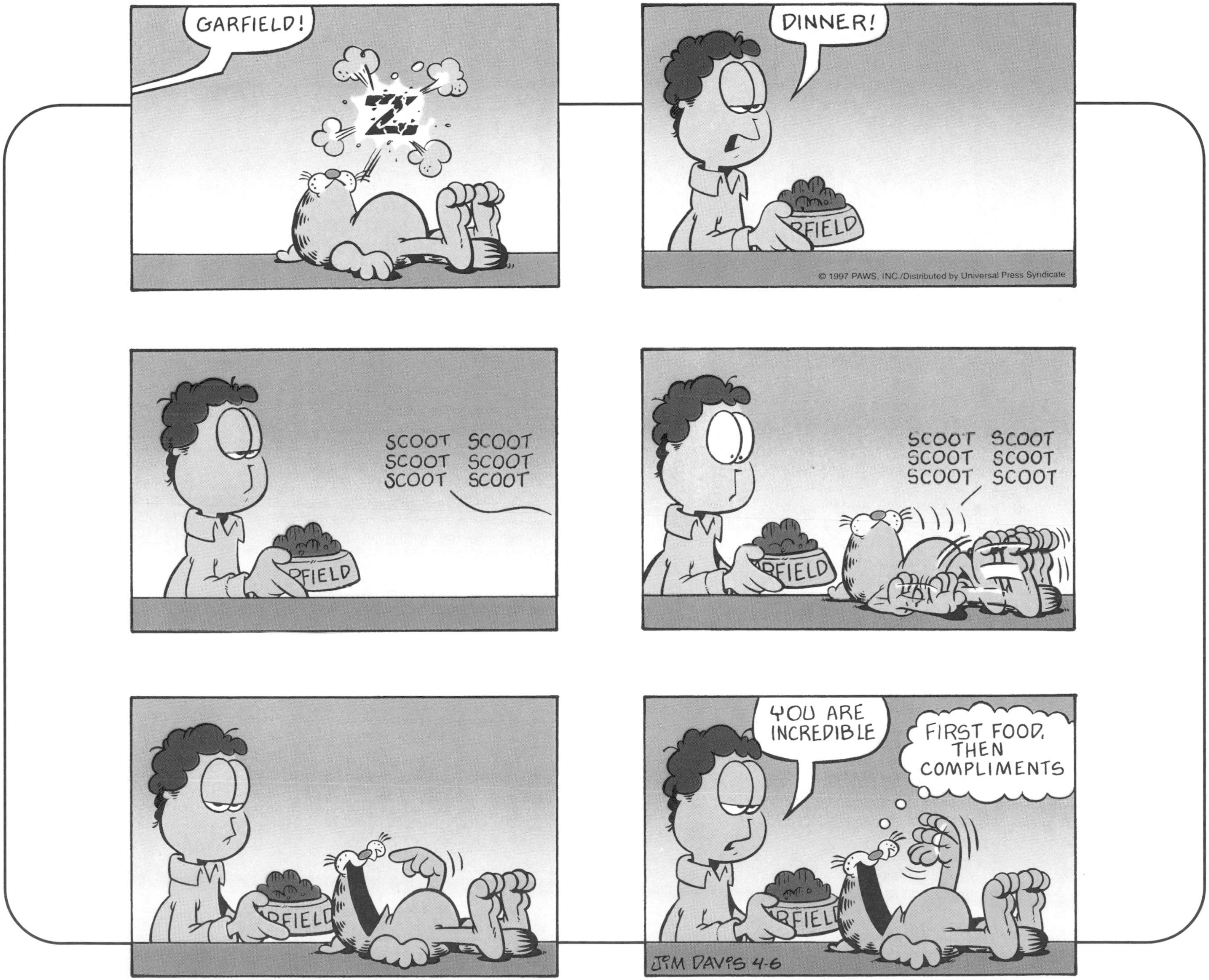
GARFIELD!
DINNER!
© 1997 PAWS, INC./Distributed by Universal Press Syndicate
SCOOT SCOOT
SCOOT SCOOT
SCOOT SCOOT
SCOOT SCOOT
SCOOT SCOOT
SCOOT SCOOT
YOU ARE INCREDIBLE
FIRST FOOD, THEN COMPLIMENTS
JIM DAVIS 4-6

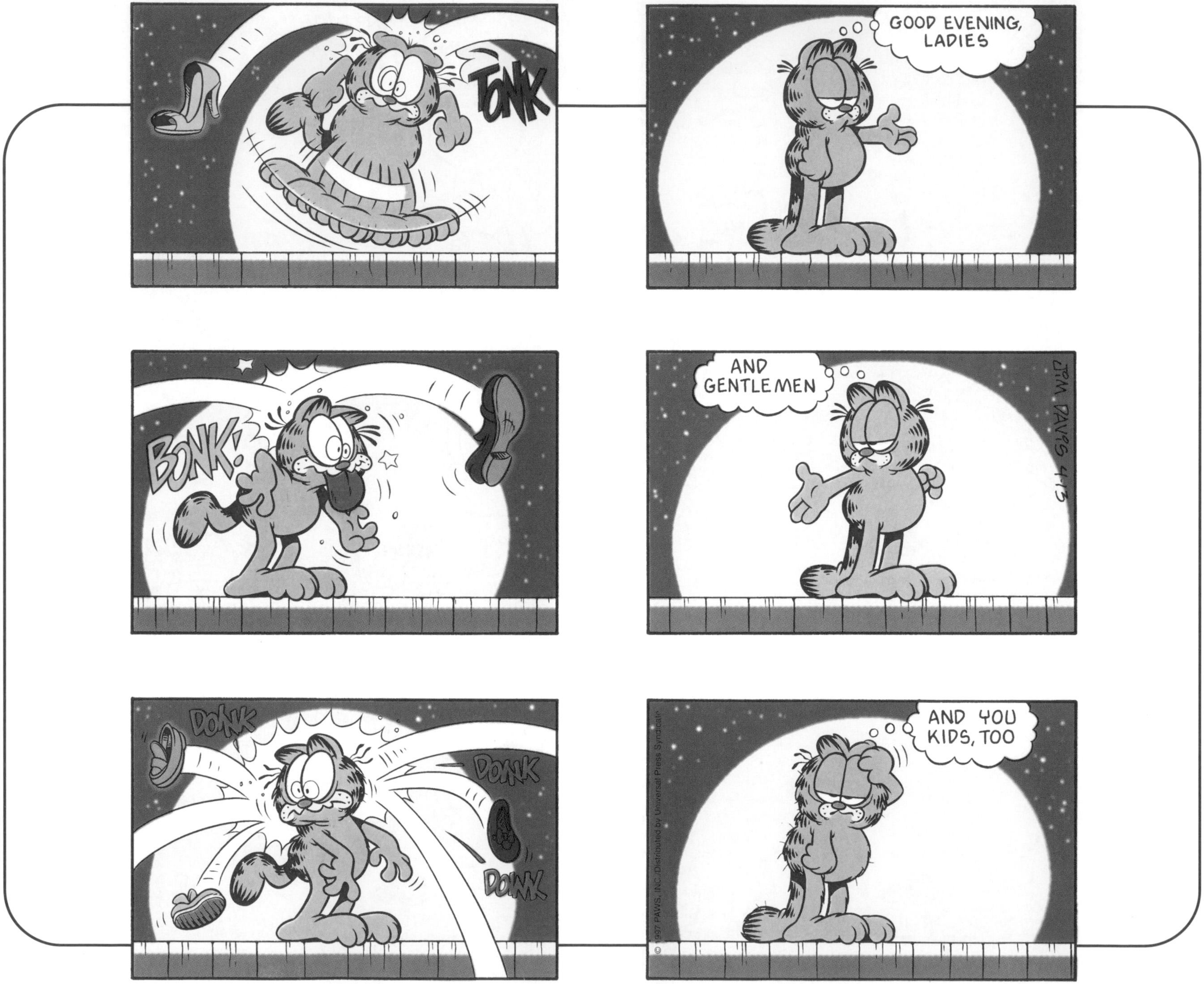
GOOD EVENING, LADIES
TONK
AND GENTLEMEN
BONK!
AND YOU KIDS, TOO
DONK
DONK
DONK
JIM DAVIS 4-13

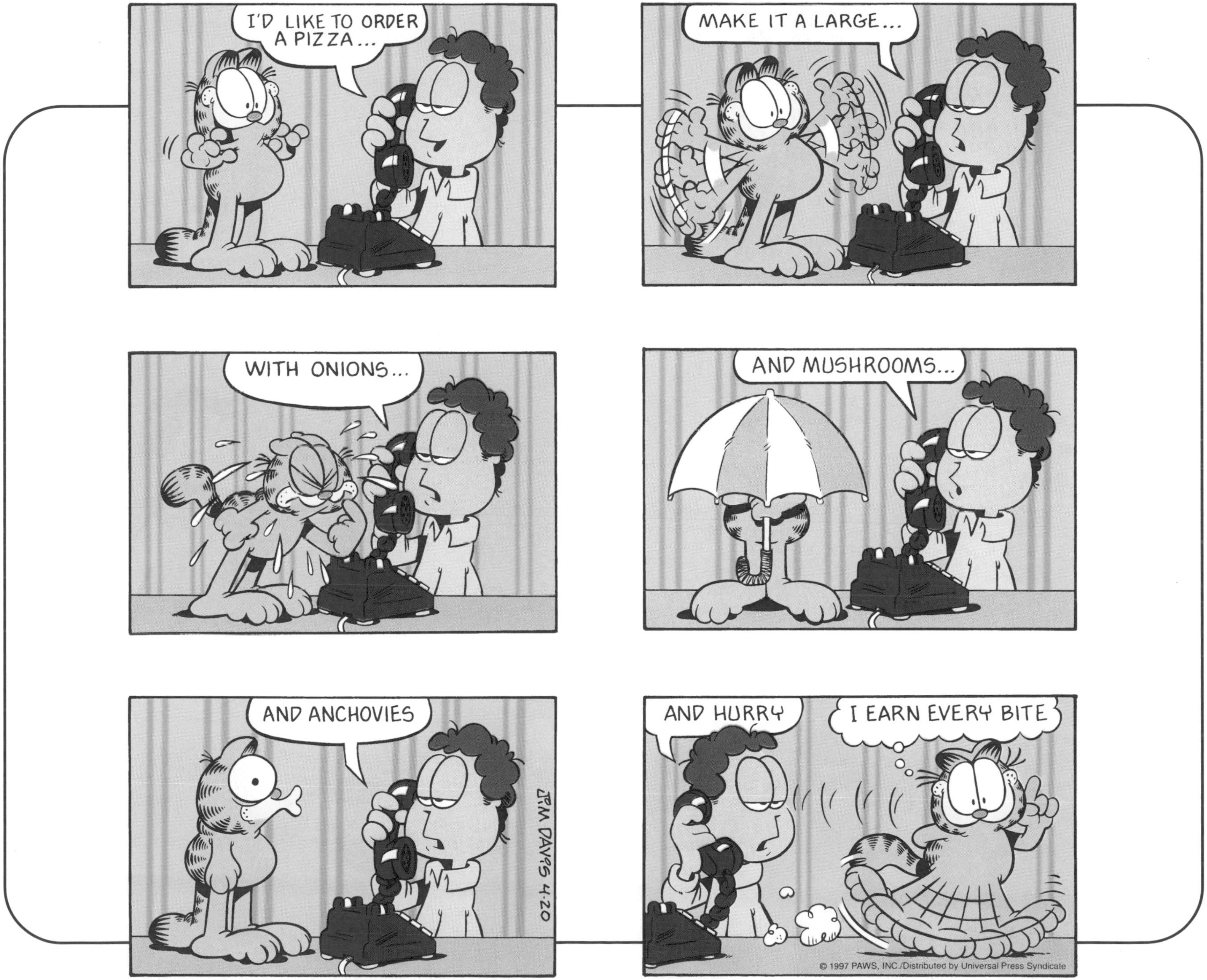
I'D LIKE TO ORDER A PIZZA...
MAKE IT A LARGE...
WITH ONIONS...
AND MUSHROOMS...
AND ANCHOVIES
JIM DAVIS 4-20
AND HURRY
I EARN EVERY BITE
© 1997 PAWS, INC./Distributed by Universal Press Syndicate

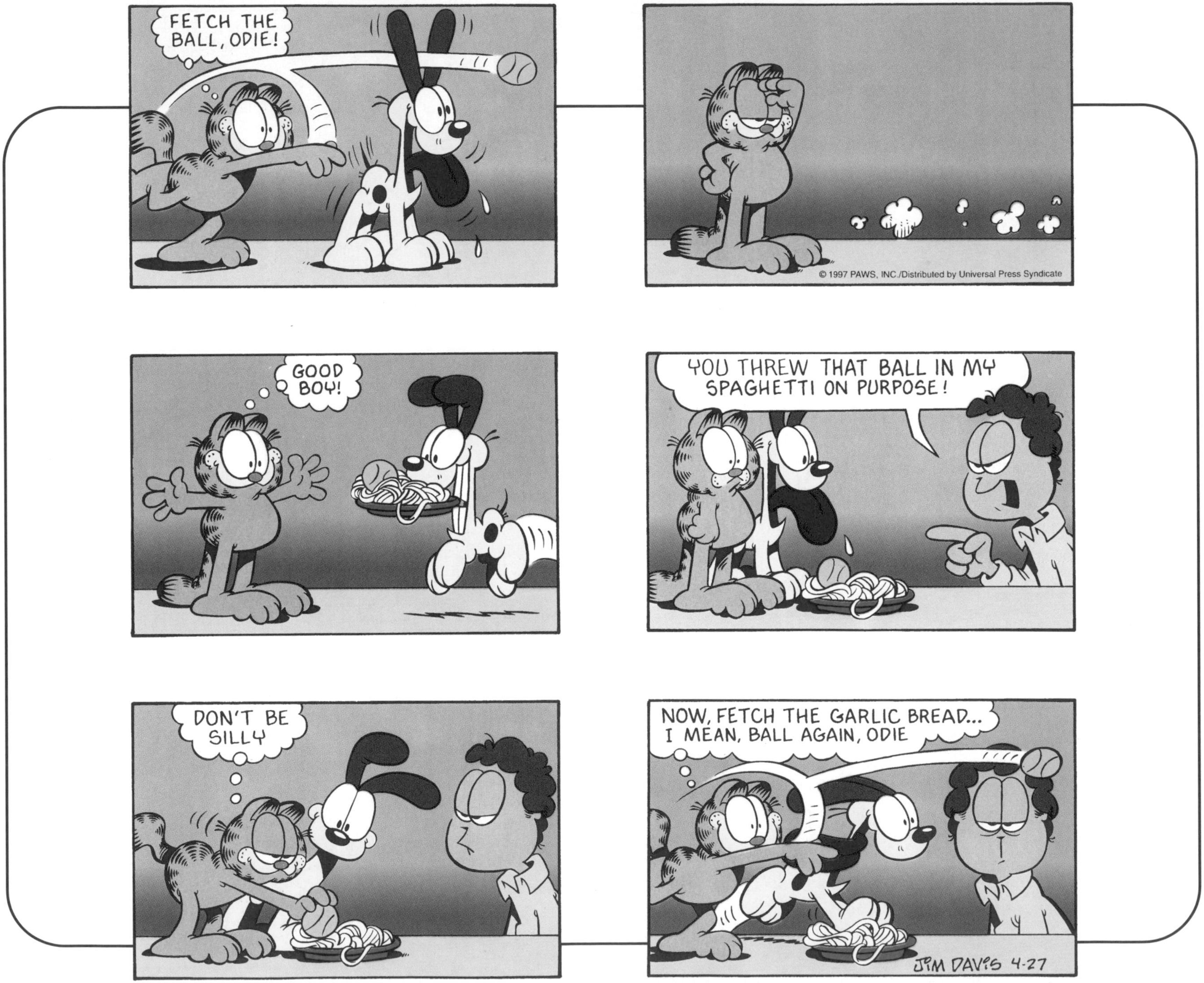

FETCH THE BALL, ODIE!
GOOD BOY!
YOU THREW THAT BALL IN MY SPAGHETTI ON PURPOSE!
DON'T BE SILLY
NOW, FETCH THE GARLIC BREAD... I MEAN, BALL AGAIN, ODIE
© 1997 PAWS, INC./Distributed by Universal Press Syndicate
JIM DAVIS 4-27

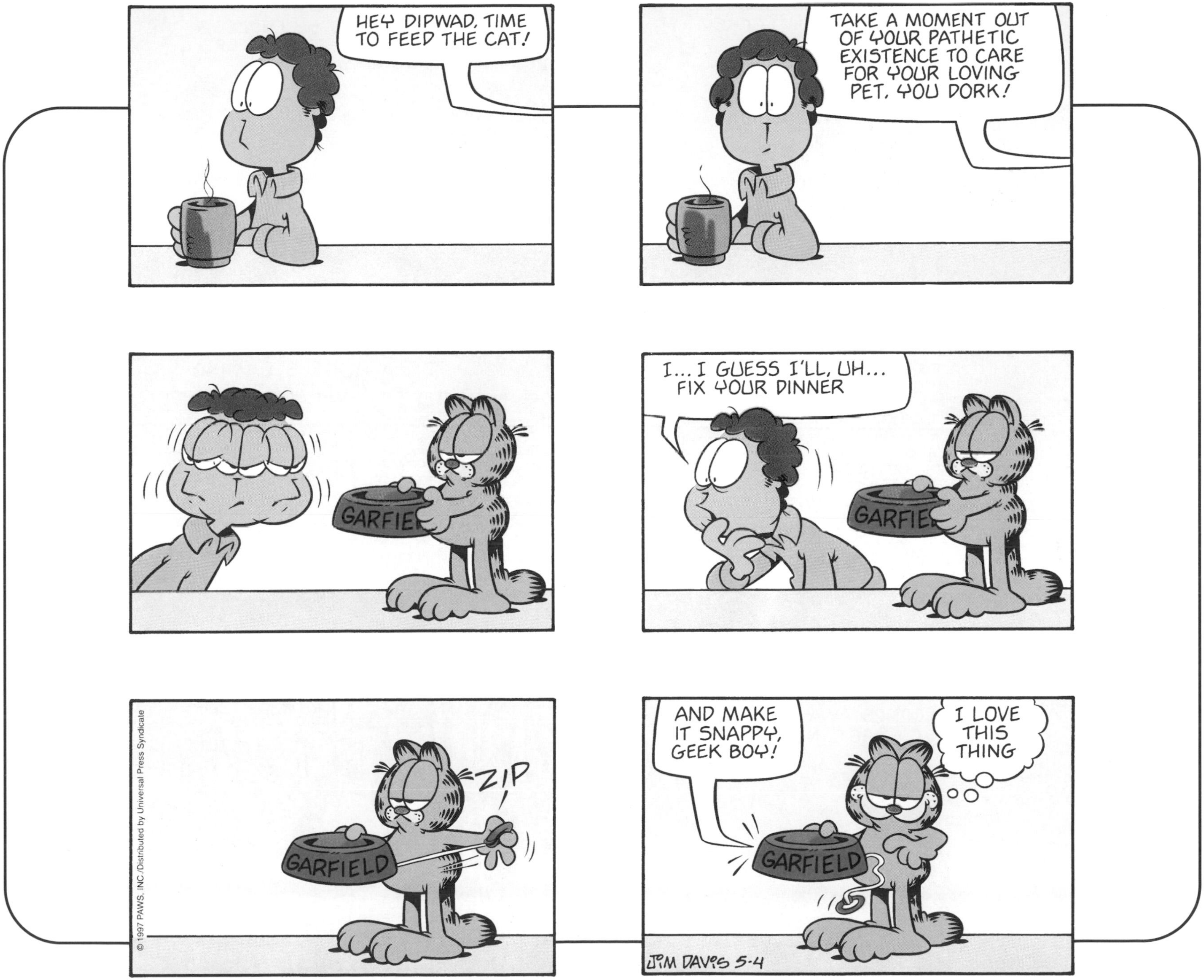

HEY DIPWAD, TIME TO FEED THE CAT!
TAKE A MOMENT OUT OF YOUR PATHETIC EXISTENCE TO CARE FOR YOUR LOVING PET, YOU DORK!
GARFIE
I... I GUESS I'LL, UH... FIX YOUR DINNER
GARFIE
ZIP
GARFIELD
AND MAKE IT SNAPPY, GEEK BOY!
I LOVE THIS THING
GARFIELD
JIM DAVIS 5-4

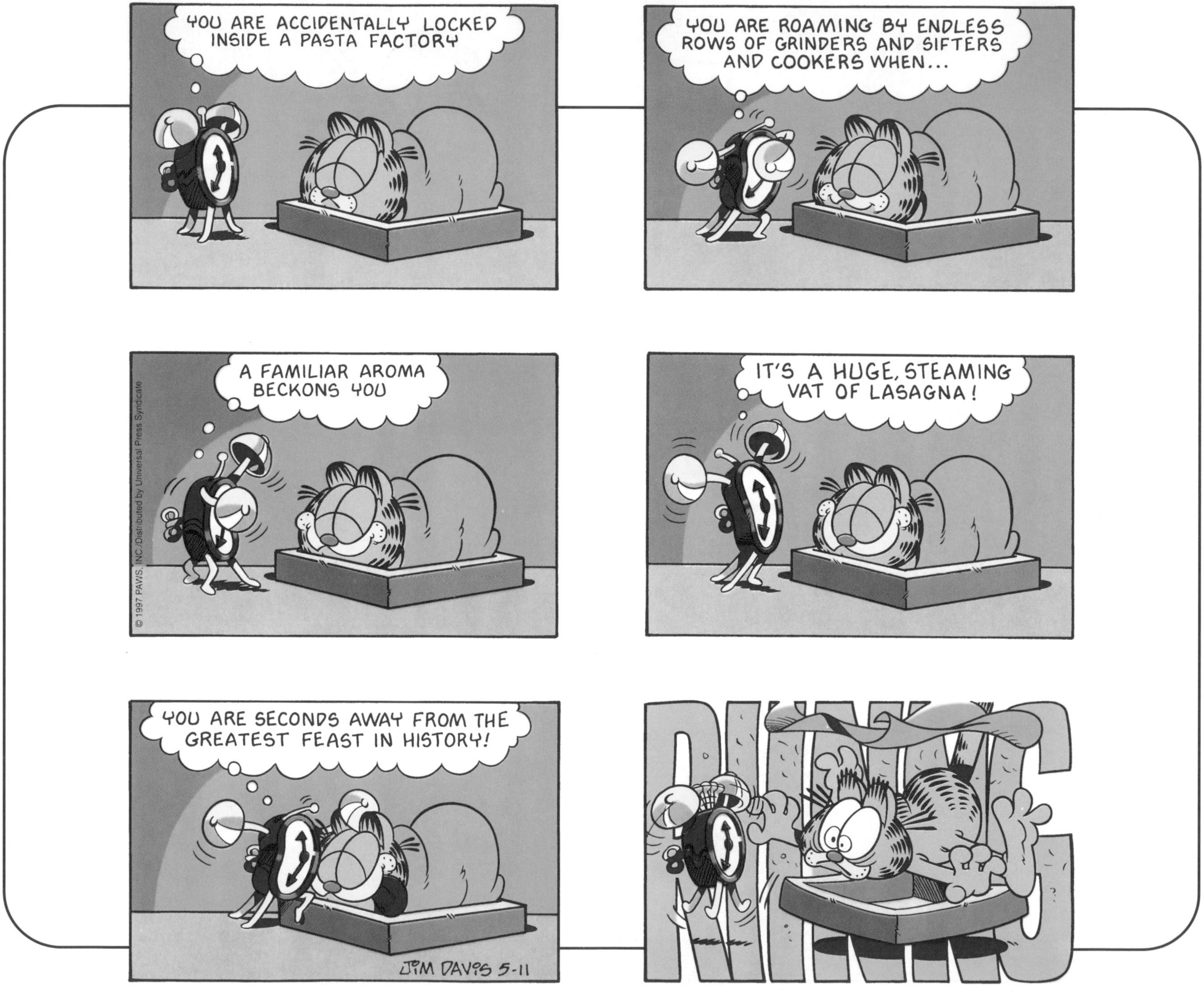
YOU ARE ACCIDENTALLY LOCKED INSIDE A PASTA FACTORY
YOU ARE ROAMING BY ENDLESS ROWS OF GRINDERS AND SIFTERS AND COOKERS WHEN...
A FAMILIAR AROMA BECKONS YOU
IT'S A HUGE, STEAMING VAT OF LASAGNA!
YOU ARE SECONDS AWAY FROM THE GREATEST FEAST IN HISTORY!
JIM DAVIS 5-11
© 1997 PAWS, INC./Distributed by Universal Press Syndicate

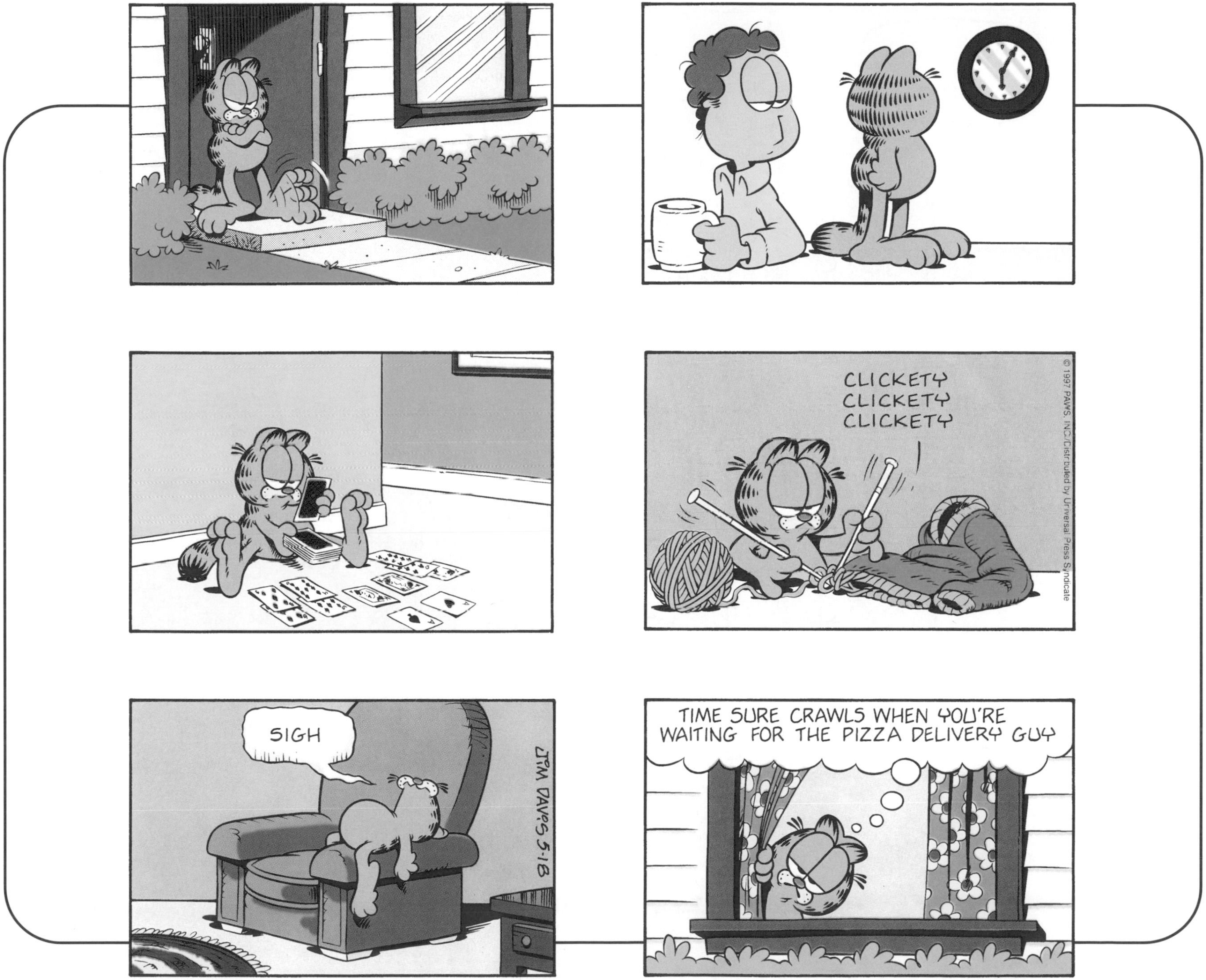
CLICKETY
CLICKETY
CLICKETY
SIGH
JIM DAVIS 5-18
TIME SURE CRAWLS WHEN YOU'RE WAITING FOR THE PIZZA DELIVERY GUY

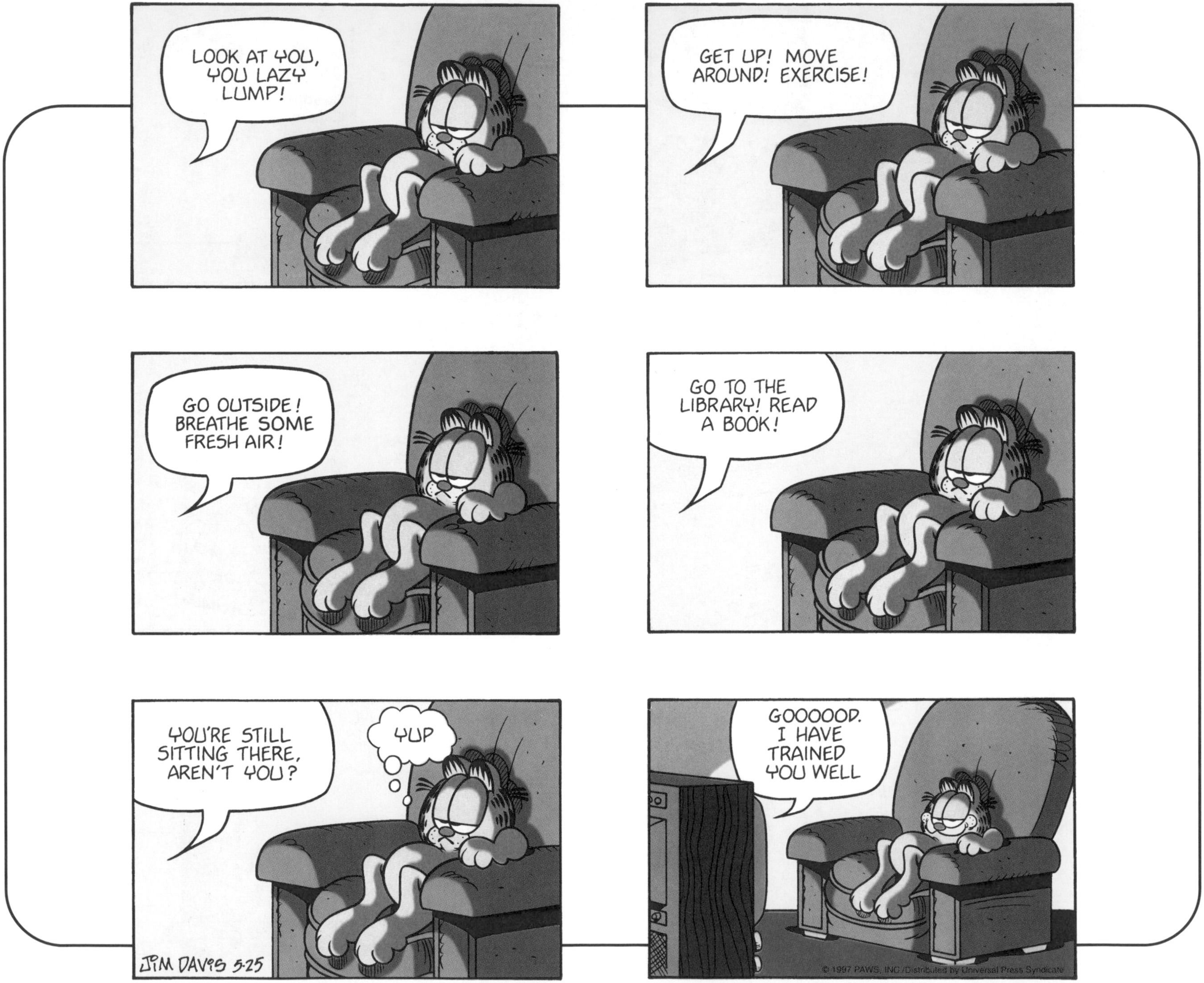
LOOK AT YOU, YOU LAZY LUMP!
GET UP! MOVE AROUND! EXERCISE!
GO OUTSIDE! BREATHE SOME FRESH AIR!
GO TO THE LIBRARY! READ A BOOK!
YOU'RE STILL SITTING THERE, AREN'T YOU?
YUP
GOOOOOD. I HAVE TRAINED YOU WELL
JIM DAVIS 5-25
© 1997 PAWS, INC./Distributed by Universal Press Syndicate

In A Perfect World...

...Stamps Would Taste Good

...You'd Never Have An Itch You Couldn't Scratch

...Horror Movies Would Be Really Scary!

...Chocolate Would Be A Diet Food

...Your Piggy Bank Would Never Run Dry